THE UNKNOWABLE IN EARLY MODERN THOUGHT

THE UNKNOWABLE IN EARLY MODERN THOUGHT

Natural Philosophy and the Poetics of the Ineffable

Kevin Killeen

Stanford University Press
Stanford, California

Stanford University Press
Stanford, California

© 2023 by Kevin Killeen. All rights reserved.

No part of this book may be reproduced or transmitted in any form or by any means, electronic or mechanical, including photocopying and recording, or in any information storage or retrieval system, without the prior written permission of Stanford University Press.

Printed in the United States of America on acid-free, archival-quality paper
Library of Congress Cataloging-in-Publication Data
Names: Killeen, Kevin, author.
Title: The unknowable in early modern thought : natural philosophy and the poetics of the ineffable / Kevin Killeen.
Description: Stanford, California : Stanford University Press, 2023. |
Includes bibliographical references and index.
Identifiers: LCCN 2022039372 (print) | LCCN 2022039373 (ebook) |
    ISBN 9781503635395 (cloth) | ISBN 9781503635852 (paperback) | ISBN 9781503635869 (ebook)
Subjects: LCSH: English literature—17th century—History and criticism. | Theology in literature—History—17th century. | Religion and science—History—17th century.
Classification: LCC PR438.T45 K55 2023 (print) | LCC PR438.T45 (ebook) | DDC 820.9090/31—dc23/eng/20220822
LC record available at https://lccn.loc.gov/2022039372
LC ebook record available at https://lccn.loc.gov/2022039373

Cover design: George Kirkpatrick
Cover image: Pieter Bruegel the Elder, *The Fall of the Rebel Angels*, 1562, painting, 117 × 162 cm, Royal Museums of Fine Arts of Belgium, Brussels

Typeset by Elliott Beard in Sabon LT Pro 10/15

For Molly Killeen and Sharon Holm

Contents

Acknowledgments ix

INTRODUCTION
1

CHAPTER 1
The Jobean Apophatic and the Symphonic Unknowability of the World
27

CHAPTER 2
The Theopoetics of Jacob Boehme
60

CHAPTER 3
Thomas Browne's Poetics of the Unspeakable
90

CHAPTER 4
The Bewildering Surface from Boyle to Cavendish
115

CHAPTER 5
Anna Trapnel's Aesthetics of Incoherence
140

CONTENTS

CHAPTER 6
Miltonic Vertigo and a Theology of Disorientation
166

EPILOGUE
Ordinary and Exquisite Bafflement
199

Notes 205

Index 257

Acknowledgments

Thanks to Cecilia Muratori, Anthony Ossa-Richardson, and Namratha Rao, for reading chapters and offering astute comments. And enormous thanks, in particular, to Richard Rowland, for going through the whole manuscript with characteristic generosity and an eagle eye, as well as for fine beers with it.

The Department of English at the University of York is a lovely place to work, in the midst of general madness, and the energy of the Centre for Renaissance and Early Modern Studies is always a pleasure—thanks to members, past and present: Brian Cummings, Tania Demetriou, Simon Ditchfield, Cat Evans, Dave Harper, Helen Hills, Ezra Horbury, Katherine Hunt, Gašper Jakovac, Mark Jenner, Tom McLeish, Emilie Murphy, Jeanne Nuechterlein, Namratha Rao, Jane Raisch, Richard Rowland, Freya Sierhuis, Helen Smith, Lauren Working, as well as our wonderful postgraduates. I have benefited enormously from giving papers here and there at conferences and seminars. Early drafts of the chapters have been commented upon and in some cases published. Jessica Wolfe invited me to the Huntington Library for a conference on Error out of which came a version of chapter 3. This was published as "The Apophatic *Garden of Cyrus*: Thomas Browne's Fleeting God," *Studies in Philology* 114 (2017): 748–67. Thanks to Reid Barbour, Katie Murphy, and Claire Preston for ideas and suggestions, and to University of North Carolina Press for permission to reprint. The UEA seminar was another outing for the ideas—thanks to Sophie Butler, Tom Roebuck, William Rossiter, and Matt Woodcock, for Rabelaisian hospitality. Conferences at King's College London, organized by Hannah Crawforth and Sarah Knight, and the Scientiae shindig in Belfast allowed me to test out the chapter on Job, while an invitation to speak at the Irish Renaissance Seminar gave me the opportunity to spend time at Marsh's Library—enormous thanks to Jane Grogan and Danielle Clarke. Subha Mukherji and Lizzie Swann gave me valuable advice on the chapter for a shorter version, towards their collection, *Devices of Fancy: The Poetics of Scientia in Early Modern England* (Palgrave, forthcoming [2024]), and I had a number of enjoyable conversations on the topic with William Franke, Cassie Gorman, Joe Moshenska, Jenny Richards, Rachel Willie, and others, here and there, that gave me ideas. A conference on German Mysticism, organized by Torrance Kirby at McGill University, and another organized by Jon McGovern at the University of Nanjing (alas, both held on Zoom) allowed me to try out material on Jacob Boehme; conversations with Cecilia Muratori, Ariel Hessayon, and Nigel Smith were very helpful. Working with Liz Oakley-Browne on a volume, *Scrutinizing Surfaces in Early Modern Thought*, was a real pleasure, and gave me the opportunity to think about the curious character of the tiny, with a preliminary chapter on "Microscopy, Surfaces and the Unknowable in Seventeenth-Century Natural Philosophy," published online in the *Journal of the Northern Renaissance* 8, https://jnr2.hcommons.org/2017/5081/. Chapter 6 was written, initially, as "Anna Trapnel, Enthusiasm and the Aesthetics of Incoherence," for the *Oxford Handbook of Early Modern Women's Writing, 1540–1700*, edited by Elizabeth Scott-Baumann, Danielle Clarke, and Sarah Ross (Oxford University Press, 2022); my warm thanks to the editors and to OUP for permission to reprint parts of this. Likewise, to Tania Demetriou, for asking me to give a talk to the Cambridge Renaissance Graduate Seminar, and to the EMoDiR (Early Modern Religious Dissents and Radicalism) network for the panels at the RSA conference in Dublin. The British Milton Seminar allowed me to try out the final chapter, with astute ideas from Vladimir Brljak, Tom Corns, and Philippa Earle, as well the organizers, Hugh Adlington and Sarah Knight.

Thanks also to Ulrika Wray for checking my German; to Kate Alderson-Smith at Harris Manchester College Library, Oxford, for help with the images; and the staff at Marsh's Library. Thanks, finally, to Caroline McKusick at Stanford, to the Press's readers, and to Lys Weiss for copyediting and Richard Rowland (again) for indexing.

This book is, like everything, for Molly Killeen and for Sharon Holm.

THE UNKNOWABLE IN EARLY MODERN THOUGHT

Introduction

EARLY MODERNITY WAS MESMERIZED BY the idea of the unknowable, what was constitutionally beyond the ability of fallen humanity to fathom, and it developed a rich hoard of terms to describe the inexpressible. "To paint a Sound," wrote the physician and natural philosopher, Walter Charleton in 1652, "is a far easier task, then to describe the impervestigable manner of *Gods operations*."[1] If the "impervestigable" is unfamiliar these days, we might also note Henry More and Gilbert Burnet, exercised with the "imperscrutable," while Richard Linche tried out "inexcogitable," and Thomas Morton played with the "indeprehensible."[2] Things, but God in particular, could be: uncogitable, indivinable, searchless, uninvestigable, inscrute. What cannot be said naturally produces a good deal of speech, and the era inherited not just a vocabulary, but an impressive intellectual machinery for thinking through those bolts of perception that eluded words, to glimpse the thing beyond.

This book looks at the failures of language and the buckling of logic when faced with an elusive object, whether skittish divinity, dumbfounding paradox, or a reality so skewed as to defy words. In particular, it explores how scientific thought dealt with this hinterland. Faced with the endemic inscrutability of the world they encountered—below the threshold of sight, before the beginning of time, beyond the parameters of reason—the response of natural philosophers was not always to suppose that better instruments, sounder logic, or more refined paradigms were the issue. Seventeenth-century thinkers believed in the generative role of the imponderable. Rhetorical, poetic conceptions of the unthinkable were a part of the early modern lexicon that natural philosophy relied upon. Early modernity was in part paralyzed by and in part energized by the gymnastics of paradox and contradiction. The natural philosopher and theorist of skepticism Joseph Glanvill, in a chapter of *The Vanity of Dogmatizing* (1661) entitled "Our Decay and Ruins by the fall, descanted on. Of the now Scantness of our Knowledge," depicts a particular protest of those who "after all their pains in quest of Science, have sat down in a profest *nescience*." This nescience has the seeker of knowledge adopt "the *Adage, Science had no friend but Ignorance*." This was by no means a counsel of despair. The cusp of knowledge, what lay beyond the visible and beyond the sayable, was a valuable intellectual resource.[3]

The thing that can be intuited but not understood, sensed but not described is, in its theological guise, termed the "apophatic"—knowing only by negation, the *via negativa*, in which God can only be intuited by what he is not or what he is, in inexact fashion, like.[4] But early modernity is not a period associated with any flourishing of the apophatic. It was, in Protestant England at least, a tainted tradition, its best professors being Catholic, Jewish, or Sufi, with their rich mystic philosophical legacies.[5] In a post-Reformation era and culture so convinced of biblical fullness, plainness, and sufficiency, the notion that God might be willfully obscure was not wholly welcome, even while the unapproachability of God was conceded: Richard Hooker lamented how "Dangerous it were for the feeble braine of man to wade farre into the doings of the most High."[6] Robert Dallington, bemoaning the "froath" of philosophy, noted that "it is a presumption to think we can pierce the marble hardness of Gods secrets with the leaden screw of our dull understanding."[7] However, we might term this mere courtesy ignorance—to be politely acknowledged, but not long dwelt upon. The period's chief theological concern was with the hard labor of doctrinal and biblical scholarship, with limited inclination for the cloud of unknowing and the gossamer semiotics of the ineffable. A great deal has been written on the religious culture of the long Reformation, and few would claim a diminution of religious experience in these most fervent of times, but mysticism, in general, has little part in it; indeed histories of mysticism have tended to "leapfrog" early modernity, to presume its heyday was past, and that what remained was its mere devotional remnant.[8]

The intellectual culture of early modernity was, however, syncretic and voracious, given to creative recycling of tradition, medieval as much as classical, that it encountered. The central idea explored here is this: early modernity inherited a rich set of rhetorical, poetic, and logic-twisting strategies for grappling at the edge of what can and cannot be said, to negotiate the unknowable, drawn from Platonic and hermetic traditions, from a scholastic engagement with *insolubilia* and paradox, and from a variety of popular and learned mystical traditions.[9] But the seventeenth century experienced the unknowable quite differently from earlier eras—at times as a puckish game, at times as a terrible hole in a sought-for reality—and it produced its very particular array of unthinkables, which included the mechanics of creation from nothing, the character of the infinitesimal, the world's intractable character and its richness beyond the merely visible. A lush rhetoric of nescience, a grammar of ignorance came down to an era obsessed with epistemological loss, the hobbled nature of fallen thought, and the painful distance to which God had retreated (though strictly speaking, it was humanity that had moved), and the era deployed this battery of techniques beyond, though never entirely separate from, the theological. The apophatic was borrowed in a scientific register of thought.

The questions asked by a culture invested in nescience were never quite the questions asked by what would become "epistemology," never quite as clean and clinical. Many of the texts explored here can be understood as natural philosophy, but sprawlingly so, wrapped up in theology or the scriptural, while others are centered in political or religious concerns: what unites them is their deployment of the apophatic in a nondevotional register. It remains important, however, that the apophatic is always in some sense about longing, as much as it is about knowledge. The unknowability of God may have been more or less a *fact* in the eyes of early modern thinkers, but only a fact in the way that love or agony could be a fact. It was not the territory of cold, hard thinking, nor was it abstract or austere in its logic. The apophatic, as a theological discipline (of sorts) depends on *how* as much as *what* one does not know, the emotional valence of a truth glimpsed and lost. The apophatic dangles its knowledge; it tantalizes and disappears, at best a fleeting truth, only briefly *really* real. In so far as knowledge of the world's inner workings, the terrain of natural philosophy, resembled knowledge of God, it suggested something unstable and unsolid. Much of what mattered was elusive, victim of a fallen world where lack of coherence was endemic, and certain things could be known only in a manner akin to the fleeting nature of how one might encounter God.

This book does not provide an orderly account of events. To borrow Rosalie Colie's quip in speaking of early modern paradox, its subject is less the zeitgeist of the seventeenth century than a poltergeist within it.[10] Its center of gravity is seventeenth-century England, though European thought was, of course, distinctly porous. It explores the philosophical sublimity of Jacob Boehme, the German shoemaker mystic, whose account of the world before time existed and the origin of the universe was avidly consumed in England. It looks at Robert Boyle and Margaret Cavendish contending over the infinitesimal, what can and cannot be seen, and the mysterious nature of matter distended in the microscopic gaze. It addresses the skittish apophatic prose of the mystic-scientist Thomas Browne and the quasi-prophetic language of the radical Anna Trapnel. It returns frequently to the event of creation, that most inconceivable of moments, the mechanics of which positively obsessed the era, in scientific writing by Thomas Burnet and others. The Book of Job, with its chaotic account of creation, provides a starting point, and Milton's nearly omnipotent forays into the eternal provide its conclusion, making the case that the vertigo of the epic, its travels in the nontime and the nonplace of chaos, owe a good deal to the early modern fascination with the unknowable and the apophatic. Some of these writers, Boehme and Browne, for instance, are more readily associated with the mystical, but others are not. In the seventeenth century, the book will show, serious and sober scientific thought could coalesce with what would come to seem outlandish speculation. Most but not all of the chapters bear on natural philosophy. Running through them all, however, is a concern with how a rhetoric or poetics indebted to the apophatic was wrought to idiosyncratic purpose, to new problems of the knowable and unknowable.

INTRODUCTION

The miscellaneous and the amorphous character of the terms that will recur here—the unfathomable, the unutterable, the unthinkable, the ineffable—will not be carefully disentangled, because the object of attention is very much how they slip and slide into new usage. Indeed, the blur is of some importance to the terrain of the book, in which the strategies of apophatic thinking and apophatic poetics are deployed beyond sacred experience and become potent intellectual tools in other domains. Its chapters do not point to a card-carrying "School of the Unknowable" in the seventeenth century. Nor is there a shared theological or philosophical position between the writers encountered here: some are on the Puritan spectrum of religiosity and some on the Anglican; some are sober and some outlandish in their scientific or religio-political thought. They share a sense that the world or ideas they describe are in some respects unfathomable, such that they not only encounter, but need to incorporate what is beyond reason. The complexity of failing to fathom the divine, and of our terrible fallenness, which so intruded in all areas of early modern thought, spread wildflower seeds of paradox and the unknowable far and wide. Straight-up mysticism, out of the medieval traditions, may not be widely discernible in Protestant early modernity—indeed, there is a deep strain of antipathy toward the mystical and enthusiastic, but its brilliant, controversial, alogical strategies of thought were still very much alive. The argument here is that these habits of thought migrated and underwent a disciplinary shift. The strategies by which apophatic theology grappled at the edge of what can and cannot be said were purloined and deployed to quite different purposes, contributing to the rhetoric and the poetics of early modern natural philosophy.

A growing body of scholarship on early modern intellectual history has attended to the rhetorical and literary character of scientific thought, its dialogic and analogical habits, and its practices of narrative construction. Claire Preston's *The Poetics of Scientific Investigation*, for instance, shows the conscious, complex alignment of style and idea in scientific writing of the era. She discerns an emergent seventeenth-century idiom in which writers sought, in their varied generic forms, the expression of a partial and provisional understanding of the world. Figures such as Joseph Glanvill, Henry More, Robert Boyle, and Francis Bacon are evidently self-conscious in their *poetics* of scientific writing, not as mere embellishment: it was a constituent part of how one could make sense of the natural world. For writers "attuned to the incomplete character of natural knowledge," a corresponding style was required.[11] Writing of these rhetorical hinterlands where the literary and natural philosophy blur, Frédérique Aït-Touati has noted how often such works turn their gaze on creation, a widespread early modern "association of aesthetics, cosmology, and poetics . . . a demiurgic game, a meditation both geometric and poetic on creation and on the Creation, a paradoxical association of nothing and everything passing from the infinitely large to the infinitesimally small."[12] An older critical legacy on this kind of cosmopoetics, in works by for example, Marjorie Nicolson, explored the shared imaginative endeavours of the scientific and the literary, and the ways in which nascent disciplinary forms readily borrowed from each other.[13] These studies register something central about the intellectual bent of the era, how readily it turns to an outsized "cosmopoiesis" in its scientific gaze. But they do not, I think, register the marked theological character of the early modern unknowable, its resort to a theopoetics for speaking about the outer edges of experience, that which could be sensed, intuited, or glimpsed at best, and it is the poetic or the theopoetic strategies of such thought that occupy this book.

While early modernity looks, in retrospect, like a vibrant era of new ideas and relations between ideas, it did not always feel so to contemporaries. Katherine Eggert depicts a sense of stasis, even stagnation, in the thought of the era, working with "a discredited knowledge system that is nonetheless the only game in town."[14] This calcified knowledge structure, understood as a concoction of sixteenth-century humanist, religious, and old scientific ideas, necessitated what she characterizes as the exercise of strategic ignorance and amnesia, whereby ideas and their vocabularies cling on, because the problems they arise from are still deemed real. She notes, for instance, how Eucharistic theologies and questions, inherited from a scholastic framework of accident and essence, come to be discussed in early modernity in terms of alchemical change and, later, Cartesian matter theory.[15] In all likelihood, this did not do much either for theology or for the emergence of physics, but as the incommensurable frames of reference collapsed under the weight of their contradictions, the character of the era's intellectual questions shifted. A Kuhnian frame of reference—the lurching nature of scientific paradigms—might be implied in this, but seventeenth-century thought often involves a much messier disciplinary slippage, encompassing theology, imaginative poetics, and philosophy, as much as the scientific, considered in any discrete fashion.[16] The sprawling nature and organizational cacophony of early modern writings, which can move from high-caliber philosophical thought to witchcraft to the apocalypse in a single work, are familiar to many readers of such texts. Ernst Cassirer wondered, for example, why the Cambridge Platonists in seventeenth-century England, though in many ways elegant of thought, wrote such ill-shapen monstrosities.[17]

The era's penchant for digression and the labyrinthine, in writers such as Montaigne or Burton, has been widely noted, and Anne Cotterill suggests that this reeling had something threatening and something energizing about it at the same time, in that it "facilitates an oblique way of seeing, an alternative perspective and hidden or peripheral or forbidden vision."[18] Cotterill's work focuses mainly on the quasi-political use of meandering, but indirection has its theological (and philosophical) lineage, as well: the apophatic is wordy and circuitous about its inexpressible object. This concern with language that fails is the subject of Carla Mazzio's *The Inarticulate Renaissance;* Mazzio notes the era's swollen sense of its own rhetorical competence and fluency, and explores a fecund underside to this, in which its speakers flunk their eloquence, where lovers, courtiers, thinkers, or lawyers find themselves trapped in a "logic of unintelligibility." She traces some spectacular instances of bad prayer, mumbling to God, thwarted speech, and the botched word. The devil goes around with a satchel collecting up mumbles, hoarding the unsaid.[19] Language, in early modernity, was damaged, and with it, knowledge. If we poor humans were prone to bumbling and babbling, we were no less prone to babble-thinking with the same lack of elegance. There is, in the scholarship I mention here, an impressive sense of the era's makeshift character, its improvised concoction of new intellectual forms and its obsession with failure of thought. And if this was true on the microcosmic scale of human interactions, it was true too on the cosmic scale. The rich disciplinary hodgepodge so characteristic of seventeenth-century thought, where science and religion are braided together, offers some of the most startling instances of thinking in the no-man's-land of what cannot be said.[20]

Cosmology and the Unknowable

What, apart from God, was unknowable? When early modern thinkers asked about the origins of the world, the precosmological, or when they sought answers to how time was bound up with eternity—and there could be no answer that was not both exegetical, dealing with the biblical, and apophatic—they had to concede that many of the questions they wanted answers to floundered in the cosmic dark. Scholarship on early modern "cosmology" has tended, naturally enough, to think about its models of the created universe, Copernican or otherwise, of the earth and its history, or about how the era understood the laws that underlie nature, its harmony and disharmony, its contingency or necessity.[21] But alongside such subject matter, often itself speculative, there was a rich seam of writing on the utterly unrecoverable. The beginning of all things, the creation from nothing, was the subject of vast amounts of commentary, theological, philosophical, and hexameral (on the six days of creation), despite its being, or because it lay, fundamentally beyond what could be known. John Sparrow, translator of Jacob Boehme, writes about the gap between the bare biblical event of creation ("In the Beginning God Created the Heavens and the Earth") and the hidden mechanisms that must have driven it, the logistics of the Word. The Bible's explanations only deepen our ignorance and leave more unanswered than they clarify: "But it no where expounds what the Beginning, God, the Creation, the Heavens, the Earth and the Light, are, nor how God did then Create, or how spake and it was done."[22] Joannes d'Espagnet, in his *Enchyridion physicae restitutae* (1623), commenting on the deep unknowable facts of physics, writes as though it were an unfortunate oversight: "I am not at present able to lay down any positive determination concerning that first Principle of things, since it being created in the dark, could never by mans invention be brought to light."[23]

INTRODUCTION

The Book of Job occupies the opening chapter of this book, and its extraordinary place in early modern thought generates some of the central ideas here. It is not so much the lamentable and put-upon Job that is at issue, the figure who would come to be at the center of biblical theodicy, but rather the book's cosmopoesis. The Book of Job features a version of the creation far longer and more detailed than that in Genesis, rolling and seething across four chapters. But unlike Genesis, in its majestic good order, creation in Job is chaotic, precarious, close up, and loud. It is at least a little apocalyptic, with end-time falling back in upon the beginning. God, it seems, strains with the immensity of holding the logic of the universe together and recalls, by way of discordant answer to Job's pain, having given birth to the messy world, containing its molten geology, and attending to the world's anarchic variety—wild seascapes and desolate land brimming with animals. The poetic vertigo of the book, its rapid changes of scale, its sublimity, makes early modern readers dizzy. Job was widely and frequently described, by virtue of this hexameral harangue, as having a capacious scientific knowledge, because the creation that God subjected him to was understood within the framework of natural philosophy. At the same time, however, Job was also castigated by the divine voice on the grounds of his encyclopedic ignorance. He cannot know what is, perforce, unknowable. Ignorance is human. Creation, narrated in God's whirlwind logic, was, it seems, some kind of response to why he should suffer so, or perhaps a roaring refusal of an answer. In the seventeenth century, the Book of Job was not only a theodicy, or a morality play. In its atonality, its noncorrespondence between Job's abjection and God's parade of painful creation, the book represented an apophatic poetics of creation, things whose meaning and order were only ever briefly glimpsed.

It is useful to probe here what early modern writers did and did not expect to find in such inquiries into the origin of the world. In one respect, this speculative natural philosophy sought, via deduction and biblical clues, some insight into the "mechanics" of creation. There was an abiding sense that scientific logic and philosophical logic were entwined with scriptural truths. But we might note also, in this respect, Terry Eagleton's comment that to treat creation narratives as a botched attempt at *scientific* explanation is "like treating ballet as a botched attempt to run for the bus."[24] Neither Job nor Genesis, nor early modern explications of them, was trying to do the very direct, running-for-the-bus explanatory thing that modern scientific thought understands as its task, to get to the point, to fathom reality, and to minimize the unknown and unknowable. Early modern natural philosophy was wholly interested in the *poetics* of biblical creation, what was beyond understanding, only to be sensed in the gap between the biblical creation narratives—both of them—and what natural philosophy could infer. To theorize the unknowable origins of the world was an exercise in wonder, as well as in natural philosophy.

When the cobbler-philosopher Jacob Boehme wrote his dazzling hexameron, *Mysterium Magnum*, he recounted the creation of the world in an idiosyncratic industrial-erotic surge, the nearest thing, perhaps, to the cacophony of Job's theopoetics. Boehme's heaving depiction of God, continually flickering into being, positively reveled in the fugitive and playful nature of God and creation—wrestling, kissing, writhing. Boehme's "anarchic vision" of a cosmogony that consists of "moral or sentient forces" and a universe that reacts in its innermost composition to the deeds and energies of scriptural actors will not allow any aspect of the world to be over and done with, to be static.[25] There is an endemic provisionality, an inwritten wrongness to any formulation of universe or God. Neither chronology nor causality is unidirectional, but hurls wave upon wave, the constituent causes of being arriving and receding, in their "Egresse of the Spirit" and the "will of the Abysse," Boehme's enigmatic *Ungrund*.[26] None of this should make sense, entirely. Insofar as it will allow itself to be understood, it is as a fleeting shadow of a truth that cannot be calibrated or captured. *Mysterium Magnum* aimed less to describe a natural philosophical state than to *exemplify* the perplexity of the surging, enthusiastic spirit, at best a momentary understanding, which rapidly decays and is replaced. It is apophatic, Escheresque, and abyssal, one thing continually modulating into another. Boehme, the subject of chapter 2, found a wide audience across an arc of Northern Europe, from Görlitz, in what is now split between Germany and Poland, to Holland and England, and many of his works were published in translation far earlier than in his native German. The chapter makes the case that his appeal to early modern thinkers (of a certain cast) lay in his kaleidoscopic attention to the unknowable origin of things, a natural philosophy of the eternal.

To address the time before time, or the state of the eternal prior to the universe, is as giddy and hubristic an enterprise as any. It is the terrain of Milton's *Paradise Lost*, a work whose tumultuous changes of perspective are Jobean in scale. Milton has something of Boehme about him and something of Job too, though perhaps, considered as "source," they constitute no more than an oblique echo here and there within the poem. Nevertheless, the seventeenth-century obsession with the unknowable, shapeless state of things before the universe is at the core of *Paradise Lost*, a work that never loses sight of the "fact" that it takes place in the nonsequential eternal, that its words are not equal to its indescribable subject, and it revels in the vertigo of this, its interpretative abyss. Its vastness of scale and perspectival shifts cannot be calibrated to any quotidian experience. It is beyond theology, and the poem deals with realities never quite accommodated to human thought. The Miltonic unknowable, subject of the last chapter of this book, links back to, indeed grows out of the book's first two chapters, not only in their shared early modern obsession with chaos, creation, and the atemporal, but in that they convey the experience of encountering what is, strictly speaking, unthinkable. The last chapter makes the case that Milton, most unmystical of writers in some respects, produces, in his shifts of geocosmic scale, a quasi-theological, quasi-apophatic plunging into the unfathomable. *Paradise Lost* is vertiginous in other ways too, in its mazy intrusions of the fallen world into the unfallen, in its doppelgänger hermeneutics, where resemblance is as often as not misleading and our hapless postlapsarian view of things is always wrong-footed. Disorientation, the poem's "delirium" as Gordon Teskey terms it, is for Milton theological in a manner quite different from the poem's "major" theological investments, its attention to free will and the justification of the ways of God.[27] Disorientation in the hinterland of logic that tries to fathom the eternal is almost apophatic, and it is yet another turn of the screw that the ineffable in the poem is encountered as much in hell and in chaos as in Milton's heaven. The poem's sublimity—that once ubiquitous term for *Paradise Lost* nearly lost in modern criticism—is theological. Perhaps the sublime, an idea that was to become a ubiquitous term of reference in the following century, might be present throughout this book, but it might have misleading, aesthetic associations, so I engage only sparingly with the idea before the final chapter.[28]

The cosmology of the creation lost to time—which both begins and concludes this book—allowed for an entirely singular mode of speculative thought, which involved divinity, poetics, and natural philosophy. But it was not the only discursive field that borrowed from the apophatic, or that traded in the poetics of the unknowable. The ordinary world in front of natural philosophers presented ample opportunities, and it is these which occupy the central three chapters of the book. There were, of course, fundamental differences between the speculative realm of cosmogenesis and the visible, tangible objects of the present, which might be perplexing, but which could nevertheless be investigated, explored, and reasoned through, notwithstanding our fallenness. The scientific culture of the seventeenth century conceded its limits, but could hardly be accused of surrendering the mundane as something beyond understanding. On the contrary, post-Baconian and Royal Society natural philosophy, and its continental equivalents in France and elsewhere, seemed, at least in their promotional rhetoric, supremely confident. Historians of science have done a good deal to complicate narratives of scientific whiggishness, perhaps most importantly in showing that thinkers in the era were well aware that there was a point at which their "objectivity" could no longer be assured.[29] Robert Boyle, writing in his *Discourse of Things above Reason* (1681), has one of its philosophers describe a set of "Priviledg'd Things," a body of "supra-intellectual" half-ideas or semi-knowable facets of the world, things that existed, but which were not amenable to philosophical discussion. This was not a distinction between the things of reason and the things of faith, but a description of the hinterland of truths that can be intuited but remain intractable, not fully thinkable.[30] The gaze through the microscope, the controversies over what was seen there and what language and visual rhetoric could appropriately mediate its strange sensory experience, has become one of the most productive areas for historians seeking to rethink the character of early modern scientific thought, and the carefully wrought poetics of subsurface discovery and perspectival mystery have been subject to some probing analysis. Alexander Wragge-Morley, for example, in a work exploring the "empiricism of imperceptible entities," looks at how the scientific culture of the era sought common strategies to perceive and represent "both infinitesimally small atoms and an infinite, immaterial God."[31]

Chapter 4 will make the case that early modern encounters with the minuscule—the vertigo of a microreality so choppy, so counterintuitive and at odds with experience—remain alert to the unknowable character of what they come upon there, on the cusp of the perceptible. In response to this frustration, that the thing sought will always remain elusive, the "last leaf to be turned over in the booke of Nature," as Thomas Browne put it, natural philosophers concocted a poetics of distortion.[32] They found their models for this, the chapter will argue, in unpalatable places: firstly, in an inheritance of mysticism where reason buckles, but equally, in the poetics of the arch-atheist of the early modern imagination, Lucretius. Nobody wanted to be indebted to Lucretius: his atomic theories, considered as "science," were largely understood to be preposterous, but he was, nevertheless, ubiquitous in early modern scientific thought, because he provided a way of thinking about disproportion in scale and perception—a poetics of the invisible. To attend to the "merely" literary and rhetorical debts of early modern science might be seen, by some, as interesting but peripheral. The chapter argues, however, that there is something fundamentally wrong in characterizing Restoration writing on microscopy as a debate primarily over the efficiency of the technology. Or rather, although there was a good deal of debate over the technology, and the use of artificial experiment, this was always preface to, or sideshow to, more fundamental questions, including the character of the unknowable in the mundane world. A natural philosopher such as Margaret Cavendish is rendered more or less incomprehensible when the questions asked of her writings are the same as those that tend to be asked of Hooke and the Royal Society. Cavendish, whose remarkable vitalism is dealt with in chapter 4, troubles the very idea of an objective observer probing the limits of the knowable, insofar as she invests matter with a kind of knowledge, alert to its surroundings. Like Milton, Cavendish is a writer who, tonally, has little of the mystic about her, but whose ability to plumb vertiginous quarters of reality is indebted to an early modern fascination with the unfathomable.

There is, then, a rich seam of early modern thought that thrives on (or wallows in) its nescience. We might, however, set this against what has been seen as the militant optimism of the era, in a figure like Francis Bacon, who rails against the defeatism of acatalepsy—the idea that knowledge of the world is impossible—and who defies the era's endemic pessimism, its working presumption that *how* we think is a product of our fallenness.[33] It is true that Bacon's projects of knowledge (and their Royal Society imitators) might seem to run counter to the thesis of this book, but I think, nevertheless, that he shares some of its scientific-apophatic approaches. Francis Bacon is a natural philosopher who seemed, once, the embodiment of no-nonsense engagement with the world. But it is a long time since he was that epitome of empirical probity and positivism, or what Paolo Rossi describes as "the completely imaginary Bacon of Sir Karl Popper."[34] The much more complex figure we know now is more gnostic, as likely to speculate on intangible, pneumatic theories of matter as to spend his time dabbling in experiment and pure induction. More recent studies have noted a kind of early modern vertigo faced with Bacon's unabridgeable "infinitie of individuall experience," and Bacon's puppy-dog excitement with particulars in the endlessly deferred search for "natures of things."[35]

Bacon's *Novum Organum,* his deranged masterpiece, a vast mining machine for digging down into the structure of reality, has as its key tool a sprawling set of "Prerogative Instances" or "Instances with Special Powers." These constitute a spreadsheet of anomalies, theoretical instances of the unknown—in particular its "forms"—and how we circumvent our ignorance of these elusive qualities, by deducing in intricate fashion, their outcrops into the discernible. The Baconian forms are not Platonic idealizations, but involve understanding the nature of such physical qualities as "yellowness, weight, ductility, fixity, fluidity" and how they function as "latent processes" in Nature.[36] There is something utterly seductive about Bacon's vast intellectual vision, his hard philosophical logic in play with his metaphorical tricksiness, all interim steps, in *Novum Organum*, to discerning the rudiments of reality, a syntax of its most impalpable attributes, to enable the natural philosopher to "slice into nature."[37] Bacon's algebra of forms involves a detailed "presentation to the understanding of all the known instances" of a thing: a key example is heat. Bacon suggests that in order to grasp something that is simultaneously so ordinary and so unfathomable, we need to tabulate the occurrences, absences, and qualities of heat, in a kind of "big data," to quantify what it might be and what it is not, by reference to where we encounter it and fail to find it. He speculates on some twenty-seven classes of prerogative instances, though this is not meant to be an exhaustive list.[38] This is his toolkit—gimlet, wrench, and pliers, to pry reality apart, to crack the safe, philosophically speaking. We might object that, far from being the "unknowable," this is merely the unknown, and yet it is not the outer teguments of heat he seeks, or its utile qualities, but some deeper nature, the nature of which is the very mystery at issue. While there seems something absolute about the "unknowable," this is not where mere humans work. Human fallibility requires that we trade in, as Boyle puts it in *Things Above Reason*, "gradual notions of truth . . . limited and respective, not absolute and universal."[39] Bacon's descanting on murky forms of an encrypted nature can border on the Faustian, and he can very often seem hierophantic in his ambition. So while his grand designs to fathom nature fall outside the parameters of this book, I take it too that he is an ally on the borderlands of the philosophical and the quasi-mystical.[40]

The key idea that runs through the book is the early modern obsession with a poetics or a theopoetics of what cannot be said, how seventeenth-century thinkers attempted to shape language, to find mitigating strategies for the brokenness of our fallen perception. Bacon, at times haughtily insistent that he attends to *res* not *verba*, things not words, also deploys some of the most dazzling scientific metaphors of the era, in whose alchemy, ideas are transported from the provisional to the solid; it is hard to argue with a metaphor, or to dislodge it, once it has established itself.[41] If this is true in scientific thought, it is also the first rule of the mystic. The mind, in its dull rationality, needed to be tricked in order to encounter a reality that was indescribable, unattainable, more than the merely real. Some truths, those of the natural world as much as those of the divine, could only be glimpsed fleetingly, in lightning flashes, as Maimonides put it, in his *Guide of the Perplexed,* a text that remained influential into early modernity.[42] The terrible correlate of this was that "truth," be it God or the character of the Eternal, could only be grasped in ephemeral form, by outwitting our rationality. The poetics of negative theology can dazzle and estrange in a manner that produces its particular illumination, but even the most adept metaphor, the most sublime analogy, which hurls you into some encounter with the divine, will begin, in time, to pale. The power of language to move is, intrinsically, mutable. Though early modern writers attended frequently, if not obsessively, to the "essence and attributes" of God, it was also conceded that little important about the divine could be represented in propositional form. This was also true of other kinds of knowledge, that they are apprehended in a kind of flash-logic. Descartes would say as much in a note, copied by Leibniz: "The seeds of knowledge are within us like fire in flint; philosophers educe them by reason, but the poets strike them forth by imagination, and they shine the more clearly."[43]

This notion, the mutable character of truth, or the perception of truth, is addressed in chapter 3, on Thomas Browne, who shares with Boehme at least some tinge of the mystic-scientist-enthusiast, but who, in his carefully crafted prose, in his learned humanism and his medical frame of reference, seems also to be from another, altogether more sober world. For all that, however, in *The Garden of Cyrus* (1658) he writes on an elegant edge of sanity. It is a text variously scientific, erudite, and scrupulous, yet batty and demented, soaring toward its mystical finale. It is hard to say what it is about, a work so diffuse, so digressive as to defy logic, a text that undertakes to demonstrate order and pattern in the world through its chaotic, ungovernable accumulation of particulars. Sometimes a natural theology and paean to the beautiful design of the world, and at times carefully scientific in its observation of the natural world, *The Garden of Cyrus* nevertheless contrives to baffle, with its quincuncial miscellanies and its puckish shape-shifting. Exploring its rhetorical style, the chapter will make the case that Browne's text mimics something essential about apophatic longing: its ravenous character, prone to inattention and never able to rest. Though not a text with much to say about the divine, it nevertheless exemplifies a poetics to the apophatic, a protocol of metaphor, disorientating, failing, needing constantly renewed attention.

Browne is a writer in whom the scientific and the humanist are combined with careful erudition. That he shares something, tonal and gentle, with Boehme, is intuitively plausible, but at the same time, the two figures emerge from very different worlds. Jacob Boehme was much admired and translated in mid-century England, but largely this admiration was centered in radical political-religious communities, disdainful of "university learning" as dead-letter thinking, cultures of enthusiasm, and spirit-infused illumination, while Browne was averse to schism. "Behmenists" (as Boehme's followers were termed) were allied with Fifth Monarchists, Ranters, Quakers, and the like, figures who almost court incoherence. One such radical, Anna Trapnel, is the focus of chapter 5. Trapnel sits still more incongruously beside Browne, but the focus of this chapter is likewise on early modern strategies for animating tired and dead language, lightning strikes of insight. One such strategy was the prophetic, which bears closely on the seventeenth-century engagements with what lay beyond words. But prophecy was also, in the minds of many, absurd and unkempt, practised by charlatans, the self-aggrandizing and the insane, making up for its senselessness with theatricality, making up for its lack of content with spurious enthusiasm. It was also political, anarchic, and class-conscious: in the view of its detractors, in the era of the civil war, in particular, it aimed primarily to overturn order, hierarchy, and education. It consisted of cheap stunts, biblical juggling, and impressed only the gullible. Though there might be agreement on this across a wide religious and political spectrum of early modern opinion that could agree on little else, nevertheless, prophecy mattered. It did things with language, and with biblical language in particular, that were appealing. It woke language up.

Anna Trapnel's prophetic episodes in the 1650s were a phenomenon, in which a self-educated, working-class woman, a Fifth Monarchist from a shipwright family, prophesied in Westminster and grabbed the attention of London in its two weeks of tumult. From a certain perspective, this political-religious event might lie outside the book's tracing of the apophatic—Trapnel involves herself in Cromwellian political drama in a manner that is a far cry from the "mystic tradition"—but to tell the tale of the seventeenth-century apophatic without attending to this seam of prophetic enthusiasm would be to miss the most potent and radical deployment of this mystical tradition, as it manifested itself in the era. There is a fairly direct line from Boehme, whose work straddles natural philosophy and proto-theosophy, to the radical sects of the English civil war. The account of Trapnel's prophecy was taken down by a stenographer as it happened; even if she reworked the text, perhaps with the help of an unknown shorthand secretary, there is nothing like it in terms of its immediacy, and few texts illustrate so well how prophecy was understood to plumb the instability of language, adopting the deranged style of biblical prophecy, with its fragmented logic, as the proper correlate to a deranged world.

Mystical Theologies

Michel de Certeau's two volumes (the latter posthumous) on early modern mysticism provide an important survey of a subject he depicts as always already lost, its best days gone by. Mystic discourse inspired both a distaste and a longing, and produced, as if by default, "a mourning . . . the malady of bereavement," a homesickness for a kind of religious experience that was no longer quite possible, and he remarks that this was "already a hidden force in sixteenth-century thought."[44] Certeau deploys the term *la mystique*, which the translator renders "mystics," as opposed to "mysticism," with a syntactic bent similar to how we might use the word "poetics." His "mystics" implies a protean reformulation of the ineffable into political, philosophical, psychological, psychoanalytic, and other forms: "hundreds of brilliant fragments remain," writes Certeau, of the tarnished discourse, with their "quid pro quos between the hidden and the shown." It is, he comments later, "a ghost that continues to haunt Western epistemology," with its resources of uncertainty.[45] Such fragments are the subject of this book, too, the remnants of an apophatic way of thinking, its spillage in an era more interested in the character of the unknowable, its black hole in fallen reality, than in the individual in his or her spiritual-mystical longing. Some of these fragments, these habits of thought, turn up in early modern natural philosophy, and some in its politics, and the era's noisy love of prophecy. I will have various occasions on which to refer back to these traditions, but this book is not about mysticism, as such. It is, however, worth saying a little about the main coordinates of this never quite orthodox strand of religious experience, one that has often aroused antipathy, but which has never quite been absent, either, from Christian tradition, and which has a rich place in Jewish and Islamic thought.

Theology is cataphatic, wordy to the core, a "verbal riot, an anarchy of discourse," according to Denys Turner, in *The Darkness of God*, writing on medieval mystical traditions, but it also suffers its own wordiness, insufficient to its divine object. It is overburdened with its borrowings, its metaphorical character, and leans heavily on its abundant nonverbal vocabulary, "its liturgical and sacramental action, its music, its architecture, its dance and gesture." The ecclesiastical gluttony for the visual and aural, he suggests, is at least some compensation for the failure of words.[46] Turner attends to an uncertainty in the "canon" of mysticism, which at times understands its character as ecstatic and experiential, the brief lightning of understanding, shot through with love, communicable only as aesthetic, para-gnostic luminosity.[47] But as often, he finds writers resisting or qualifying the experiential, and deploying a more speculative mode of thinking about unthinkability, a dialectic of excess, the hobbled soul's ascent requiring an undoing of logic, a derangement. This is a useful distinction and qualification of how mysticism is understood. Though some of the topics explored in subsequent chapters here might be characterized as experiential, on the whole, seventeenth-century thinkers are interested in a more speculative dialectics of bafflement.

The traditions of negative theology came down to the Protestant seventeenth century tainted, because they were so often associated with Catholic mysticism and devotional practice, with dubious visions, pilgrimage, and the testimony of devout anchorites and anchoresses. And it was tainted too because its speculative theological character was so often opaque. This is a vast and unwieldy heritage, one that can hardly be outlined in any brief fashion. We can perhaps usefully divide it, following Turner's ideas on the experiential, into the popular-devotional and the philosophical-speculative strands of mysticism, though they are not, of course, clear-cut categories.[48] A good deal of the animus toward mysticism in early modernity is predicated on what was seen as its popular, concocted, marketplace nature, dangerous both because it was sponsored by Catholicism and because it was not sufficiently corralled and tamed by the church, having something anarchic about it. Popular mysticism, associated with meditation and devotion, was deeply rooted in the religious cultures of medieval Europe.[49] It was both firmly institutional, associated with popular piety and cults of saintliness, and existed on the dangerous fringes of Lollardy, and sometimes on the dangerous fringes of gender battles, in the writings of Marguerite Porete, Margery Kempe, and Teresa of Ávila, to name but a few. To these, we might add John of the Cross, the author of the *Cloud of Unknowing*, Richard Rolle, Walter Hilton, and others who recount their experiences—pious, tortured, sexual, profound. Although any such canon of mystics is a later construction, they remained in view in early modern England.[50] As with Ignatian spirituality, there was a deep ambivalence, both impressed with and suspicious of its devotional claims. Those persecuted in pre-Reformation Europe—Porete was burned and Meister Eckhart was hounded to death—could, by default, be coopted as Protestant proto-martyrs.[51]

Alongside this history of "practical" mystics, so to speak, whose domain stretched from the heretical to the quite orthodox, there were other streams of mystical and apophatic theology—Platonic and patristic—that were harder for Protestantism to ignore or disparage. There was an august patristic heritage in, for instance, Gregory of Nyssa's *Life of Moses*, and in Pseudo-Dionysius or Dionysius the Areopagite, the most astonishing theorist of the character of language in relation to the divine, and a figure to whom later chapters will return. The ninth-century Irish scholar, John Scottus Eriugena, translator of Dionysius into Latin, and author of *Periphyseon (Division of Nature)*, honed what Deirdre Carabine terms a hyperphatic theology of superaffirmation, every predicate empty in itself, yet metaphorically electric. In tandem with the writings of Aquinas and other medieval luminaries, Hugh of St. Victor's *Didasalion* did much to establish the monastic-meditative expectation that the study of the world and of natural philosophy were not only compatible with the devotional and mystical, but proper conduits through which to know and not to know God.[52]

From the fourteenth and fifteenth centuries onward, this Christian intellectual-spiritual inheritance was intertwined with the revival of a Platonic strand of mysticism in the Florentine humanism of Pico della Mirandola and Marsilio Ficino, and proved very attractive, not least in the latter's edition of and annotations on Dionysius the Areopagite, whose authenticity was later to be put through the wringer. Ficino's *Platonic Theology*, together with the era's recovery of or new attention to Philo, Plotinus, and Proclus, produced a rich neo-Platonism, with elaborate imagined lineages of ancient theology, the *prisca theologica* of Mosaic "Egyptian" hermetic knowledge, which, interwoven with Greek neo-Platonism, fed the hermetic thought of early modernity, centered most notably in England on the amorphous and prolix Cambridge Platonists.[53] Less often, accounts of Jewish and Islamic mysticisms and their medieval heritage were noted, but were not on the whole given much sustained attention in the sixteenth and seventeenth centuries.[54] Nicholas of Cusa, a writer of delirious breadth, produces some of the most important late medieval revisions to the tradition with his notion of a coincidence of opposites, his quasi-mathematical demonstrations of how irreconcilable ideas can, from the perspective of the infinite, be reconciled.[55]

Although the presence of neo-Platonism, philosophy bordering on mysticism, is well-enough established in early modern historiography, a working presumption is that the era has limited patience with the more practical and popular mysticism, that it was more or less routed in the Protestant North during the Reformation. Such a view is not meant to imply that the numinous and the holy played a reduced part in the clearly intense individual religious experience of the era, but Protestantism's recrafting of corporate religiosity brought a different set of issues to the fore, doctrinal and ecclesiastical matters, and above all, one's engagement with scripture. This narrative has been challenged and nuanced by several scholars, including Sarah Apetrei and Liam Temple, who trace the persistence of a well-theorized Catholic devotional mysticism and its opponents, and recount how this jigsawed with radical Protestant mysticism—Quakers, Philadelphians, and others—whose spirituality was frequently labeled as enthusiasm and tarred as irrationalism, with accusations of trafficking in obscurity and religious charlatanism.[56]

A large part of the story of mysticism in early modernity revolves around the prophets and enthusiasts, radicals and mystics whose engagement with the apophatic "canon" is considerable, but whose demeanor—rhetorical as well as social—has little of the contemplative, devotional character of medieval mysticism. For these porous and protean communities—Quakers, Baptists, Fifth Monarchists, Ranters—God's engagement with reality was political, in the way that the prophets of the Bible were political. I will not have much to say about the taxonomies of their political-religious radicalism, though it is important enough. What I do address, however, is their engagement with the unthinkable. Theirs was a theology, Nigel Smith comments, in his *Perfection Proclaimed*, "predicated upon an intensely rhetorical understanding of Scripture language and indeed of the world generally, despite the radical castigation of learned rhetoric."[57] This rhetoric is fissile, unstable, and it speaks to a sense of the mutable self, shaped in its mold of scripture. The language of these radicals can be shocking and can border on incoherent—this is a rhetoric aware of its own aesthetic, crafted to the mangled reality in which the cold present of England in the seventeenth century was only one coordinate of being. They lived, at the same time, in the technicolor of Revelation or the sometimes feral biblical prophets (Ezekiel baking his bread upon dung, Isaiah going naked for a sign, Hosea's sexual-political marriage antics), through which lens, time was chopped and nonsequential, and through whose poetics, the world was intrinsically a skewed half-reality. The motley prophets of the seventeenth century, in their large numbers, can hardly be said to *interpret* the scripture they so inhabit. There is little sense of an objective hermeneutic, which is applied in this or that literal, typological, or figurative fashion. Rather, it seems that they are *inside* the scripture, rattling its bars. They are its syntax. They are the connection between its parts, Old and New, bitter and sweet.

The connections between English radicalism and this mystical tradition are reasonably well established; Smith's work, for instance, notes the translations of John Everard, Giles Randall, and others into English of something like a mystical canon, and Ariel Hessayon has explored figures such as Jane Lead and TheaurauJohn Tany, in their truculent idiosyncrasies.[58] However, it is also the case that the radicals just do not sound like medieval mystics. Where the older devotional adepts might commune quietly toward an annihilation of self, into which purged space God may move, the sectarians are all noise; too political, too raucous and wild-eyed. The early modern prophetic responded to a reality that could not be fathomed, but which was resolutely political. They could, they were sure, see clearly how the theological, the cosmic, and the political structure to things was imploding, the turmoil of an eternal wrath surging into temporal being. No words but mad words could correspond. The "chopped and minced" prophetic style, both biblical and early modern, was a kind of nescience, an apophasis, responding to a chopped and minced reality.[59] It is a style, at once scriptural, borrowed, and crafted to outrage. The rapids of prophecy, their quick-fire spate of divinely infused language, in early modern sectarian writing, was a poetic hunting of truths that changed as soon as you found them.

Alongside and in response to such raving, there was a deep-seated seventeenth-century skepticism about the ruses of mysticism. Abraham Caley's *A Glimpse of Eternity* (1679), for example, characterizes the insubstantiality of the apophatic, and the emptiness of so-called mystical experience; he cites Cornelius à Lapide who comparing mysticism to a German magician's feast for "Noble Persons, who while they sate at Table, received good content, and fared deliciously to their thinking, but when they were departed, found themselves as hungry as if they had eaten nothing at all."[60] Mysticism, in such a view, looks tasty, superficially, but is entirely insubstantial. The vast and scholarly survey of mystical vocabulary by the Dutch Jesuit, Maximilian Van der Sandt (Sandaeus), *Pro theologia mystica clavis* (1640), irked some readers, even while it impressed them in its thoroughness. Edward Stillingfleet, noting with Sandaeus that mystical writers might be "obscurus, involutus, elevatus, sublimas, abstractus, & quadem tenus inflatus" (rendering the latter term "flatulent"), added that "there were some, who (not unhappily) compared them to Paracelsian Chymists, who think to make amends for the meanness of their notions, by the obscurity of their terms."[61] The problem with mystics was their courting of the opaque and the ambiguous. The premodern reader, on the whole, did not love polysemy and plenitude of meaning, but sought rather clarity, with the possible, but quite cordoned-off, exception of the Bible—ambiguity, argues Anthony Ossa-Richardson, tended to signal for early modern thinkers a lack of control, an excess and fault in language, rather than an opportunity for polysemy.[62]

Again and again, writers voice their irritation with this theological legacy and those who would reanimate it. Stillingfleet goes on to despair over Dionysius the Areopagite, in response to Carolus Hersentius's 1626 commentary on him: "God would never require from men the practice of that . . . which it is impossible for men to understand, when it is proposed to them."[63] Louis Ellies Du Pin, in his vast *New History of Ecclesiastical Writers* (1693), writes of Nicholas of Cusa's *De docta ignorantia* that the "Work is very abstract and obscure" and of his subsequent *Apology* for the work, that "the two Books of Conjectures are yet less intelligible, and less useful, and contain nothing but Metaphysical Notions, which are of no use."[64]

If early modern thinkers were alert to what might be called, in modern philosophical parlance, bullshit, or what Meric Casaubon called "mere Gulleries and Impostures to get money (as is practised to the day . . .)," the suspicion surrounding the mystical tradition was also a philological one, in a culture alert to forgery. Casaubon's attack on enthusiasm, published in the 1650s, when it was a highly fraught and politicized issue, has relatively little to say about his radical enthusiastic contemporaries, but reserves its venom for "Ancient *Theologues* and Poets, pretending to Divine Inspiration," in particular, "*Dionysius Areopagita,* the first broacher of it amongst Christians."[65] Dionysius, who is lush and poetic, but not the Pauline figure he insinuated he was, attracted serious ire, firstly for the misattributed authorship, uncovered by Lorenzo Valla and noted by Erasmus, but equally for his obscurity. Writing on Dionysius's "*Mysticall Theologie* against which I think too much cannot be said," Cauaubon finds it "apt to turn all Religion and all Scripture (in weaker brains) into mere phansie, and Teutonick Chimericall extravagancies."[66] Meric Casaubon's more famous scholar father, Isaac, had, a generation earlier, been part of the unmasking of Hermes Trismegistus, lauded by Marsilio Ficino as the conduit for this Mosaic wisdom, albeit Hermes may have been the collateral damage in Isaac Casaubon's more pressing aim, to demolish the genealogy of Catholicism in Cesare Baronio's *Annales ecclesiastici*.[67] Such hostility speaks at least in part to the dangerous appeal and pliability of mysticism, broadly construed, in an era when religion was inextricably interwoven into early modern natural philosophy as well as politics. [68] If the Reformation had exposed the Catholic proclivity to mysticism as ruse and chicanery, mystification and charlatanism, the suspicion was that the revival of its apophatic bag of tricks in the political arena, by Quakers, prophets, and radicals, was new mountebankism designed to lure the gullible and procure disorder.[69]

In his introduction to a modern edition of Pseudo-Dionysius the Areopagite, Jaroslav Pelikan cites Bertrand Russell's "celebrated *bon mot*, that he had difficulty telling the difference between a paradox that veils a profound truth and one that is simply nonsense."[70] The ambivalence we find in early modernity toward mysticism—suspicion and attraction—bears at least brief comparison with contemporary philosophical thought. The suspicion aroused by negative theology is that the runaway apophatic begins to seem a bushfire of negation, a contagion of the unutterable in which "God's name would suit everything that may not be broached, approached or designated in an indirect manner. Every negative sentence would already be haunted by God," writes Jacques Derrida, a concern that the pathological negation threatens to tether together negatives that have nothing in common.[71] John Caputo, commenting on the plurality of negatives in the apophatic, writes not only of its ruse of turning into the cataphatic—all talk, verbose and profuse—but equally of its crafty twist by which it becomes more certain than any affirmative, how it "drops anchor, hits bottom, lodges itself securely in pure presence and the transcendental signified, every bit as much as any positive onto-theo-logy," even while it insists it has, ostensibly, given up on all "representative paraphernalia."[72] There has been a substantial and sustained interest in negative theology in critical theory and contemporary philosophy, not quite post-God, but understanding the resources of the apophatic to speak to the profane much more widely. William Franke, whose writings form an important part of this, talks in his *On the Universality of What Is Not* of the "apophatic turn in critical thinking," across a substantial, modern disciplinary span. If this is the case in mystic contemporaneity, it comes with a long history of outright hostility.[73]

It is in the context of this multiform suspicion of the apophatic that the subject matter here emerges, a depiction of early modernity fascinated with the idea of the unknowable, but wary of the spiritual-intellectual lineage in which it was couched. Neither the intense personal spiritual helter-skelter of devotional writing nor the hermetic-Platonic philosophical tradition is the subject of this book, though they constitute its intellectual, and its poetical-rhetorical, background. It is not, in itself, a chapter in negative theology, and neither does it constitute forgotten episodes in the history of mysticism. It is rather about the adaptation of the apophatic, its rhetorical habits, its tropes, and its poetics, wrought to other purposes—political, natural philosophical and literary. And it shows how the seventeenth century encountered the unknowable anew, at a moment when the parameters of natural philosophy were being redefined.

CHAPTER I

The Jobean Apophatic and the Symphonic Unknowability of the World

THE BOOK OF JOB PERPLEXED early modern readers, but not in the way that it has perplexed writers in the twentieth and twenty-first centuries. Our bafflement tends to center upon a perceived rank injustice, that God and Satan *bet* on the integrity of wealthy, happy Job, blighting and playing dice with his life. Early modernity, attuned to the fathomless ways of providence, did not presume to haul God to the bar. For seventeenth-century readers, the book's difficulty and illogic lay less in its problematic theodicy, than in its creation, which recounted in its whirlwind theophany what happened at the origins of the universe not as the orderly, sequential unfolding of events, but rather as an anticreation narrative. The Book of Job was the chaotic and raucous twin of Genesis, a model of the unintelligible and of the symphonic unknowability of the world, designed to baffle and skew mere human logic, which would buckle under the weight of its contradictions. "God penned the book in such a style as Sadducees & Epicures should not care to understand it," wrote Hugh Broughton, his Sadducees and Epicures representing a skeptical and rationalizing cast of mind.[1] The Book of Job in early modernity characterized something important about scientific endeavor.

Writing of Job's being weighty with all manner of natural philosophy, Francis Bacon, in *De Augmentis scientiarum* (1623; rendered, if not quite translated, as a nine-book version of *The advancement and proficience of learning* [1640]), comments:

> So likewise that *excellent Book of Job,* if it be revolved with diligence, it will be found full and pregnant with the secrets of *Naturall Philoso-*

phy; as for example, of *Cosmography* and the roundnesse of the Earth in that place, *Qui extendit Aquilonem super vacuum, & appendit Terram super nihilum,* where the Pensilenesse of the Earth; the Pole of the North; and the Finitenesse or convexity of Heaven, are manifestly touched.²

Though in *Novum Organum* Bacon is skeptical of those who "build natural philosophy on the first chapter of Genesis, the Book of *Job,*" here he appears wholly seduced and elaborates on the "great elegancy" of its astronomy, its fullness in "Matter of Generation of living Creatures" and "Matter of Minerals."³ That Job's concern was creation, at its most capacious, was a widely shared idea in early modern thought. John Spencer, the Cambridge Hebraist, similarly asserts the breadth of its scientific framework, writing in 1663: "We find the Almighty poseing of *Job,* almost through every science," and he details where the Book of Job produces its natural philosophy "In Geometry . . . In Natural Philosophy . . . In Opticks . . . In Astronomy . . . In Arithmetick . . . In Natural History."⁴ In an era deeply invested in the idea that the Bible enfolded natural philosophy within its fabric, writers cite Job on the geocosmic and on the primal chaos, on magnetism, mining, and atomic theory. The idiosyncratic Richard Franck, in his *Philosophical treatise of the original and production of things* (1687), speaks of Job, "that famous, and most accurate mathematician," who, Franck explains, had an unparalleled understanding of the scientific: "whose Library was the Firmament, and every Star an Author, whereby he mentally inspected the Orbs; consequently the Constellations, and Machine of the Creation."⁵

This latter is a startling claim for Job's knowledge of and glimpse into the very mechanics of the cosmos, startling first in its hyperbole, but also because Job is thoroughly lambasted by God precisely because he does *not* know the secrets of the "machine of the creation": "Who is this that darkenth counsel by words without knowledge?" (Job 38.2). Over the course of four splendid, terrifying chapters, God shows Job, again and again, his outsized ignorance. Biblical theophanies—those moments when God's voice is heard directly—are typically brief. The speaking

God tends to axioms rather than the voluble. The exception to this, however, when God is positively loquacious, is his answering Job from out of the whirlwind. Job, as Franck continues, was among those select and privileged few "who personally discoursed his Creator, as did *Moses;* but confused, and astonished, as appears by his Writings."[6] Across the long slow finale of the Book of Job, the divine torrent announces how human thought can only buckle in the face of a creation intricate and incomprehensible. In a wholly sublime poetics of the unknowable, God recounts the warp and woof of the world and its complexity, to puncture the insolence and the temerity of Job's complaint at his treatment.

This, then, leads to an important paradox: Job, who is the epitome of ignorance, serves also as the epitome of knowledge for an era that took the scriptural seriously as a source of natural philosophy, in a way that earlier and later centuries could not, even while, as some had to admit, it was occasionally wrong, when speaking about natural philosophical subjects. Early modern readings of the origin of the world—Genesis, overlaid with Job, Psalms, and Ezekiel or 2 Esdras—were, very frequently, intended as something of an *anticreation* narrative, announcing not what happened, but the insufficiency of humans to grasp it. This was a Testament of the unintelligible. Scholarship on the early modern period has been alert to the Fall, and the catastrophic epistemological effects it was deemed to have had on Adam, Eve, and their progeny. But it has not, as far as I know, attended at all to the quite different scale of ignorance posed in Job.[7]

This chapter, then, pursues two ideas: in its first half, it will show the pervasive presence of Job in discussions of creation and how early modern readers discerned there our constitutional human ignorance of its processes. In its second half, the chapter argues that when early modern natural philosophy turned, as it frequently did, to the premundane physics by which the world took shape or to the nature of primordial chaos, what it sought there was something quite counterintuitive. It was not "science," in any meaningful fashion, even by early modern standards. The mechanics of creation was deemed simultaneously to be a proper object of natural philosophy and beyond human speculation.

What occurred at the creation of the world, or how it occurred—the physics of creation—was unknown and lost in time, but the intellectual encounter with the unknowable, facing our puny human limits, had something sublime about it.

Apophatic Natural Philosophy

The tale told in the Book of Job (at least how it looks in the twenty-first century) centers on a man who lives contented and prosperous in the land of Uz, but who becomes the object of celestial attention when God boasts of Job's upright nature. In what might be seen as a temptation, Satan, who flies to and fro around the earth, a celestial prosecutor rather than a hell-chained devil, suggests a game: only allow him to make Job suffer, and his godliness will not last. The bet made, Job's children are killed, his worldly property is taken from him, and he is smitten with boils. His wife in despair suggests he "curse God and die" (2.9), and though he initially rejects this, as the book continues, he comes close to doing so. After the dramatic opening, the book consists of his three comforter-tormenters misunderstanding his suffering and looking for its cause in his sinfulness, while Job refuses to concede anything to their logic, their insistence that the severity of his downfall must indicate the immensity of his failings. The back and forth of accusations continues in some of the most haunting poetry ever written, on suffering, injustice, and theodicy, with a fourth "comforter" entering the fray late on. In the strange conclusion of the book, God intervenes, speaking out of the whirlwind, and while he dismisses the comforters, he also insists that Job has no grounds on which to question, to doubt, to demand explanation for his wretchedness, the proof of which is the sheer impossible beauty and immensity of creation.

Not only was the creation of the cosmos, in its own terms, unimaginable, but equally fathomless was its place in the theodicy of a book that had to wait for the adjective "Kafkaesque" to capture its very particular warp, by which Job's accusers assert, with prosecutorial venom, that the depravity of his punishment proves his guilt. Discordance and misdirection of speech is the modal form of the book: the answers of Job and those of his comforters are consistently mismatches to the questions that prompt them. The charges against Job are never revealed to him or his accusers, only speculated upon, and God's final set piece (out of the whirlwind) is the most sublime dissonance, seemingly divorced from what has gone previously, with its fog of category error, its elusive and rapid shifts of subject from one matter to another, insisting on Job's perspectival ineptitude. Though the early modern era never quite understands the Book of Job to be putting God on trial—and I will return to what it does make of the book—it nevertheless "strikes a Discord in the Readers ear," as Richard Franck puts it.[8] The lawyer, William Clark, in his set of *Poetical exercitations* (1685), attempts with his paraphrase to rectify the discontinuous fabric of the book, having "endeavoured to connect the several Texts in continued Discourses, notwithstanding of the abrupt transitions from one Subject to another."[9]

That early modernity understood Job in relation to scientific knowledge and human ignorance had important effects. Natural philosophy was some kind of answer to suffering, or at least, natural philosophy in the key of discontinuity and atonality. The dazzle and the sublimity of these final chapters in the Book of Job emerges, in part, from their sheer categorical chaos, even while, after a fashion, the taxonomy of the speech as a whole is orderly. The theophany proceeds from the churning of earth into being, out of chaos, the monumental division of the sea from the land and the creation of the elements (chap. 38), on to the intricacy and cornucopia of animal beauty in its delirious variety (chap. 39), and the close-up magnificence of the Behemoth and Leviathan (chaps. 40–41), in their awful and mysterious complexity. This is hexameral structure, following the sequence of creation in Genesis. Accounts of the geocosmic and gravitational hanging of the earth upon nothing (chap. 26) and the geoterrestrial underearth, with its deep mines (chap. 28), only added to what the era understood as the scientific comprehensivity of the book. Everything and more from the six days of creation was here, and early modernity was attuned to the notion that this was a structure proper to the scientific study of the world.[10]

And yet to note its hexamera does not really convey its poetics of the impossible—the shuttling of metaphors, by which the animate is constructed from the inert, and the immense is rendered minuscule. The

CHAPTER 1

Book of Job may describe the same once-only event as Genesis, but it does so in so alien a mode as to render the creation strange and horrific. Job's whirlwind theophany tells the tale of what happened at the origins of the universe not as the orderly unfolding of events, but rather as cosmic paradox, impossible geologies tumbling into being: less what occurred, than the insufficiency of humans to grasp its complexity.

The voice from the whirlwind in the Book of Job offers a version of creation as a process of divine chaos and spawn, of monumental geo-architecture, the uncontainable toppling of materials out of chaos, whose process was no less than a birth:

> Where wast thou when I laid the foundations of the earth? declare, if thou hast understanding. . . . *who* shut up the sea with doors, when it brake forth, *as if* it had issued out of the womb? When I made the cloud the garment thereof and thick darkness a swaddlingband for it. (38.4, 8–9)

In quoting Job, it is important to include the Authorized Version's italics—they indicate editorial intrusions, words that are not there in the Hebrew, but which have been inserted to render the probable sense in English. The force of the poetry is at least in part dependent upon considering the verses *without* the fillers, and the syntactical oscillation and leap by which we produce the sense. This God knows what it is not only to give birth, but to give birth to the stoniness of ice, and this may or may not be metaphor. God may or may not, in Job, be using the womb as a simile. Later we return to this same cold impossibility: "Out of whose womb came the ice? And the hoary frost of heaven, who hath gendered it?" (38.29). This is the God who both contains and lets loose: "*who* shut up the sea with doors, when it brake forth."

While the disorderly waters of this birth-deluge looked, to early modernity, as though it might be a natural history, it was an order of nature in which strangeness, the sheer dark unthinkability of making the world, was also at issue. The world was a reproach to our ignorance:

> [Who] brake up for it my decreed *place*, and set bars and doors, And said, Hitherto shalt thou come, but no further: and here shall thy

proud waves be stayed? . . . Hast thou entered into the springs of the sea? or hast thou walked in the search of the depth? (38.10–11, 16)

God, in the Book of Job, suffered in the making of the world. Creation was agony. And even accepting that none of this was literal, that it was accommodated to human intellectual insolvency and insufficiency—nevertheless, the theophany renders creation as exquisite pain. It is not just that Job cannot grasp the mechanics of creation, its feats of geological engineering; these chapters are about the ache of creation. The God who is impassible, unsuffering, unchangeable, records creation for Job not from the serene and distant perspective of the cosmic viewing deck (which viewing deck we are safely on, in Genesis), but down where the turbulent work was being done. This creation is violent and Blakean. It is catastrophic and risky, and Job, or the reader, is made to experience it close up. Its forces, the sea, the chaos, the oozy foundations of intractable matter are threatening, and almost animate. If this is the same event as stately Genesis, it is a very different poetic.

But the theophany is disorienting as much by its vertiginous shifts of scale, that the God who calibrates gravity in the hanging of the earth must also attend to the stupidity of the ostrich: "Which leaveth her eggs in the earth . . . And forgetteth that the foot may crush them, or that the wild beast may break them" (39.14–15). He has to take care of empty space as much as fullness. Who, God cries, has responsibility like his, "to cause it to rain on the earth, *where* no man is; *on* the wilderness, wherein *there is* no man; To satisfy the desolate and waste *ground*" (38.26–27). Creation was as much about capturing this unreckonable scale of things, this divine incommensurability by which the maker of worlds would attend also to the breathy snorting of a warhorse: "He paweth in the valley, and rejoiceth in *his* strength: he goeth on to meet the armed men . . . He saith among the trumpets, Ha, ha; and he smelleth the battle afar off, the thunder of the captains, and the shouting" (39.19–25), what God pre-imagines as the thrill of war from a horse's perspective—an equinethropomorphism or theohippothropomorphism, perhaps.

It is quite difficult for us to recover the strangeness of Genesis 1, its cosmic scale, its sublime. It is so well-trodden a text that it can come to seem banal or stubbornly straightforward, but this was not how early modern commentators encountered it. Genesis depicted a stately, musical ceremony of creation, what William Franke calls the "measured, cadenced unfolding of the event."[11] This was what good order felt like, a neatness and precision of natural philosophy at its most majestic, a creation whose logistics and loveliness were military and mathematical in their fine timing. Readers were inordinately proud that Moses was praised in Longinus's *On the Sublime* in counterpoint to Homer and Hesiod, even while classical natural philosophy, evidently more sophisticated than the Hebrew, was accused of cribbing its genius from Moses.[12] Theophilus Gale comments: "Pagan Physicks, or Natural Philosophie . . . seems evidently traduced from the first chapter of Genesis, and some Physick Contemplations of Job."[13] This fact, that Genesis itself was understood as balletic and majestic, rendered Job still more discordant.

While Job's hexameral order looks momentarily as though it is a natural history (at least early modernity certainly sought natural history there), it is an order of nature in which strangeness, the sheer dark unthinkability of constructing the world, plays an essential part. This idea, that Job embodied the unknowable, and that nature would always, ultimately be encountered as enigma, was widespread in seventeenth-century comment on the book. John Vincent Canes, for example, in his *Fiat lux* (1661), discusses the "Obscurity of nature," how the internal logic of the world's workings is bafflingly opaque, and how the theophany of Job 38–41 demonstrates repeatedly "the mode, method and chain of operation utterly hidden," going on to note that

> our ignorance of nature is sufficiently insinuated and evinced . . . The whole world is an immens intangled gordian knot which the wisest of men could never yet untye, or discern the intermingled series of the many voluminous causes concatenated therein.[14]

William Clark has God lambaste Job's inability to plumb the obscure, or to grasp what should be, comparatively, straightforward: "Sure thou who understand'st not what is light, / Which every day is obvious to thy sight, / Canst never understand *obscurity,* / A thing that's not perceptible by th' eye."[15] God from the whirlwind makes language buckle under the paralogical strain of failing to comprehend. To think oneself into the mind of God is to implode, and writer after writer concedes that they are in the presence of the unthinkable: "Can a Man behold God in the vast Works of his Creation, and not be self-debased, and as it were *self-annihilated* thereby," writes Matthew Barker.[16] Natural history and natural philosophy merely skim surface reality: "Man is ignorant, as well of what is obvious, as of what is hid," notes George Hutcheson, going on to consider Job's scientific master class: "The scope also of those *Instances* being to point out the *Incomprehensibleness* of the *Counsels* of God."[17]

For early modern readers, however, there was also purpose to this illogic, and to its runaway metaphors. Natural philosophy that would attend to the scriptural origin of the world understood its task to be at least in part a matter of understanding the varied *poetics* of Job and Genesis. Joseph Caryl, writing in his multivolume and at times quite lovely *Exposition upon the Book of Job*, discusses this midwifery of a turbulent creation, and suggests that the waters of Job, the numerous contradictory representations of the sea, its tumult and its calm, at once icy and natal, gives a glimpse, albeit partial, of the divine. According to Caryl, "The Sea hath in it a representation of God himself in his divine perfections," or more particularly the divine unfathomable, his "hiddenness and unsearchableness," which we can only glimpse in the paradoxes that scuttle our abilities to reason: "there is not line enough in the understanding of Men and Angels to reach the bottom of God; he is a sea without banks or bottom."[18] Not only does the creation demonstrate our ignorance, but it says something too about God's strangeness, his utter alterity.

The poetics of the whirlwind returns repeatedly to the baffling causes that lie unrecognizably behind things. Natural phenomena, says Caryl, announce their own unfathomability: "The sea is a clear emblem of all obscure and unknown things, especially of those ways of God which are too deep for our discovery, and lie beyond the reach of our knowledge." We are, the argument goes, constitutionally baffled: "The Lord would have us satisfie our selves in the ignorance, or rather nescience of those natural things which he hath not made known to us."[19] Discussing

God's zigzag of madcap accusations, Caryl notes of the question, "Hast thou entred into the springs of the sea?" that among the etymologies, some "derive the word from a root, which signifieth to be infolden or intangled; and so they render it, Hast thou entred into the perplexities or intricacies of the sea?" And he derives from this a picture of human perplexity, that there is an invisible knottiness in the confluence of many springs, such that they cannot and will not be distinguished. The water in spate leaves no trace of its cause and origin. It is the vast effaced evidence of the divine, on which Caryl part-cites and comments on Psalm 77: "His way is in the sea, and his path in the great waters, and his footsteps are not known. Goings upon the water leave no print behind them, we cannot observe a track in the sea."[20] Job is, for early modernity, a text that proffers a brief, frenzied divine epistemology, the creation of a thing of such strangeness that only the book's wild poetic can approximate it.

Thomas Burnet's *Telluris Theoria Sacra* (1681), his *Sacred Theory of the Earth*, one of the most controversial and influential scientific works of the late seventeenth century—measured at least in terms of vehement response—has some quite thoroughgoing observations on the Book of Job as a model of scriptural style when it addresses matters of natural philosophy, commenting that

> the Divine Writings, upon the Origin of the World, and the formation of the Earth, seem to me to be writ in a stile something approaching to the nature of a Prophetical stile, and to have more of a Divine Enthusiasm and Elocution in them, than the ordinary text of Scripture; the expressions are lofty, and sometimes abrupt, and often figurative and disguis'd.[21]

Burnet's deployment of "Divine Enthusiasm" might cause some to bristle. Enthusiasm, generally a term of abuse, implied delusion, fanaticism, and frenzy.[22] Biblical prophets—and this is enlarged upon in chapter 5—were not generally said to *enthuse*, as such, even while they were the generic model for those who pretended to divine inspiration: but the "Prophetical stile" certainly involved something inflamed. The prophets gush and rage in uncontrollable supralogical torrent; they are beyond and outside themselves. They are figures though whom the inchoate and ireful Word pours, channeling anger and threat in broken allegory and wild metaphors. The implication was that the divine message produced in the merely human vessel of the prophet a kind of seizure of word and a crumbling of logic. The reader needed to be correspondingly sober and prudent in reading the prophets whose characteristic mode is hyperbole.

In describing the Book of Job and its whirlwind account of creation as being written in a prophetic style, however, Burnet is referring to God's words, not his conduits. While the prophets, negotiating the anger of kings and the blockheadedness of people, needed to shock and outrage, the divine voice surely did not need such strategy, such subterfuge. But it becomes clear that what Burnet has in mind here is the mode of *interpretation* that the reader adopts in approaching the work. Burnet's account of the properties of scripture describes the need for at least a little enthusiasm in the exegete. Scripture demands polyphonic interpretation in response to its cacophony: "Philosophical descriptions in Sacred Writings, like Prophecies, have often a lesser and a greater accomplishment and interpretation," and the reader is required to allow both of these intentions to coexist:

> And it commonly happens so in an Enthusiastick or Prophetick stile, that by reason of the eagerness and trembling of the Fancy, it doth not always regularly follow the same even thread of discourse, but strikes many times upon some other thing that hath relation to it, or lies under or near the same view.[23]

The "thread of discourse" in Job is tugged and stretched, both from verse to verse and across the book more fully. It is out of sequence, and we need to connect some one thing in the text to "some other thing that hath relation to it." This in turn bears on its diffuse scientific content, the parts of a jigsaw puzzle that needs to be reassembled. When the scriptures are opaque, Burnet suggests, it denotes a need for interpretative ingenuity: "So as, all things consider'd, what might otherwise be made an exception to some of these Texts alledg'd by us, *viz.* that they are too obscure, becomes an argument for us: as implying that there is something more intended by them, than the present and known form of the Earth."[24] Burnet's text is remarkable—a splendid, demented farrago of the biblical and the scientific, a full-blown account of natural history and geomorphosis, and I return to it briefly at the end of the chapter. Here though, I cite Burnet less in his role of natural philosopher than as subtle exegete, as he often is, in his understanding of the poetics of Job, having something of the prophetic about it, with its vertiginous leaps and its disorientation in the fabric of the world.

Early modern writers were very much aware of the musicality and grandeur of the cosmology of Genesis. But they understood it in relation to the cacophony, the atonality of Job, its style as a function of creation poetics that circumvented, that short-circuited human logic. William Hodson, in his *Divine Cosmographer* (1640), speaks of the description of the Leviathan exemplifying the aesthetic of Job, "which for acutenes, vigour and majestie of style doth farre exceed what ever we can fetch from the schools of Rhetoricians," while Edward Reyner, writing on its "lofty and elegant Stile," notes that "Job stretched all the veins of his wit in an eloquent way, to express the greatness of his grief."[25] Another account comments on the biblical poetic and prophetic books: "yet the Matter is most sublime . . . the Style more elyptical, concise, and abstruse," going on to note its discontinuities "in many places, without any Connexion of Antecedents and Consequents."[26] Such descriptions speak to a sense of unease at the illogic and disjointedness of a work that was sometimes attributed to Moses, albeit tentatively and on the basis of traditional rabbinic speculation.[27] Why would Moses or whoever had written the Book of Job, they wondered, produce a work so at odds with the clarity of Genesis?

The scientific edge that the Book of Job acquired in seventeenth-century thought is not the full story, of course. In an era so besotted with soteriology, with the causes and causelessness of damnation, with questions of the foreknowledge, forewilling, and predestination of events, the Book of Job was an essential work. It might serve, for some, to mitigate the despair engendered by the era's harsh theological options, when a figure who looked for all the world conspicuously damned could prove in the secret accounting of God to be righteous, after all. Job was a book of comfort in one's trials. For others, of course, it might engender despair, that good and bad fortune were so arbitrary. The Book of Job was a significant text in the formation of Protestant understandings of character and selfhood, and an emergent theodicy of the period.[28] It received extensive attention in the explications of Calvin, Beza, and other theologians, in works that dwarfed the book itself, as well as significant older commentaries by Gregory the Great and Aquinas.[29] Among the still larger exegetical projects in the seventeenth century, George Hutcheson produced 316 lectures, constituting his *Exposition of the book of Job* (1669), while the multivolume work of Joseph Caryl, *An exposition with practical observations upon . . . the book of Job* (1643–53), mentioned previously, was issued in twelve vast and phenomenally popular volumes.[30] On top of these, and working to quite different ends, there were numerous poetic "paraphrases" or elaborations, such as Arthur Brett's 150-page *Patentia victrix, or, The book of Job in lyrick verse* (1661) or William Clark's 370-page *The grand tryal, or, Poetical exercitations upon the book of Job* (1685), as well as versions by Du Bartas, George Sandys, Zacharie Boyd, and others.[31] Suffering Job, it has been noted in studies by Hannibal Hamlin and Victoria Brownlee, may be a model for King Lear, or at least King's Lear's impression of himself.[32] Job had, in addition, a steady place in the homiletic literature of the early modern sermon culture.[33] These more evidently theological facets of the Book of Job are essential to its place in Christian thought—Job might be a type of Christ or a model of the vehement, suffering martyr, who refuses to surrender his faith, a broken man who nevertheless produces his resonant declarations: "Oh that my words were now written," he proclaims, "oh that they were printed in a book! That they were graven with an iron pen and lead in the rock for ever! for I know that my redeemer liveth and that he shall stand at the latter day, upon the earth" (19.23–25). This understanding of Job runs down the Christian centuries, and Job in Jewish thought is wretched in other ways still.[34]

    The book's role as a pivotal work of natural philosophy, in contrast, is more idiosyncratic to early modern exegesis. Few places of scripture struck such a geocosmic chord as the verses of Job on the erection of the world in empty space, pinioning the formless abyss with geographical specificity: "Hell is naked before him, and destruction hath no covering. He stretcheth out the North over the empty Place, and hangeth the Earth upon Nothing" (Job 26.6–7). Even those keen to disavow any too literal an understanding from this could not but speculate on how to apply it: "I have wondred much at the Curiosity (how learned soever) of some who undertake to set downe the subterraneous Geography of this place," writes John Gregory, of attempts to second-guess the entrance to hell. He goes on, "The North here is not to be taken for the Terrestriall Globe, as the Jewes would have it," but this leads him only to a greater cosmological framework: 'The North is meant of the Heavenly Expansum . . . And though the North onely be nam'd, yet the whole spheare is meant."[35] At issue here was the enigmatic word *Tohu*, the "nothing," or "confusion," that occurs both in Genesis and here in Job. Gregory clarifies (if that is the right word): "God in the beginning (as Mercator deviseth) strucke a Center in the Tohu or Inane, indued with that quality as might call unto it the congeniall parts of the Chaos, which immediately applying themselves gathered into this Globe."[36] The careful and ongoing management of this act was to be seen in the "magnetical vigour," which was the essential force of the earth's continual stillness with respect to the cosmic gravitational tug, so that "if by Staticall impulsion as Archimedes undertooke" the earth is pulled one way, it rights itself.

Thomas Browne, writing with Vallesius's *Sacra Philosophia* (1600) in mind, similarly considered it to bear on geomagnetism, while he also refers his experiments on the congelation of water and the qualities of mineral formation to Job, noting that it "well accordeth with that expression of God, Job 38."[37] Writing of the creation's "excellent expression," John Arrowsmith, in 1660, describes the pendent world in terms that sound like a cosmic party trick: "God hath so made it, as to make it admirable to our understandings; that . . . a body so heavy, should yet be able to hang, as it doth, in the midst of the air!" But the sequential unfolding of the world in Genesis had its very particular heuristic purposes: "God could have done all things in a moment, yet it pleased him to be six dayes about this great work."[38] Job had a part to play in scientific argument from astronomy to atomism. Kimberly Hedlin writes on the use of Job by Diego de Zuñiga, in his *In Job Commentaria* (1584), in astronomical arguments to support heliocentrism.[39] William Clark, a lawyer with a bent for natural philosophy, transposed God's Jobean works into an atomic puzzle:

> Dost know how every Atome doth support
> Each other in *that Mass* in such a sort,
> As no part upon any part doth rest,
> Nor are light parts by heavy parts deprest,
> But altogether solid, firm, and sure,
> Ly in one lump, by *Aequilibrature:*
> And for the *Air,* that subtile, fluid, thing.[40]

God's dressing down Job, "Where wast thou when I laid the foundations of the earth?" (Job 38.4), conceals within it, for Clark, an atomism, a physics of planetary gravity, by which the earth hangs, miraculously: "how a thing / Of so much weight, i'th' open air can hing [sic], / Without some Nail."[41] If a figure such as Clark is undistinguished in his scientific credentials, Robert Boyle is a far more substantial natural philosopher, and he too addresses how we can apply the physics implicit in the scriptures. In his physico-theology, *Of the High Veneration Man's Intellect owes to God* (1685), Boyle lists a medley of dazzling qualities of earth and cosmos in spin: the character of motion and churning fluidity, its surge of whirlwinds, the velocity of bullets, and the whirl of the earth's vortex, citing Job as God's claim to the mathematics of vortices and the authorship of all tumultuous motion.[42]

The attribution of scientific acuity to Job was both thoroughgoing and, at the same time, honorary, in the sense that it might be granted to be true, without having any serious consequences—Job might have known things, but he did not commit them to posterity. And, some noted, the natural philosophical knowledge of biblical antiquity was, by early modern standards, quite rudimentary. If Job was outstanding, it was only by comparison with the "vulgar Israelites." The "penmen of Scripture," writes John Wilkins, "might yet be utterly ignorant of many Philosophicall Truths, which are commonly knowne in these dayes." Even Solomon ("strangely gifted with all kinde of knowledge") and even Job might have been impressed with the erudition of someone like Wilkins himself:

> 'Tis likely that *Job* had as much humane Learning as most of them, because his Booke is more especially remarkable for lofty expressions, and discourses of Nature; and yet 'tis not likely that he was acquainted with all those mysteries which later Ages have discovered.[43]

Responding to Wilkins, Alexander Ross, who plays the role of intractable Aristotelian in the exchange, expresses exasperation that Wilkins does not distinguish between the ordinary unknowable, those questions which, though difficult to know, are not theoretically impossible, questions which are googleable (I paraphrase), and that which is God's "hid and unsearchable" domain. Ross rails:

> what should be the cause of his [Job's] stupidity, and of your [Wilkins's] quicknesse of apprehension? Alas! how doe wee please our selves in the conceits of our supposed knowledge, whereas indeed wee have but a glimmering insight in Natures works, a bare superficiall and conjecturall knowledge of naturall causes?[44]

Twentieth-century readings of the Book of Job are very frequently aghast at how previous eras seem to miss the scandal of the theophany almost entirely. God may insist Job has no right to ask for explanation, that the reasons are not to be probed, and his providential edicts must be met only with human patience, because he cannot know the complexity of things; but while Job may be ignorant of the cause of suffering, the reader is not.[45] God's reason for permitting the evil and Job's exquisite pain, is very plainly his whimsical bet with Satan, his divine boast about his servant Job's incorruptible nature. God was, we might say, seduced and tempted by the wily Satan to allow Job to be the playground for the divine wager. Job is the apple. The Book of Job, seen this way, is a testament to cosmic peer pressure. It is abyssal and a too-beautiful abomination, the book of the Holocaust and the atheist's first article of evidence. Job, says Simone Weil "struggles like a butterfly pinned alive into an album . . . nailed to the very centre of the universe."[46] Why, we might wonder, did earlier exegesis not attend to the work synoptically, structurally speaking? Why does it not return to, or be outraged by the very fact of, the bet? The answer is no doubt that, according to early modern lights, this must be a misreading, because to posit thus of God is so plainly not the action of a just God. If some readers noticed that Satan could goad God with Machiavellian cunning, they did not commit that to writing. If we gasp at the blind spot of such readings, however, it is worth noting that seventeenth-century readings are not so dissimilarly aghast at those who, almost willfully, would not see the intricately crafted natural philosophy of Job.

The "creation" sequence of the book—with its jagged logic, its categorical incongruity, and its cosmic nescience—might to a modern eye seem conspicuously, gratuitously at odds with what has come before.[47] The cause of Job's suffering, the question that has animated the book's searing dialogue between comfortless comforters and Job, remains unexplained. God does not sheepishly concede it was a bet, and no early modern account that I have found suggests any outrage at the divine flippancy. Even while, occasionally, the creation theodicy—suffering or evil being as inexplicable as the mechanisms of creation—is simply excluded from a paraphrase or commentary, on the whole, post-Reformation readers were agreed that God in the theophany is chastising human impertinence for even addressing his divine and volatile pleasure.[48] Job himself undergoes the whirlwind of divine wrath, the mighty blast of the infinite, for his temerity, and yet he is deemed to have satisfied God, to have won him his wager, presumably. On the basis of a comment in the New Testament (". . . for an example of suffering affliction . . . Ye have heard of the Patience of Job" [James 5.10–11]), Job came to exemplify and embody patience. This is very frequently the leitmotif of exegetical works, even though the book itself does not mention the term and many readers, early modern ones among them, recognized that Job seems conspicuously impatient with his lot, that after his initial shock during which he sits traumatized on a dunghill, he is not really a suffer-in-silence type.[49] God's refusal to answer in any terms beyond citing his own greatness cannot but be disturbing. Accused of injustice, he changes the subject. Early modernity routinely cites God's privilege and providence as the message, and I have not found any evidence of readers supposing the bet to be unseemly, but that is not to say readers did not feel uneasy, or did not have qualms. Hugh Broughton, bringing his philological and linguistic expertise to the work, suggested that the book's twisted logic served to undermine the vanity of worldly readers, but he concedes that he too has difficulty, in part with the Hebrew (unlike any other in dialect) and in part with the theology: "And of my selfe I wil say, that the tongue, in proprietie and trope and sequeles of arguments, hath ben harder to me, then all the rest of the Bible."[50]

Early modern exegetical practice was attuned to the idea that incongruity was there for a reason. Robert Boyle, in his defense of the scriptures, writes: "Sometimes, nay oftentimes, the Inspir'd Discoursers seem to say things not onely Incoherent but Contradictory."[51] That one text stood in baffling or obscure relation to another, however, merely tasked the reader with reconciling the discordant texts—the Bible's multiperspectival quality was a bedrock hermeneutic presumption. Job demanded that Genesis be read as intractable. Lucy Hutchinson's retelling of Genesis, *Order and Disorder* (c. 1664), for example, insists on what seems a duty to the unfathomable, that the majestic order be tied to its sublimity and its mystery, the elaboration of Genesis prefaced and punctuated by frequent references to Job in its biblically annotated margins, but its implicit reference is fuller still; for her, creation is shot through with our inability to comprehend it:

> Easier we may the winds in prison shut,
> The whole vast Ocean in a nut-shell put,
> The Mountains in a little ballance weigh,   Es. 40.12
> And with a Bullrush plumm the deepest Sea,
> Than stretch frail humane thought unto the height
> Of the great God, Immense, and Infinite,
> Containing all things in himself alone,   Job 38
> Being at once in all, contain'd in none.[52]

To contain the "Ocean in a nut-shell" was a near-proverbial trope of things beyond "frail humane thought," in the face of the creation dissonance of Job.⁵³ Hutchinson describes a bleak stew of primordial chaos, in which place was indistinguishable from place, in which the formless earth was mere churning dark potential:

> The Earth at first was a vast empty place,
> A rude congestion without form or grace,
> A confus'd mass of undistinguisht seed,
> Darkness the deep, the Deep the solid hid:
> Where things did in unperfect Causes sleep.⁵⁴

This Jobean seething of chaos is not just preplace, but precausal, with even its riddle and mystery not yet formed. When Hutchinson says, "Darkness the deep, the Deep the solid hid," she has the verb "hid," at the end of the phrase, governing both of these clauses (the rhetorical trope of hypozeugma), so that the darkness hid the impenetrable deep, inside which was hidden the solid: nested incomprehensibility, boxes inside boxes, out of which chaos the world was produced. This crawling deeper and deeper into the unfathomable is the gambit of the Book of Job, which is recalled, frequently, and whose tropes and metaphors are woven into the descriptions. Hutchinson's account of the world's origin is explosive:

> Th' allforming Word stretcht out the Firmament,
> Like azure curtains round his glorious Tent,   Psal. 104.2,3.
> And in its hidden chambers did dispose
> The magazines of Hail, and Rain, and Snows,
> Amongst those thicker clouds, from   Job 38.22,23.
>   whose dark womb
> Th' imprison'd winds, in flame and thunder come.⁵⁵

That the firmament is the product of "allforming Word" from the Gospel of John suggests its various enigmatic theologies of language as the propulsive energy of creation. Here, though, God stretching out the skies in the manner of a spectacular tapestry or superb laundry, serves to envelop and enclose the dramatic act. At the crucial moment, a curtain is drawn round—we might be reminded of the bad magician from *The Wizard of Oz*—and within his "hidden chambers," God produces the all-dizzying storm-force, and hectic elements, "th'imprison'd winds" and electric animation. This creation is never quite finished, in the sense that it is enmeshed in and prepared for its future, both in its pulsing fecundity and in the reference to its "magazine," a military storehouse for cosmic ammunition of hail, rain, and snow. The Jobean presence in creation epic is, of course, far from unrecognized, and the final chapter will take this up in relation to Milton. Job serves, again and again, not merely to elucidate the cosmic mechanics by which the chaos and the nothing are wrenched into being, but rather to announce the inscrutable and the impenetrable nature of that process. Gazing into the wellsprings of the book of nature—that most bidden task for early modern natural philosophy—produced only intractable noncomprehension.

Creation Poetics and Mosaic Cosmology

These disorientating uses of Job—poetic, prophetic, and "scientific"—throw light on the era's obsession, a more or less insatiable passion, with cosmological, geological, and animate creation. Scholarship is well attuned to the differences between the seventeenth-century "literal" understanding of the creation story—which was shared more or less without demur by scientists, scholars, and philosophers—and the stony biblical literalism that developed in the nineteenth century as a response to Darwinian ideas, insistent on the inerrancy of the Bible's undigested word, its surface, its lexical shell. The "literal" can mean many things.[56] Early modern writers very often imagined creation in concert with, rather than in opposition to, natural philosophy. Nevertheless, we can still plausibly wonder what kind of truth thinkers thought they were getting when they theorized the origins of the earth, the creation of Genesis, or the creation of Job? The counterintuitive answer, I think, lies in the very unknowability that baffled human efforts to comprehend things. Seventeenth-century writing returns frequently to creation as the cold plunge into nescient awe, a bracing dose of unknowing. The era understood the scriptures to be both poetic and literal, at the same time—they were unimpeachably true, but they were also fantastic and ungraspable.

Early modern scientific and philosophical thinkers were at home with, indeed insistent upon the notion that natural philosophy was not only compatible with the biblical, but deeply entangled with and indebted to the mesmeric clues offered by the scriptural, beyond anything the meager resources of human reason or experience could discover alone; science at its cutting edge, in matter theory, in cosmology, in mathematics, in natural history, was there *in utero* in the scriptures, awaiting dilation.[57] The Bible was not by any means deemed a repository of ungainsayable detail. Moses could even be cavalier with mere fact, and it was not uncommon to note how limited the Hebrew parameters of knowledge were, often with the caveat that this was accommodated to the capacity of the audience. Yet writers also insisted that the Bible mattered in understanding natural philosophy, with such discussion becoming ever more detailed over the course of the seventeenth century. This "Mosaic philosophy" can, in its sixteenth-century form, seem quite blunt and crude. Moses, commanded to describe "the beginninge of the worlde, and creation of all thinges," writes Lambert Daneau, "is either a vaine fellowe, or a lier, if the knowledge of naturall Philosophie be not conteined in the holy Scripture." The "Mosaic physics" or "Mosaic Cosmology" that ensued involved a complex symbiosis of exegesis and natural philosophy [58] As things moved on, however, the scientific became more palpable, more sophisticated, more outlandish—atomic, Cartesian, geological readings of the scriptures—while refusing to concede it was thereby less literally scriptural. So outlandish is the *physica sacra* of the era that it is often difficult to imagine it as "literal" interpretation at all. But, as Peter Harrison has shown, such flights of physics were literal, or "modifications of the literal," in that they referred to the physical realm, not the allegorical or the spiritual.[59]

Even the most devoted of exegetes might be expected to concede that there was not actually much there in the Bible, by way of science, but in general, readers were still more impressed with its concision, what they imagined was folded in. Samuel Gott's *The divine history of the genesis of the world* (1670), a text that relates its exegesis with some enthusiasm to advances in "Mechanical Arts," was impressed with the brevity through which Genesis communicated its natural philosophy: "in this

Divine History, we have the *Genesis,* and System of the whole World, in one Leaf, yea one Page, delineated as in a Mapp."[60] Indeed, he was keen to counter the idea that God's primal action was confined to the role of mere producer, and he traduced those who, in reading the beginning of Genesis, "say he made only Matter and Motion" or that "this Spectable World from a Chaos, or from Matter only diversified by its own Motion, Figure, and the like; whereas God expresly declareth that he Produdced [sic] it out of a Chaos in the Six Days Works."[61]

There was, alongside this, some resistance to such exegetical excess. George Hughes, writing his *Analytical exposition of the whole first book of Moses,* comments on what he takes to be the all-too-common imposition of the scientific on the scriptural: "If it fall into the hands of a supercilious Philosopher he may think it strange, and possibly be angry too that the author should passe over the 3 first Chap. and not . . . vent some new Hypothesis to the world." The problem, Hughes implies with fine-tuned sarcasm, was the effort to entangle contemporary science and the biblical: "what body of Physicks should by a divine right take place and be entertained, either the elementary, Globular, or the newly revived Corpuscularian. And that great Phainomenon be resolved whether Moses were not altogether Cartesian." Neither was the issue confined to Genesis, and Hughes went on to argue against the idea "that either these Chap. or the books of Job, the Psalms and proverbs, &c. were designed by the Spirit to furnish the world with a body of Physicks."[62]

There are quite a large number of texts that apply mundane physics to the world in the process of becoming, that imagine the alchemical workbench or the building site at the origins of the world. In some respects, this has a venerable patristic and scholastic heritage: Augustine's seminal principles are a comparable explanatory mechanism, and the hexameral tradition often domesticated Aristotle to such purposes. But the premundane, pretemporal cosmologies of early modernity have their own character, not infrequently affecting a Cartesian framework, as plausible submechanisms of and divine strategies undergirding biblical creation, literal after the manner of seventeenth-century hermeneutics. Thomas White, the "Blackloist" Catholic philosopher, working in the orbit of Kenelm Digby, attached to his *Institutionum Peripateticarum* an extensive *appendix theologica de Origine Mundi* (1646), which offered alternating philosophical and scriptural explanations of the world's coming into being, hexamerally speaking. The first two days, with their cosmic underarchitecture, are properly unknowable and distinct from the "works of the other four days," which might be more amenable to mechanical analogy, moving from the laboratory to cosmology, to retro-imagine the origins of the world.⁶³ Miraculous it may all have been, but one could still infer the engineering feats of God, how the earth was hung in the firmament, by a process analogous to fire drawing up "crasse *Oyls* and *Oyntments;* nay even Salts and very Gold it self."⁶⁴ White theorizes the dazzle and the mass of the glassy firmament, lit by heavenly bodies, which served to light up the beautiful earth, at which point the temporary furniture of the universe—the glow of the angels, like construction site lighting—could be withdrawn: "Wherefore, were they set & moved in a convenient site to the Earth now inhabited, they might alwaies more or lesse enlighten it: nor would there be any longer need of that vast light made by the Angels."⁶⁵ White is not an author who seems driven by any criteria of idle loveliness, but his picture here, of a string of angels serving to light the scaffold of the skies till the wiring of the cosmos could be put in place, is at least accidentally lovely.

This 'philosophical' reckoning of the primal origins is followed for each day by "An Explication of Genesis concerning the same." On the third day, for instance ("And God said, let the Waters which are under the Heaven be gathered together into one place, and let the dry Land appear"), White explains it as our induction into the theory of attraction and conglobation in the postexistent, law-bound world: "Here is the first mention made of *gravity* . . . that we may see *Gravity* is not a motion towards any particular *Site,* but towards the *unity* of a body; and that it was made out of the Order of the Universe now *establisht.*" Not only gravity, but the world's oceanic circulation was established by explicable process, through the moisture sweating and swelling out of the earth, "by the permixtion of hot water," which he substantiates by noting that "*Job* 38 'tis said, that *the Sea flow'd, as it were, out of a womb.*"⁶⁶

Géraud de Cordemoy's 1668 *Copie d'une lettre* in defense of Descartes aimed to show both that the latter's theories were not theologically dangerous and, moreover, "that this systeme of M. Des Cartes . . . seems to have been taken out of the first chapter of Genesis," as the title runs. De Cordemoy insists that his will be a literal interpretation, albeit one must transpose, generically speaking from the perspective of Moses as historian, to that of Descartes as philosopher, both training their holy eye upon the beginning of the world. Where Moses notes the *fiat lux* as a historical event, a Cartesian commentary allows one to consider the physics of light, in relation to the first day. Descartes's vortical matter theory posited the primal light-matter in vehement motion, so "that there were formed divers *Vortexes* or *Whirl-pools* of these little round Bodies" whose spin produced luminosity, and in turn, "so that this pressure of the *Globules* made Light in all those places, where was found a sufficient conflux and heap of subtle matter."[67] In turn, these vortices separate masses of different density, water from earth and the waters of the firmament from those below, all the time compatible with a strict scripturalism: "that M. *Des Cartes* hath always followed *Moses*."[68] This can certainly sound like nervous apology rather than any fulsome sense that natural philosophy should be derived from the scriptures, and may well be so. But the efforts to reconcile natural philosophy with Genesis were thorough-going, and not notably more evident in Protestant than in Catholic thought.

At times, they attended to the geology of the earth—the melting, congealing, crystallizing, and chemical work of the Holy Spirit upon the face of the deep. At times, the same Holy Dove would brood, gestate, or hatch the world, in avian analogy, or its seeded explosive fecundity would burst into being in the fireworks of seminal principles, the world seeded with the almost Platonic, latent "ideas" of creation, waiting for existence. At other times, these writings were elaborate versions of element theory, how matter was derived from the composted watery primal matter, how chaos was sublimed and condensed. The chemico-physics of the laboratory or the alchemical studio might by analogy serve as the model for the submechanisms of the divine Word. A cornucopia of sacred-scientific theories of origin occupied writers from the most serious of natural philosophers and theologians, to the most elaborate allegorists of mystical creation. Two common threads link these writings.

One is that they tend to situate themselves in counterpoint to classical error, whether Aristotelian, on the eternity of the universe, or Lucretian-Epicurean, on its chance production. Second is the working presumption that, while scientific reason could and must be applied to thinking about cosmic origins, at the same time, creation *ab nihilo* could not be subject to the same "scientific" or philosophical reason that governed the creation *after* it came into being. One had to concede and incorporate a core of the unknowable into one's theorizing. The world came into being by a different physics, by rules inexplicable, and through a Jobean physics of the Word. This produced some remarkable epistemological quivers.

Early modernity inherited a scholastic tradition of discussing this unknowability of the moment of creation in terms of voluntarism: whether God was bound by the rules that structured the universe—the rules of logic and of physics—or whether he was intrinsically unconstrained. The seventeenth-century manifestation of this occurs in debate on miracles and the suspension of the natural order. However, while this remained significant, thinkers were often as interested in the human state of encountering that sublime possibility of contradiction.[69] These twinned notions—that the biblical creation *ab nihilo* scotched classical philosophy and that its logic was beyond human capacity to imagine—are found in Edward Stillingfleet, writing on "the Origine of the Universe" in his influential *Origines Sacrae* (1662), which characterizes the arguments of the ancients as coming constantly upon the same dead end: "For we finde by these *Naturalists* who thus asserted this *principle* [that nothing can be produced out of nothing] that when they go about to prove it, it is only from the *course* of *Generations* in the *world*, or from the *works* of *art,* both which suppose *matter praeexistent,* and from these short *collections* they form this *universal Maxime.*"[70] That creation *ab nihilo* was outside of the order of things, was a proposition defended vehemently against the amorphous threat of atheism. Ralph Cudworth, in *The true intellectual system of the universe,* devotes considerable space to it.[71] This was one of the philosophical and hermeneutic sinkholes in any account of things, that necessarily, the conditions of divine creation-from-nothing defy the logic of the created world, and the very conditions of the thinkable. As Stillingfleet explains it: "they apprehend *God* only as an *Artificer* that contrives the world first into a *platform,* and then *useth instruments* to erect it, and consequently still suppose the *matter* ready for him to work upon." This is the ancients' unbendable logic, thinking from the world as it is, now, and its physical laws, as eternal, preceding even their creator. Stillingfleet, like others, insisted that one had to disable one's knowledge of the laws of the world to enter into the alien (and Jobean) logic of creation.

In support of this, Stillingfleet goes on to quote an extensive passage of Maimonides from his *Guide of the Perplexed* (2I.7), which captures the difficult nub of unthinkability in creation-apophatics. Maimonides, the twelfth-century polymath and rabbi (known also as Rabbi Moses the Egyptian, Rabbi Maimon, and Rambam), was significant in many areas of early modern thought, not least in his presentation of the scriptures as resolutely, exactly true in their account of the divine, while nevertheless being irreducible, without idolatry, to any terms explicable to mere humans.[72] As with the unthinkable God, so it proved with the unthinkable origins of the world. Imagine, says Maimonides, a baby whose mother died, and who was left in the care of his father on an isolated island, with no women, and on which he had never seen a female animal. When he asks his father about existence, he is told about pregnancy, growth inside the body of the mother, and birth. In amazement, the child asks whether the being within the belly eats, drinks, breathes, and excretes. And when he is told no, he detects a trick, because clearly this is impossible. If we don't breathe, we die, and how then could one exist cooped up in the space of a solid body? In Stillingfleet's rendering, the boy opines:

> If one of us, saith he, should swallow a little bird, it would presently dye as soon as it came into the stomack, how much more if it were in the belly? If we should be but for few days without eating and drinking, we could not live; how can a childe then continue so many months without it?[73]

The dubious child continues to think through the impossibility of not eating, not breathing, not shitting, never mind the body's miraculous opening up to allow the child to escape, and he concludes that it is *a priori* nonsense, lacking evidence beyond the "authority" of his father.

The boy's perplexed inability to credit the tale of origins is, we discover, our situation in relation to the origins of the world. "Much after this way, saith that excellent Author, do Aristotle and others argue against the production of the world; for if the world were produced, say they, it must have been thus and thus, and it is impossible that it should have been so: why? because we see things are otherwise now in the world."[74] The physics of the Word, of the "first matter" and of scriptural *ab nihilo* creation, are so utterly unlike anything we can experience in the postcreated world that any statement about the origin of things has to include this caveat, that its laws and its conditions are unthinkable, distinct, and unlike any laws we might formulate of the perfected world: "You ought to memorize this notion. For it is a great wall that I have built around the Law, a wall that surrounds it warding off the stones of all those who project missiles against it," writes Maimonides.[75] This is the final bulwark against overnaturalizing the scriptures. It is at this lacuna, where the thinkable fails, that the apophatic steps in.

Stillingfleet's account of sacred origins is a sprawling text (also changing shape across its editions), and as with many such synoptic works defending Christianity from the ground up, the structure is at least a little hard to discern as it shifts its scale and finds its many unnamed ancient and modern enemies, atheists and enthusiasts. As its subtitle has it, it is "a *Rational Account of the Grounds of Christian Faith*," an early example of the many Restoration texts determined to reestablish an exegetical orthodoxy against the rising tide of enthusiasm. It is in this context that *Origines Sacrae* moves its capacious history of ancient philosophy, gentile theology, and religious teleology, to a discussion of biblical prophecy, true and false.[76] This can strike the reader as digressive, but Stillingfleet needs to accommodate the contradiction that is present in much of the era's biblical cosmology. One cannot know anything about the creation of the world—we are Maimonides's doubt-struck boy—but one's attention to that gulf of what we do not know must be encountered rationally, not enthusiastically. We must allow the clarity of Genesis and the fog of Job to coexist.

I cited earlier and will conclude with one of the most remarkable and controversial pieces of biblically derived natural philosophy of the era, Thomas Burnet's *Telluris theoria sacra,* written in 1681, translated into English in 1684 as *Theory of the Earth* and augmented in subsequent editions. It traces the world, considered as a geological entity, from creation through to, in later editions, Apocalypse. It is a remarkable work for several reasons. It is urbane and stylish, such that Coleridge reckoned Burnet among the great prose stylists of the seventeenth century and considered rendering the work into blank verse.[77] It engaged and sparked numerous geocosmic responses that characteristically traverse the biblical and the scientific; Burnet engaged in correspondence with Isaac Newton, and his work has a formative place in histories of geology, albeit it remains remarkable also because it is so wholly bizarre an argument delivered in so sumptuous a prose.[78]

Burnet's attention to the Book of Job and his arguing for its "Enthusiastick or Prophetick stile," that Job's poetics might be the cracked lens for natural philosophy, sits oddly with the fact that the *Sacred Theory* was presented as a literal and thoroughgoing rationalization of the geohistory of the world. But his pristine earth looked like nothing anyone had really imagined before in the Judeo-Christian tradition. The world of Eden was entirely smooth, without mountain or crag, without shoreline or rocks. Adam and Eve lived on an egg. Insistently literal, and scrupulously scriptural in the premises it started out from, Burnet's natural history is so far removed from the Bible that it prompts the question again: what did thinkers think they were describing when they attended to the creation of the world, and to what end? In critical commentary on Burnet, whose landscapes and whose ideas are so vertiginous, compelling, and impossible, the sublime is often invoked, but the Burnetian sublime is Jobean, in its violence and tumult.

His argument proceeds from the idea, developed with some care, that there was insufficient water in the circulation of even the densest rainclouds to do more than inundate the lower grounds, and not enough to submerge the mountains of the world, such as they were. Mere oceans could not, physically, naturally, have produced a universal destruction.[79] This in itself was not a new observation. Thomas White, for instance, had brought the same cluster of biblical texts together, noting the difficulties in finding a sufficient volume of water, naturally speaking.[80] Dismissive of any claims that it was a mere localized flood, or that it should be attributed to the direct, miraculous intervention of God, Burnet elaborates over the course of his two long and lovely books the notion that pristine earth had to be flat in order for the deluge to be total. Describing one of several section-diagrams of the earth, he notes how "the Exteriour Region of the Earth is as the Shell of the Egg, and the Abysse under it as the White that lies under the Shell." His idea takes metaphorical form in relation to the classical *"Mundane Egg,"* whose unruptured, oviform, and pristine surface was without blemish of water channel or rocky hillock. Burnet undertakes, as he himself explains, to "proceed upon this supposition, *That the Ante-diluvian Earth was smooth and uniform, without Mountains or Sea,* to the explication of the universal Deluge."[81]

The work is thus based on the idea that the necessary water for the flood was contained *within* the bowels of the egglike earth, which at the flood cracked open, and that, afterward, the water seeped back under, leaving behind its rubble and rubbish of rocks and gorges, crevices and trash-heaps of littered mountain chains befouling the earth's postdiluvian surface. The key to this geocosmic insight on Burnet's part was the fleeting clue in Genesis 7.11, on the "breaking open of the Fountains of the Abysse" ("great deep" in KJB), allied to a set of other scriptural clues to creation, not least God's enigmatic insistence in Job that it was he "who shut up the sea with doors when it brake forth, as if it had issu'd out of a womb," which set of verses, Burnet notes, have "more propriety and elegancy, if they be understood of the first and Ante-diluvian form of the Earth, than if they be understood of the present."[82] Paolo Rossi's *The Dark Abyss of Time* comments on Burnet's being attuned to the idea that nature has an ancient past, even within the short space of biblical chronology, and within which "the postcatastrophic world was seen as without order or proportion—a sort of new chaos."[83] On this basis, Burnet has his strange place in the history of geological thought, and also in the annals of late Restoration science. Burnet is Cartesian in his presumptions, his frames of reference, and his intellectual debts. His working premise was that the Bible's account of creation was amenable to, indeed properly demanded, mechanical and mathematical attention, working out the volume of water necessary to drown the world. If one was to figure this with the mountains and valleys of the existent world included in one's calculations, the amount would be intolerably large, but with Burnet's flat-egg earth, it was just about manageable. While some of the responses attacked his mathematics, others took issue with his exegesis. Others still objected to his aesthetics.

There have been two broad approaches to Burnet's work: first, to see it as a work of Restoration science, albeit one tied in its biblical thought-shackles; and second, to account it a gothic theology of the pre-Romantic sublime. These are not necessarily easy to reconcile. Margaret Nicolson's *Mountain Gloom and Mountain Glory* exemplifies the latter of these strategies, understanding the work to have emerged in response to a very particular aesthetic horrified by mountains with their rocky debris: "though it be handsome and regular enough to the eye in certain parts of it, single tracts and single Regions; yet if we consider the whole surface of it, or the whole Exteriour Region, 'tis as a broken and confus'd heap of bodies, plac'd in no order to one another, nor with any correspondency or regularity of parts . . . a World lying in its rubbish."[84] A focus on the aesthetic, the wistful, mournful, and pedantic sense of untidy nature, is hard to resist, and Burnet's account of the geocatastrophic process by which this carnage came into being only adds to the sublimity, by which we stand back from the mere planet and watch its opening up, the heft of destructive waters calamitous and tumbling through its cracks, drowning everything in its torrent, plunging with death everywhere and divine proto-apocalypse.

This is horror like no other, except perhaps like the Book of Job, amplified with the more cataclysmic parts of Isaiah and Ezekiel. Burnet's account of the world is more or less the opposite of physico-theology, so important a stimulus to natural philosophy in the era. It did not look at the world and see the divine therein, but gazed rather at what it took to be a broken catastrophic wreck of the Alps and other scars, the decimated work turned inside out, ripped open like a burst football. If Job is Genesis inside out, the story told from the dangerous job-site under construction, Burnet's account produces a picture of the current world that makes it sound like just such a ruin. Indeed, Burnet's caverns measureless to man, which so horrified him and so entranced other readers, were quite consciously Jobean. In one of his many follow-up tussles with those who objected to, but were nevertheless enamored of, his work, he makes considerable play of how his own breaking up of the earth "is elegantly exprest in *Job,* by the bursting of the Womb of Nature."[85]

Burnet seems to have reveled in the controversy, answering tract after tract in detail, with expositors such as John Woodward and William Whiston offering counter-theories of flood-physics, and others objecting to his hermeneutics.[86] One that throws light on Burnet's purposes is his careful and extensive reply to Erasmus Warren's *Geologia*. Warren criticized Burnet's insistence that before the flood, the world lacked deep seas. Where, then, would the Jobean whale, the Leviathan, sport? Not, surely, in the shallows, but if not, Warren suggests, Burnet must imagine that the whale was in the under-Abyss with its waters, inside the unburst globe. Ever willing to embrace the impossible, Burnet concedes that maybe this notion is right, that in the Jobean beginning, the Leviathan was housed in the underaquarium of the world, and he does this by referring the matter to the trope that Stillingfleet had used some years earlier: "this minds me of the saying of *Maimonides: That no man* ever would believe, that a child could live so many months, shut up in its Mothers Belly." Just as the child would not believe this, so Warren is unable to conceive of anything outside his immediate experience, Burnet suggests in turn. Perhaps the Leviathan burst into mammalian, air-breathing being only at the point when the earth cracked open, born like the child who was so unimaginable to the island-orphan: "They might have some passages, in their body, open'd, (at the disruption of the Abyss) when they were born into the light and free air, which were not open'd before. As we see in Infants, upon their birth, a new passage is made into their lungs, and a new circulation of the bloud, which before took another course."[87] Burnet's evocation of this story is a trick. Where, in Maimonides, it represents the essence of the unknowable, Burnet takes it as license to unalloyed invention. He literalizes Maimonides's embryo, who (we recall) would certainly suffocate according to the boy-human who could not understand God's ways. But Burnet has Job's Leviathan in the belly and womb of the earth freed from its cavern, after its geological gestation, its lungs inflating in spectacular birth. It is hard to suppose Burnet is being serious here, although from another perspective it is also quite hard to suppose that any of the *Sacred Earth* controversy was serious, but clearly it was.

Burnet's is a vast paradoxical terrain of inquiry, whose only precursor in scale, in hubris, in sublimity, is the Book of Job itself. Burnet positively embraces the paradox of proving something that was evidently not there in the scriptures, the unbiblical oviform world derived though sleight of hand and sleight of science direct from its pages. The sublime of Job may be different from the sublime of the *Sacred Theory*, but both demand that the reader accede to the unfathomable. To some early readers, this suggested not the Job who was the epitome of knowledge, but the Job who represented the height of ignorance and presumption. Herbert Croft damns the *Sacred Theory* by first comparing it to the science fiction of Francis Godwin, and damning him further for his Jobean impertinance: "God asks him [Job] a question, *Where wast thou when I laid the foundation of the earth? Declare if thou hast understanding.* So I may well say to this Man [Burnet], Where wast thou when I brought a Deluge upon the Earth."[88]

The presumption that natural philosophy could be deduced and elaborated from the scriptures runs deep in the seventeenth century, but it was more or less never untethered from the interpretative demands, both that the scriptures be accommodated to the knowledge of its unfit Hebrew readers and that its poetics, its resonances, needed careful attention. The Book of Job has an aesthetic like no other, an emotional undertow, riptides that utterly unmoor the reader's every certainty. And in large part, these are created by its recurrent, unsettling poetic motifs. The idea that early modern science remained indebted to religion is well established, but there is a poetics of exegetical and religious thought that intrudes into and may underlie the nature of that relationship; the biblical, insofar as it bore on natural philosophy, was a wild poetic terrain. Early modernity, religious to its core, took seriously what to modern readers of Job seems preposterous—that if one sought to plumb the theological paradoxes of the Book of Job, its study of pain and patience, one had to consider its account of creation. Natural philosophy was a strange answer to unfathomable questions. The next chapter considers one monumental attempt to understand God's impenetrable being, in the bowels of eternity, and the nature of the world in the temporal—Jacob Boehme's *Mysterium Magnum* of 1623.

CHAPTER 2

The Theopoetics of Jacob Boehme

> For the Essence in the Tree of the knowledge of Good and Evill, and the hunger of the desire in Adam, were alike; what he desired was represented unto him by the Fiat; Adams Imagination was the Cause of it.
> JACOB BOEHME, *Mysterium Magnum*, 17.40[1]

> Albeit selfe-Reason might heere cavill at us, and say, we were not by, when this was done: yet we say that we in a Magicall manner according to the Right of Eternity, were really there, and saw this: but not I, who am I, have seen it; for I was not as yet a Creature; but we have seene it in the Essence of the Soule which God breathed into Adam.
> JACOB BOEHME, *Mysterium Magnum*, 9.1[2]

FRANZ ROSENZWEIG, IN HIS MIND-BOGGLING *The Star of Redemption*, a philosophy in descant in the beleaguered aftermath of World War I, writes that, as well as a negative theology, we need what he calls a "negative cosmology." In negative theology, the fugitive divinity, the *deus absconditus*, conditions our longing for what we cannot know, even as he vanishes. But the world performs the same disappearing trick. It appears to surround us, objectively and self-evidently there, but it dissipates no less easily than the absconding God: "We are in it, but it exists within us too. It penetrates us, but with every breath and every stirring of our hands it also emanates from us."[3] This is a world teeming, endlessly renewing itself, plunging from the particular into the universal, but a world too in terrible slumber, such that its inner and outer natures are disjunctive and incompatible, "a world inwardly infinitely wealthy, a colourfully irradiated, overwhelming cascade which ever renewed, ever renews its clarity and placidity in the still depths which gather in it, but a world outwardly weak and impoverished." Rosenzweig's "strange masterpiece" is breathless and beautiful, but it is not peerless.[4] Its long-lost twin in negative cosmology, where the elusive nature of the *deus absconditus*, and the elusive nature of the physical world, had something in common, is Jacob Boehme's *Mysterium Magnum*, written in 1623.[5]

The reader coming to Boehme's *Mysterium Magnum, oder, Erklärung über das erste Buch Mosis* (1623), translated into English as *Mysterium Magnum, or an exposition of the first book of Moses called Genesis* (1654), encounters early and pervasively a churning of time and the eternal, and what we might call a physics of the Johannine Word. It involves an apparent culinary-chemical transmutation of the divine Word to produce the outward World, an outward World that "is all onely the expressed Word [*das ausgesprochene Wort*]: which hath so coagulated it self in its re-conception to its own expression."[6] Though he disavows too outright a deist inflection to this coagulation ("now we cannot say, that the outward World is God"), it is also the case that the Holy Spirit as Word does not so much bring something distinct from itself into existence (*ex nihilo*) as thicken into being; it cooks and caramelizes and continues, vitally, to infuse what it has bloomed into. The breathy *"verbum fiat"* pulses, distills, and condenses. Perhaps this is just Boehme's way with chemical metaphor. But the metamorphosis is understood in a strong sense: a stone is made of Word, and within it still "the eternal speaking Word" remains quiveringly active, with its "spiration [*Aushauchen*]" suffusing the object in real presence.[7] The Word in fact (so to speak) precedes and produces the essence and the material being of the stone: "it is the *Formed Word*; and the *working Word* is its life, and incomprehensible: for it is without all *Essence*; as a bare understanding onely, or a Power that bringeth it selfe into *Essence*."[8] Boehme is a writer who explains, in some great detail, not just the six cacophonous days of creation—a mere hexameral bagatelle—but the nature of the uncreated world, shimmering outside of existence still, how God came into being, sucking himself out of the nothing, the *Ungrund*, in an act of unbridled divine lust.

Jacob Boehme, the cobbler-mystic from Görlitz in Silesia, remains an enigmatic figure far too little known in early modern anglophone literary-political-historical studies. He is a writer whose borrowed and original ideas were Heath-Robinsoned into complex philosophical-theological works. He was by no means unlearned, for all that there was a romantic tradition that liked to see him so, but he was in essence self-tutored, and all the more brilliantly so for it. Boehme, born in 1575, reported having had a luminous vision in the year 1600, whose transcendent afterglow and meaning he attempted to formulate into spiritual-philosophical form some twelve years later, in a work that was to become his *Aurora oder Morgenröte im Aufgang*. But when word leaked out about the local shoemaker's writing, the pastor of Görlitz, Gregor Richter, got his hands on a copy of the manuscript and, under a threat of exile, ordered him to cease, which for some years he did—or at least, *Aurora* was left unfinished, and it was not until 1619 that Boehme took up his pen again. In a five-year burst of activity before his death in 1624, he wrote copiously, during which time and in the early tumult of the Thirty Years War, Richter, a Rottweiler for orthodoxy and social probity, pursued "the shoemaker and rabid enthusiast." [9] Boehme has a longstanding association with a German philosophical-mystical tradition stretching back to Meister Eckhart, but he is also idiosyncratic within it, not least in that he is less preoccupied by, indeed at times almost indifferent to, the self, and one's own relationship to an elusive God. What matters is the cosmos and everything in it: this is a mysticism that attends to the world within worlds, to the condition of eternity and its relation to the created universe. It is the wildest of apophatic writing, baffling and seductive to an early modern culture alert to the idea that the veiled and opaque scriptures incorporated arcana of both God and nature.

Little of Boehme's writing was published in his lifetime, but a large body of his work was rendered first into Dutch and then into English in a feverish twenty years in and around the interregnum, albeit less lavishly illustrated than some of the beautiful (though later) continental editions, in Dutch and German.[10] Boehme was widely admired in English radical circles—traced by Nigel Smith, Ariel Hessayon, and others.[11] Though the nature of his influence remains elusive, there is good reason to think that it was his scriptural gymnastics that most endeared him to these radical and "begodded" readers.[12] Alongside these Boehme enthusiasts (in both senses of the word), he was also the object of the condescending, but nevertheless serious attention of Cambridge Platonists and members of the Hartlib and Oldenburg circles.[13] The taint of enthusiasm hung to Boehme tenaciously, however, and there was a considerable period during which his reputation was not high, before a belated reanimation of interest in the philosophical character of his thought among German Romantics (in Schlegel, Novalis, and Schelling) and, in England, by Coleridge and, in particular, William Blake, whose churning philosophical-prophetic cosmologies are thoroughly Behmenist (as the adjective goes), even while Boehme is not ostensibly mythopoetic or mythodramatic in the manner of Blake. There is a different kind of volcanic rolling and recurrence of idea upon idea.[14] This tentative interest reached its culmination in Hegel's attention to Boehme and mysticism, since which time, he has retained his place in the German philosophical pantheon, with Nietzsche, Heidegger, and others owing something to him.[15] Attention to his philosophical reputation in the seventeenth century has, until recently, been sparse, in large part, no doubt, because he proved so baffling, although there has been some important reassessment in recent years.[16] Boehme's writing, however, has a poetics or a theopoetics about it that defies most efforts to corral him to any philosophical tradition, and if he is a writer of metaphysics, it is in a prophetic-metaphysical mode of his own devising.

Early on in *Mysterium Magnum,* Boehme describes how matter, wrought in the physics of eternity and turned out into the cool of time, retained about it something of the immanifest within its material being. Here he is looking at a stone or a clod of earth, in a passage that, it seems clear, appealed to William Blake:

> When I take up a stone or clod of earth and look upon it; then I see that which is above, and that which is below, yea, the whole world therein; onely that in each thing one property hapneth to be the chiefest and manifest; according to which it is named: all the other properties are joyntly therein; onely in distinct degrees and centres, and yet all the degrees and centres are but one onely centre.[17]

A stone or clod may be made of crystallized Word, the "*Verbum Fiat,*" but that stone or clod is also made of everything else. Boehme thinks of objects in the way that white light contains all colors—all of them simultaneously present always, but occluded, such that the visible property of a thing represents a failure of hiddenness.[18] He suggests the idea that the visible world is constituted by subtraction and severance from its more "pullulating" whole.[19] Reality throbs in its fullness below the threshold of the visible, and what we get to see of the world, of temporal nature, is at best partial. When, then, he takes up his stone or clod, he sees not only the world in a grain of sand, but the stone brimming, crackling with eternity.[20] The spiritual takes place within exactly the same coordinates as the material: "one world is in the other: and all are onely one," an inseparable, distinct, at times antagonistic and symbiotic intertwinedness, *alles in allem*.[21] Boehme's poetics and theology of co-occupancy is thoroughgoing; everything is to be found within everything else, and he follows the logic and illogic of this relentlessly.

Mysterium Magnum, in its weave of the biblical, the philosophical, and the apophatic, is perhaps the most important and impressive work of Boehme's vast output, in scale and ambition. It fitted within, and appealed to readers steeped in, the early modern Genesis commentary tradition, hence no doubt its avid readership in the Netherlands and England in the mid- to late seventeenth century. Critical literature on Boehme has not had a great deal to say about early modern understandings of Genesis and natural philosophy, but there is much to be gained from viewing this most synoptic of Boehme's works through this lens, related to, albeit distinct from, the traditions of Mosaic sacred physics. The account in chapter 1 of Creation as estrangement, that Job and Genesis read in concert were understood to demand a nescience, an unbridgeable gap in logic, is a dynamic that is wholly at work in Boehme's depiction of the origin of things. For all that there may be generic similarities, however, there is no other commentary like *Mysterium Magnum*, with its elaborate metaphysical equipment addressing not only the unfathomable divine concoctions of the world, but all its subsequent tales of patriarchs and covenant in concert with a seething creation, a chapter-by-chapter rendering of his theophysics.[22] This scale and scope is important. Boehme puts his natural philosophy, with its elaborate ontology, to work not only on the Fall and its theodicy, but on the slow unfolding covenant, of Noah, of Abraham, Isaac, and Jacob, in all of whom, the eternal is still going on. The biblical figures are to be understood as representing a state of internal-eternal energy, in a way not entirely distinct from how the stones and clods burn with the combustible Holy Spirit. So too, Boehme insists, must the reader be enthused, to read the inward figure, not the outward husk of the words.

Boehme's carnivalesque hermeneutics turn the scriptures inside out, urging that they be understood (by those capable of understanding) with the animated Spirit in spate precisely because the universe consisted in just such a mechanics, in which every physical material, element, and attribute consisted of this surge, the essence always animating the manifestation. Pneumatic reading—in the rush of the spirit—was not just a cheap shortcut to pretended knowledge, as the accusation directed against enthusiasm would have it; for Boehme, it was the very structural dynamic of creation in its ceaseless fire, the vibrating of the manifest world with the throb of the eternal.[23] Nothing takes place simply in itself. There is no merely literal event, which is not at the same time shot through with its meaning in the *nunc stans*, vehemently Christological, occasionally eschatological, to be figured inwardly, and outside of time.[24] Cyril O'Regan, in his *Gnostic Apocalypse: Jacob Boehme's Haunted Narrative*, notes what he terms Boehme's "erotic, kenotic and agnostic anamorphosis of biblical narrative," his "disfiguration-refiguration" of the scriptures, so relentless a process as to provide a "grammar of derangement."[25] Cecilia Muratori, pursuing this idea in the Romantic imagination, writes of Boehme's *poesie* and imaginative energy as "the vitality of unstructured energy."[26]

Mysterium Magnum, with its vast scale, hovers between natural philosophy and theology. But it is neither. It is, in a way that few other seventeenth-century texts are, a work of theopoetics, understood as writing around and athwart the unreckonable and the unknowable. It is a way of thinking about God that accepts its ruses will never dent the armor of divine incomprehensibility, but that aims to avoid a state in which things remain "*merely*, rather than apophatically, unknown," as Catherine Keller puts it.[27] Theopoetics, as a modern antihermeneutics, reacts to the lawyerly texture of both systematic theology and scriptural exegesis, by asserting wild poetic logic, which belies reason. Reformation "magisterial" theology, with its grand architecture of ideas, can certainly seem to display what John Caputo calls a "militant logic of omnipotence," even while it may defer to the hiddenness of God: "theology in the strong standard version belongs to the sovereign order of power and presence and favors a grammar of great omni-nouns and hyper-verbs."[28] In one sense Boehme's monomaniacal explanatory scheme might seem to be wholly fraught with omni-nouns, and yet it has long been clear to readers of Boehme that his is a theology that programmatically estranges and that dissolves to the touch.[29] *Mysterium Magnum*, in its *resemblance* to hexameral commentary and as an exposition of Genesis, is uncanny, fraught, and unpredictable. It has what was in Reformation Europe (both Catholic and Protestant) the familiar architecture of a biblical commentary and orderly explication, but it is literal in all the wrong places. Its Alice-in-Wonderland poesis shrinks and swells in its relentless inner and outer, created and uncreated. It is chemically unstable.[30]

Boehme's concoctions of creation physics and biblical exegesis, which dazzle even while they defy and revel in defying logic, need to be understood as a poetics of the unknowable that responds to the very character of scripture, which "in most of the *Mysteries* thereof... remaineth very dark to *us,* we having so little knowledge of the *things* it speaketh of," as its seventeenth-century translator John Sparrow puts it, in his preface to *Aurora*.[31] Early modernity was open to the idea that the Bible was both opaque and dazzlingly plain. As Boehme describes this hermeneutic quandary in *Mysterium Magnum*: "The words of *Moses* concerning the Creation are exceeding clear; yet unapprehensive to reason [*treflich klar, aber Vernunft unbegriffen*]."[32] Boehme's account of Adam is of particular interest, and will occupy the central part of this chapter. While one could speak of his theology of Adam, it would be almost as accurate to suggest that Boehme writes a physics of Adam. The Fall is multidimensional, taking place in and out of time, in what is, temporally speaking, a nonsensical brew of cause and effect, but whose poetics of time is quite beautiful and utterly strange. Something should be said of Sparrow's translation. Here and there, he misrenders Boehme, most notably in his eliding the Ungrund and Abgrund as "Abysse." But Sparrow, like the King James Bible, is sumptuous and wonderful even when wrong. On the whole, it should be said, he sticks fairly closely to the German, but there are some conspicuous oddities that I will point out, where the ideas are so bewildering that he seems not to trust the words in front of him. However, while there might be philosophical contexts in which a more strictly accurate and modern translation would be better, it just would not capture the lilt of the early modern English Boehme, and the rhetoric of the unknowable in England. I do not pursue the reception history of Boehme in any detail, beyond noting at the end of the chapter some of the early reaction. There have been some very good studies of this reception, but there has been nothing like a close reading of Boehme's most startling, poetic, and apophatic text.

The Components and Cogs of Systemless Thought

Writings on Boehme necessarily have to attend to the "system" of thought that can be derived from across his works. This "system," a concocted mystical physics, here alchemical, there typological, is multifaceted and thoroughgoing, and can seem both laborious and elaborate: it describes the constituent principles, forces, and spiritual dynamics of the universe. As various commentators on Boehme have recognized, even after explicating the components of his thought piece by piece, we are merely left differently baffled. "The true context of the terminology," writes Andrew Weeks, in his useful intellectual biography, "is not a philosophical system in the usual sense, but rather the sacramental and absolute mystery of presence and transcendence."[33] It consists of a lava of terms rolling over each other, whose energy is in their refigurative instability, their shift from one to another category.

Boehme's terminology is Protean, musical, and cacophonous. It develops a detailed lexicon that straddles natural philosophy and theology, and is continually reconfigured across his many writings, from the vast *Aurora* that began his writing career, though to its capacious correlate, *Mysterium Magnum,* close to the end, between which there were many reiterations and elaborations upon the vocabulary. In part the delirium and sublimity of his terminology reflects the gargantuan scale and Hesiodic poise of his projects, in which he explains, unperturbably, all things. It is a language that is variously animate-reactive-alchemical—

the metallic underclang of substance as it clatters into being—and yet the universe is also emotional, and Boehme develops a corresponding vocabulary. Boehme produced, or was persuaded to add, a series of appendices to a number of his writings, providing glossaries and various tabular presentations (which "he wrote therefore for the satisfaction of his loving friends"), translated as *Clavis* (1647), *Four tables of divine revelation* (1654), and others.[34] These elements of Boehme's thought, gathered into tables, attest to the era's investment in the logic of correspondence and analogy, but they are at least something of a trap, with their passing impression of order and structure, which the texts in their endless surging (and enthusiastic-prophetic) reformulations so belie.[35] To say so is not to chastise Boehme's cacophony, though many have done so. It is to make the claim that Behmenist knowledge is twisted and twists, and has one foot in the unknowable at all times. The distinction has been noted between Boehme's *Vernunft* and *Verstand*, intuitive understanding and discursive reason, with its cavilling objections, and these correspond in turn to inner and outer knowledge.[36] Boehme remains continually alert to those "wiselings [*Klugen*]" who (he knows) will be critical of his writing, trapped in their historical-literal frames of reference, and to a quasi-personified "Reason," prone to mockery, hole-picking, and reviling, incapable of admitting contradiction, paradox, and mystery. It is necessary, however, to lay out the recurrent terms, at least in brief, though, heaped together, they are (and I think are meant to be) exasperating.

Among the difficulties in Boehme's arsenal of terms is that some of them relate to the created and some the uncreated realm, their relationships seeming at times causal, at other points intended to dispute and undermine causality.[37] The reader is led back and forth through this wormhole, whose realities coexist and inform each other. The Ungrund, rendered "Abyss" at times in early modern English translations (as noted earlier), and "Eternal Nature [*die ewige Natur*]" are key configuring features in talking of the ungraspable divine, beyond and inaccessible to created nature.[38] Seeking in his opening chapter "What God is" produces its apophatic regression of ever deeper unknowables, exuding, dividing, unstable from the tainted viewpoint of fallen createdness, an

Abyss described as "the *Nothing and All things*," the hidden and the invisible, God who does not yet know he is God.[39]

In *Mysterium Magnum*, we reach the twelfth chapter before we get to the first day of creation, and discover that the already well-developed language of enkindling, coagulation, and desire from the will of the abyss barely describes created reality at all. Wisdom and the Word are constituent, but not identical forces of being, modally altered forms of the Ungrund, itself "a nothing, a stillness without substance," the divine in its blackest of black holes.[40] Eternal Nature is not temporal nature—it is vigorously different—but it is constituted by Desire, and it bears on the manifested world, "bring[ing] into the divine the possibility of evil, if not evil itself, and existence as the restlessness for being, rather than its realization."[41] The stark but pervasive understanding of God's anger being a constituent element of the world is alien to most Reformation formulations of humanity's guilt for the Fall, but for Boehme, there is a psychology in the physics of the universe.

There are Two Principles and Three Principles, the latter category operative only in the realm of the created. In the uncreated world, the Two Principles, ("viz, God's Love and Anger: of Darkness and Light") underlie and enkindle being, in agonistic relationship, manifestations and inflections of the divine qualities, the source and surge of being, an "essence of corporeality" without being corporeal itself.[42] That these are not tinged as Manichean is important to Boehme's complex theodicy: God is both love and wrath.[43] Alongside these Two Principles is a corresponding set of Three Principles, the third being the manifestation of God's darkness and light in the outward world—matter, men, beasts, and things. The triad has its Trinitarian correspondence or valence, and echoes also in the three primary elements, or *tria prima*, of sulfur, mercury, and salt. This triad works in turn in offbeat concordance with the four elements—more properly the stuff of the created world. In scheme upon scheme, analogies of sevenhood accrue—the seven properties, the seven spirits of God or powers of nature, corresponding in multiformous fashion to the days of the created week, to planets, to metals, to alchemical resonances, to a map of psycho-emotional and sensorial states of external and internal nature; and the seven qualities (*quellgeis-*

ter) of Virgin Wisdom or Sophia.[44] It is thoroughly exhausting. When, in *Aurora*, he apologizes for the simplicity of his scheme, it is hard to tell if he is serious.[45] Among the less elaborate of charts, tallying up the components, we have the following, in *Mysterium Magnum*:

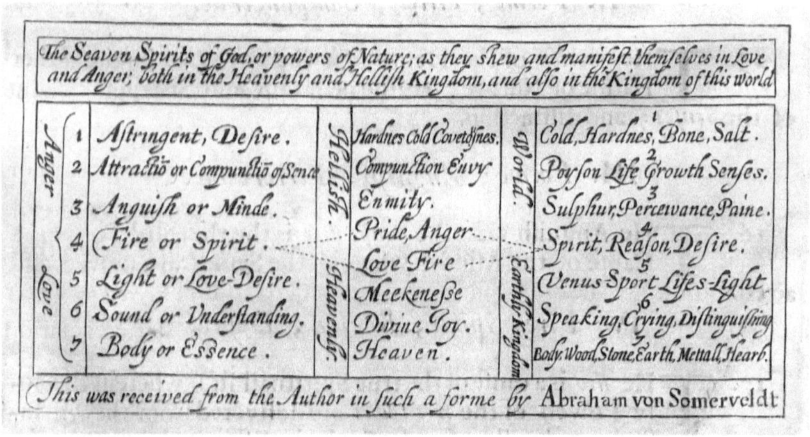

The Seaven Spirits of God, or powers of Nature; as they shew and manifest themselves in Love and Anger; both in the Heavenly and Hellish Kingdom, and also in the Kingdom of this world

Anger	1	Astringent, Desire.	Hellish.	Hardnes Cold Covetdsnes.	World.	1 Cold, Hardnes, Bone, Salt.
	2	Attractiō or Compunctiō of Sence		Compunction Envy		2 Poyson Life Growth Senses.
	3	Anguish or Minde.		Enmity.		3 Sulphur, Perceivance, Paine.
	4	Fire or Spirit.		Pride, Anger		4 Spirit, Reason, Desire.
Love	5	Light or Love-Desire.	Heavenly.	Love Fire	Earthly Kingdom	5 Venus Sport Lifes-Light
	6	Sound or Understanding.		Meekenesse		6 Speaking, Crying, Distinguishing
	7	Body or Essence.		Divine Joy.		7 Body. Wood, Stone, Earth, Mettall, Hearb.

This was received from the Author in such a forme by Abraham von Somerveldt

FIGURE 1. "The Seven Spirits of God, or powers of Nature," from Jakob Böhme (Boehme), *Mysterium Magnum, or an Exposition of the First Book of Moses called Genesis* (1654), 18. Courtesy of Harris Manchester College Library, University of Oxford. Reprinted with permission, F1654/2.

The table, in its multidirectional shifts, describes the seven spirits and qualities of anger and love, of the hellish and heavenly.[46] But, we are required to recall, none of this is "real," in the sense of the temporal, visible world, but rather refers to its eternal doppelgänger. The corporeality of objects, writes Andrew Weeks, "was only a foreground aspect, beneath which illocal forces communed."[47] There is, alongside this, a prominent Kabbalistic substratum and symbolism—which often involves prizing open the syllables of biblical terms, usually as Boehme encounters them in the German, to unearth their inner and constituent meaning.[48] The alchemical terminology, derived largely from Paracelsian vocabulary, runs deep, although it has less purchase in *Mysterium Magnum* than in other works, reaching its fullest acrobatics in *Signatura Rerum*. Then there are a set of bedrock elements of divinity, elusive, propulsive, and creative: the *salliter*, or fundamental divine substance;[49] the *Tinctur*, or mysterious energy which sublimates and transforms things, but in a manner that resists causal definition. The Limbus is the fine clay and quintessence out of which humans were formed, which drives and embodies "desire," in elements, matter, and cacophonously constituted humans.[50] The calculus involved in resolving so many elements in continual change is considerable, though in many respects, these constituent elements of a reality-before-creation are only the beginning. We can hardly understand the dynamics of Boehme without attention to the lost androgyny of Adam, and the Fall's precipitation of gender.[51] Moreover we are asked continually to understand these quasi-physical forces within a typology and Christology, to which they are resolutely subservient. Nothing in Boehme fails to be biblical beneath the physics. The fugal accrual of symbols is always at bottom hermeneutic.

Theopoetics: Seething in Eternity
One of the problems with an account such as that given above, aside from any other shortcomings, is that moving between multiple texts of Boehme neglects how his thought changes, how concepts, metaphors, and emphases change, even over the few short years in which he produced all of his writing, barring *Aurora* (which, for instance, does not feature the Ungrund, a concept that becomes so crucial a notion in his later writing). However, this is not necessarily the major problem. More significant (and underlying my focus on *Mysterium Magnum* alone) is that in explaining Boehme's ideas *across* texts, we fail to experience the discontinuity, the tumble between one and another category, the aggressively discontinuous explanatory frameworks, knitted and knotted in several kinds of indescribability. Boehme is labyrinthine, but his somersaults are disorientating by apophatic design, rather than by philosophical clumsiness. A poetics of the irreconcilable and chronic paradox governs the work, in which there is no solid mooring that is not rendered illusory as the book progresses; neither God, nor the world, nor even so formative a "fact" as the Fall, will stay still. But there is a poetic logic in the curve of individual works that is quite distinct from the philosophical logic of following terms across his oeuvre.

God's separation of his self from the Nothing of the Ungrund, one of Boehme's most celebrated, fecund, and baffling ideas, sounds in mere human language like a beginning—that the divine came into being, or some sort of different being, at least, even while God's essence is permitted to remain resolutely unchangeable. The black hole of the Ungrund, in its absolute and infinitely other negation lets neither light nor paradox out, but God, an "Eternall nothing [*ein ewig Nichts*]," emerges from its swamp.[52] There is, Nicolas Berdyaev points out, in a classic essay, a "dynamic process" of God, a battle against nonbeing that figures "the inner life of the divinity."[53] Not only the cosmos, but God coagulated out of Will and Desire—a will to discern his-her-its own divine character. In a rich unfathomable act of the Uncreated lurching into being, the hungry Nothing consumes itself into something:

> For the *Nothing* hungreth after the *Something,* and the hunger is a desire: *viz.* the First *Verbum Fiat:* or Creating Power: for the Desire hath nothing that it is able to make or Conceive: it conceiveth it selfe; and impresseth it selfe: it *Coagulateth* it selfe: it draweth it selfe into it selfe: and comprehends it selfe: and bringeth it selfe from *Abysse* into *Bysse* [*vom Ungrunde in Grund*]: and overshadoweth it selfe with its *Magneticall attraction:* so that the *Nothing* is filled, and yet remaines as a *Nothing* . . . it yeeldeth obscurity unlesse something else, *viz.* a Lustre, doth fill it.[54]

The desire, the hunger, is God's, in a tomcat prowling of what is not yet a world, but merely an obscurity (and God is the Nothing, the Ungrund, too), out of which Creating Power, the *Verbum Fiat,* fills its own whole nothing, its abyss and universe of womb, with Lustre. The indescribable tumbling here will never resolve, not only because we cannot find the right words for the paradox of eternity producing time—"The Eternal one is not yet," as Alexandre Koyré characterizes the paradox—but because the insistently dynamic nature of Boehme's cosmos is still undergoing the change.[55] The Ungrund did not cease to be, and nor is it some placeless, ancient irrelevance. While it was a given in early modern hexameral writing that the nature of divine action in pre-creation operated according to a different set of laws, a no longer accessible physics, Boehme differs in that he will have that unthinkable physics continue *after* creation, parallel within creation infusing its matter, infusing humans. Eternity, dark still with the Ungrund, suffuses the material world, while being indifferent to it, a negative cosmology within time.

The creation in Boehme's work is by turns industrial and emotional. The world and the pre-creation before it are products strongarmed into existence and wrought into some kind of reality by the smelting and smoking of wrath and desire, metals pained into agonizing being:

> This outward world is as a smoake, or vaprous steame of the fire-Spirit and water-Spirit, breathed forth, both out of the *holy* and then also out of the *dark* world; and therefore it is evill and good; and consists in Love and anger; and is onely as a smoke or misty exhalation, in *reference* and respect to the spirituall world.[56]

The exuberance of this, the spiritual bubbling into acrid physicalities, with a Blakean industrial tyger grinding still in the invisible heart of it, is bound up with the fact that eternity and its chemico-spiritual-physics continues to rumble. It continues, for Boehme, to be the starkest of facts that the outward world is permeated by the spiritual abyssal energy. The infusion of the eternal in the mundane, and the return of the mundane to the eternal is the fundamental gesture of Behmenist metaphysics, and has its correlate everywhere.

Even while the mechanics of the visible world are somewhat more amenable, theoretically, to understanding than the eternal (never mind the more primal Ungrund), it remains opaque and mysterious, and Boehme deploys a language attending to the *emotional* origins of the physical universe as the product of desire. This is not a God who deploys compasses and mathematics, as a medieval deity sometimes does; neither is the universe an architecture affair, with strutted firmament and a moat of waters, crystalline and beautiful in the heavens. Existence, in Boehme, is at least in part a throb of God, painful, sexual, a little mean: "The first Property of the Desire is Astringent, Harsh Eagerly-impressing, Conceiving it selfe, Overshadowing it selfe; and it maketh, first, the *Great Darknesse* of the *Abysse*."⁵⁷ Boehme presents God, or one modality of God, as darkness, even evil. God's wrath and God's love are the underlying principles of being:

> For the God of the holy world, and the God of the darke world, are *not two* Gods: there is but *one* onely God: he himselfe is the whole Beeing; he is Evill and Good, heaven and hell, light and darknesse, Eternity and time, Beginning and End: where his love is *hid* in any thing, there his Anger is *manifest*: in many a thing Love and Anger are in equall measure and weight; as is to be understood in this outward worlds Essence.⁵⁸

Philosophical readings of Boehme have been quite taken with this divine complexity and darkness as a kind of theodicy, but in early modern culture, attuned to, if not worn down by the rhetoric of fallen human depravity, this proximity of contraries and this suggestion of God that "he is Evill" as well as good, is startling.⁵⁹ Even if we understand this within the apophatic tradition, with its established habits of having God embody contradiction and paradox, this rarely embraces its full dark potential.

These dynamics, of things thickening into reality, are pervasive. In the fall, for example, the Dragon-Lucifer "was spewed out with the Creation of the Earth: for even then the Enkindled Essence (which with the Enkindling did Coagulate it selfe into Earth and stones) was *cast out* of the internall into the externall."⁶⁰ This opposition posits a shimmering reality of the spirit punished into externality. Bodiless Being begins to thicken into the external world, ejected, "cast out," of angelic disembodiment, with its purer essence, into the opacity of "earth and stones," and quotidian, visible reality. These "worlds" exist at close quarters and at the same time are wholly alien to each other. Another important example of this occurs in Boehme's angels, and the strange psychogeographies that result from the "thickening" of fallen angels, who can occupy the same space as unfallen angels, and yet the two be unaware of each other: "Thus we are to understand; that the *evill*, and *good* Angells dwell neere one another: and yet there is the greatest immense distance [betweene them]: for the *heaven is in hell*; and the *hell is in heaven*: and yet the one is not manifest to the other." The altered substance produces an altered spiritual sight, and they become oblivious to each other, coexisting without meeting: "the Angells see not the darknesse, for their *Sight* is meere light of divine Power; and the Devills sight is meere darknesse of Gods Anger."[61] This is the mechanism by which devils carry hell inside themselves. It is also, indeed, why humans cannot see the angels among us ("neither have they the *property* of the externall world on them: but each Spirit is cloathed with his owne worlds Property wherein it dwelleth").[62] Readers of Milton will recognize this throng of angels who thicken as their spiritual substance worsens, who endue their outward world with their own inner properties, the sludge of Satanic fallenness. Milton's monist metaphysics, as described so impressively by Stephen Fallon, may be less a response to Descartes and Hobbes than to Boehme.[63]

Frequently, Boehme pulls the reader up, and returns their attention to the ungraspable character of what he is saying: "Reader attend, and marke aright: I understand here with the Description of Nature, the Eternall, not the Temporall Nature."[64] This is a remarkable maneuver, demonstrating a pervasive dynamic of the universe, the inner and outer wrestling with each other, grappling or in harmony, "seeing his manifestation of the Eternall and Externall Nature is in *Combate*."[65] Equally significant is Boehme's consistency in this—it is not just a quality of the physical world, but has its correlate in any act of scriptural interpretation, that there are simultaneous inner and outward figurations of the text. Each part of Genesis, it seems, needs to be shot through with a Christology (and sometimes a Christological physics) that explains how the event makes sense in eternity. Boehme is scathing of interpretation (by "Reason") that "is *onely* learned in the externall Colour, and *prateth* of the painted worke of the outside and shell."[66] In the dazzle of eternal simultaneity, Adam's catastrophic Fall is counterbalanced by its redemption. The pace of earthly pain is a delusion. And it is this, I suspect, that makes Boehme so amenable to his early modern English radical readership, whose agile exegetical-prophetic style—discerning the husk and the nub of texts—mirrored Boehme's hermeneutic maneuvers: "the Spirit cannot be written down, being no Creature, but the moving flowing boyling power of God," he writes in *Aurora*, although the translation here exceeds Boehme's German in its adjectival enthusiasm (*. . . sondern die wallende Kraft Gottes*).⁶⁷ This speaks not just to an insufficiency of language, but equally to another complication: that the divine is knitted into and (in a mysterious way) constituted in language.

Whatever we find in the outward world has a provisional, inchoate quality. It represents something of God, not in his full divine unity, but in "modalized" form. God teems in how we think, and how we reckon the world in all its created variety:

> Thus man hath now received Ability from the invisible Word of God to the re-expression: that he again expresseth the hidden word of the divine Science [*Göttlichen Scienz*] into formation, and severation: in manner and forme of the Temporall Creatures; and formeth this spirituall Word according to Animals, and Vegetables; whereby the invisible wisdome of God is pourtraied, and modelized into severall distinct formes.⁶⁸

The opening phrase of this incorporates a recurrent dynamic that the Word and the mind of God in creation are reiterated both in human speech—its "re-expression" of the invisible Word—and in our perception of the natural world, that the hidden word is reiterated "in manner and forme of the Temporall Creatures." This is not a passive deism, evoking psalmlike praise. Boehme's God is not so much diffused through creation as viral within it. The Word is "modalized [*gemodelt wird*]" into animals, into creation, "*lebhaften und wachsenden Dingen*." The nature of the Word, uncontainable and eruptive within everything, continually displays the divine anew: "All whatsoever hath life, liveth in the *Speaking Word*: the Angells in the Eternall Speaking; and the Temporall Spirits in the re-expression or Ecchoing forth of the Formings of Time."⁶⁹

This eruptive dynamic—"*eine bewegende Wallung*" of the divine—emerges from the idea that creation is replete, *alles in allem*, everything pulsing in everything else, except that one quality is manifested more fully in the outward nature of a thing.⁷⁰ It can appear one way, or another, at his divine pleasure. "Where his love is *hid* in any thing, there his Anger is *manifest*," we hear, in relation to angelic and diabolic nature.⁷¹ Of the cursed earth, poisonous with thistles, we find: "The

Curse is nothing else, but the Holy Element hiding of it selfe, *viz.* the holy *Ens*, which budded forth through the Earth, and bare fruit, and held the property of the foure Elements as 'twere captive in it self; [did withdraw or closely conceale it selfe]."[72]

Over and over, things pulse thus. The six days throb in each other: "Now the first day with the manifested word did *convey* it selfe through the other five dayes-workes even into the day of *Rest*; where the beginning entreth againe into the End; and the End againe into the beginning."[73] This idea of days that convey themselves through and coexist with the days following, alive in them, echoes the relationship between time and eternity, resonant of, if not strictly Platonic in its formulation, "For the Eternall dwelleth not in time . . . albeit it be *cloathed* with the Essence of time."[74]

Everything loops, the first day pulsing through the following six, and the seventh pulsing again in the first: "*God created all things in six dayes* out of the Seven properties, and introduced the six dayes workes of the manifestation of his Creature into the *Seventh* . . . and out of the Seventh day the first day hath taken its Originall and beginning."[75] The regressions of logic and time, when it comes to God, are one thing, but Boehme does not stop there, and a similar dynamic runs across the whole of Genesis, with no part more counterintuitive than his account of Adam.

Adam, Fallenness, and the Persistence of the Eternal

In the epigraphs to this chapter, I cite one of Boehme's temporal impossibilities. Adam is, in early modern commentaries on Genesis, routinely piled high with sins that may have accompanied the apparently more mundane fruit scrumping (pride, lust, idolatry, ingratitude, idleness, avarice, infidelity, to cite a few), but never elsewhere, so far as I know, is he accused of being the *cause* of the interdicted Tree of Knowledge of Good and Evil, by which he fell:

> For the Essence in the Tree of the knowledge of Good and Evill, and the hunger of the desire in *Adam,* were *alike*; what he desired was represented unto him by the *Fiat; Adams* Imagination was the Cause of it.[76]

In this remarkable statement about the nature of Paradise, Boehme has reached a point in the warp of his argument, by which the tree from whose bough Adam and Eve ate the deadly fruit proves to have been created directly as a *result* of the fall— "*Adams* Imagination *war Schuld daran.*" Perhaps there is some ambiguity here in what, exactly, his imagination was the cause of—was it his desire, rather than a quality of the tree?—but if so, this is clarified. Adam infused and poisoned the very earth out of which the tree grew:

> For Adam was guilty therein, seeing he was yet in Paradise, when he lusted after vanity, and brought his Imagination into the Earth, *viz.* into *that Essence,* whence the *limus* of the outward body was extracted; and desired out of his mother to assay of the *Enkindled vanity* which the Devill had inflamed, thereupon the *Fiat* drew him forth such a Plant out of the *Matrix* of the Earth, whence also it had extracted *Adams* body, so that *Adams* hunger, *had* to eat.[77]

I cite the first sentence of this quotation from a 1965 "reprint'" of Sparrow's *Mysterium Magnum,* which silently emends the curious, if not incomprehensible, phrasing of Sparrow, in both the 1654 and 1656 editions, "For it was long of *Adam,* when he was yet in Paradise" for the straightforward "*Denn Adam war Schuld daran, als er noch im Paradeis stund.*" The influential "Law Edition," ostensibly reprinting Sparrow's text, has "For it was occasioned by Adam, when he was yet in Paradise," which while closer to the German, still equivocates on the idea of "guilt." It seems that the translators are so flummoxed by the ideas that they can hardly trust Boehme's actual words.

In the seething nature of reality, where substance was the mere manifestation of inchoate desires, properties, and principles, the tree was the crooked product of Adam's imagination. Boehme's Adam *thinks* himself into the earth, out of which he was formed (the limus or clay), and produces in that earth (his mother) his own "enkindled vanity." In so doing, "the *Fiat* drew him forth such a Plant out of the *Matrix* of the Earth." Adam, it seems, had a role in the character of the divine *Fiat* on the third day, to bring forth the "fruit tree yielding fruit after his kind."[78]

This maneuver on Boehme's part, in its logical and temporal oddity, serves his theodicy. It circumvents the charge that God baited Adam, that he set up the First Man for the first fall in an act of judicial entrapment:

> Reason saith [*Die Vernunft spricht*]: *wherefore* did God suffer this Tree to grow seeing man should not eat thereof? did he not bring it forth for the *Fall* of man? and must it not needs be the *cause* of mans destruction? This is that, about which, the high schooles contend, and understand it not, for they goe about to seek and apprehend the *inward* in *the outward,* and it remaineth hidden and dead unto them, they understand not what Man is.[79]

Against such objections, Boehme has Adam, like Lucifer before him, trap himself in the physics of the universe, his "selfefullness" bringing about his fallen condition. Because God knew Adam would fall, he was always already fallen, always a modality of "the Wrath of the anger of God."[80] Adam leached the venom into the tree that poisoned him and produced that very venom. The fall was asequential, eternal, and its catastrophe happens in simultaneity with the Christological salvaging of that cosmic calamity, wrath balanced and righted with love. It is not that Boehme rejects time and sequence, but that his seethingly erotic eternity—desire and wrath co-involved and kaleidoscopic—is of greater philosophical importance.

Genesis 3 was, by some distance, the most fraught text in early modernity. Salvation, damnation, theodicy, misery, misogyny, death, animality and any number of other subjects could be traced to it, but by most readings, Genesis 3 is straightforward in its interdiction against eating from the tree, followed by Eve's and Adam's disobedience. Boehme would have time reversed rather than God impugned. The moment of the Fall recedes, and recedes continuously in a cosmos where eternity is tied in knots with time. Adam's perfect balance of principles at the creation (the dark, the light, and their external manifestation) becomes unaligned, maliciously so and through his own fault, and that fault echoes back. Not only did he generate the tree, but his Fall was responsible for the birth of Eve—in that order. Androgynous Adam ("Adam was a Man and also a woman, and yet none of them [distinct]") "fooled away" their hermaphroditic innocence, for which they were punished by the sleep and severance of Eve, his womb:[81]

> *Venus's Matrix* was taken from *Adam,* and formed into a *woman* . . . *Eve* was halfe the *Adam, viz.* the Part wherein *Adam* should have loved and Impregnated himselfe; the same, when as he stood not, was taken from him in his *sleep,* and formed into a woman.[82]

The hermaphroditism of Adam is an idea that is relatively familiar in early modern thought, albeit often referred to rabbinic speculation, but the temporal distortion we find here is unique. Not only has the instant of the Fall been traced back in time, so that Adam can create the tree of his own downfall, but Adam's fall occurs *before* the creation of Eve who tempted him. His fallenness is the cause of her. Back and back, Adam is guilty before the fact, in his tainted essence. Alexander Koyré speaks of the "optical illusion" of sequentiality in relation to God and the emergence of the divine Principles, and this goes not just for the birth of the universe, but for the "meaning" of biblical characters in *Mysterium Magnum*.[83]

It is not the case, for Boehme, that the biblical story did *not* happen as written, but rather that that constitutes only the *outward* order, which may at times be wholly estranged from the real, the internal. So when, for instance, he is describing the expulsion from Eden, he begins: "The Speech of *Moses* concerning this Mystery, is wholly hidden to the Earthly Man." We simply cannot apprehend the tale ("for *Moses* speaketh of an *Angel, and Sword*"), even though its Mosaic description is entirely accurate "and albeit the Outward figure was even just so (for so was *Adam* driven out) yet it hath far another A. B. C. *internally*."[84] This internality involves, by default, the simultaneity of events from the perspective of eternity, and while, in one respect, this is a hermeneutic gambit native to exegesis (the Augustinian *nunc stans*), for Boehme, it functions at the level of both typology and ontology; the eternal is at work in Adam, not only caramelizing him into corporeality at the Fall ("whereupon the flesh became grosse hard thick and corruptible"), but acting out the whack of the eternal bruise and its healing: "But the breaking [or dividing] of *Adams* Essence, when the woman was taken out of him, is the breaking or bruising of *Christs body* on the Crosse, from the sixt houre unto the ninth."[85]

From the perspective of eternity, all is not lost in the Fall of Adam, though it remains lamentable. Unfallen Adam, we find, would have given birth himself: "not by a sundry peculiar *issue* from *Adams* body, as now; but as the Sun through-shineth the water, and rends (or teares) it not."[86] Had Adam not fallen and thickened into earthliness, the structure of the universe would have been different. Indeed, Boehme takes a chapter to imagine how it would have been. In a particularly Behmenist bending of the pictorial trope by which unfallen Adam and Eve are surrounded by playful animals, who after the Fall would become fierce, Boehme pictures the pair with some lovely metals to play with:

> The Tincture of the Earth had been their delight and passtime; they had *had* all metals for their play *untill* the time that God had changed the outward World: *no* feare or terrour had been in them, also *no* Law from any thing, or to any thing.[87]

The outcome of the Fall: we do not get to frolic naked with sulfur in the garden. Boehme's language of play is thoroughgoing. The reason behind creation is less praise, as contemporary theologians have it (or forced *Halleluiahs*, as Milton's Mammon complains), but is rather for the playtime and entertainment of God, "for the Delight, and play of the divine Power: so that the invisible might play with the visible."[88]

Genesis and the Hermeneutics of Eternity

Mysterium Magnum is not only hexameral. It is a commentary on the entirety of Genesis. Chapter by chapter, it proceeds through histories of Cain and Abel, Noah, Abraham and Sarah, Isaac and Rebecca, Jacob and Esau, and onward. This analysis, however, proves no less strange and distended than the account of Adam and Eve. Protestant hermeneutics was at ease with typological, Christological, and eschatological readings of the scriptures, albeit they swore blind that their engagement was literal and unencumbered by allegorical misdirection. Boehme routinely deploys typological maneuvers ("the whole *Old* Testament is a figure of the New, and the *New* a *figure* of the future *Eternall* world"),[89] which gambit in post-Reformation exegesis permits the reader to attest to the historical, literal probity of the text, while also allowing it to signal a wider scheme of Christological history. But what Boehme does is quite distinct from this. He is fairly indifferent to the "historical" meaning, insofar as it is merely the shell for what the text means on the inside. The Bible continually empties itself of mundane meaning, to refer instead to wilder, kenotic-prophetic spheres of being. The Word goes rogue, and the "outward meaning" of the text becomes a Pharisaical distraction, for those who understand only "in the husk, viz. in the outward letter, what God hath spoken."[90] Relentlessly, Boehme dissolves and dismisses the narrative logic, and even the covenantal coherence of Genesis.

As in his time-defying explanation of Adam's being the fallen cause of the tree by which he fell, in tale after tale, the commentary demands an exegetical shift of gear. Sometimes, it refers back to the alchemically derived language and cauldron of pre-creation. At other points, it refers, in "prophetic" fashion, to a Christological eternal. Of the fire and brimstone that rained on Sodom, for example, Boehme speculates on its relation to "the inward hellish fire, which at the *End* of dayes shall *purge the Floar*," but concludes that the fire was created at the very origin of time, ready for its destructive purpose: "The Originall of the brimstone, and fire was generated *in Turba magna* in the third Principle: it was onely a *Sword* of vengeance." But then again, he goes on, the text may not indicate fire in the outward sense at all: "although it be no palpable matter or substance; yet it is a *spirituall* substance."[91] The matter, for Boehme, is not a question of "naturalizing" the scriptures, explaining their fantastical and miraculous events by reference to plausible, nonmiraculous mechanisms, so as to maintain the literal integrity of the text. Boehme refers biblical events back to his natural philosophy with some frequency, but his natural philosophy is hardly literal, either. It refers on the whole, with its spiritual sulfur and mercury, to the nonmanifest world.

Equally often, Boehme's reading of Genesis is *prophecy*, by which he understands the "modalizing" of the story into the eternal. Anything less, anything more literal, is merely a *"child-like History."*

> And know for certain that this *first* book of *Moses* was written wholly from the Prophecy of the *Spirit,* intimating what each Act, or sentence of the History holds forth in the figure, and whosoever will read, and rightly understand these Acts [of the Patriarchs]; he must modelize or represent in his minde, the old and new man; and set *Christ* and *Adam* one against the other; and then he may understand *all,* and without this, he understands nothing hereof but a *child-like History*; which yet is so rich and full of *Mysteries,* that no man from the cradle unto the longest age, is able to express them.[92]

It would be hard to place Boehme's exegetical practice on any standard spectrum from Protestant to Catholic. But one thing seems significant: the person, as a distinct entity, even Adam, even the reader, is not particularly the unit of thought.[93] Boehme's world has more important things going on than the sovereign individual. This proves to be the case across the commentary. It is not that he disregards its history-of-the-individual and his and her covenantal relationship to God, but that is not how the universe works, and how the universe works is his subject. Genesis is, for Boehme, an electric storm of the temporal and eternal; things that may matter on the small human scale prove insignificant. Inside things (be it a clod, or Adam, or the reader) the eternal remains electric. What is most shocking about Boehme is his consistency on this point, that it trumps narrative logic, that while, on the one hand, he seems to accept that most essential of Protestant tenets—the foundational importance of the Bible—he does so with the proviso that reality is supple. The story keeps reformulating itself, every explanation churned into another explanatory framework. What something is in its essence—and that includes biblical characters—is entirely different from what it is in its manifestation, its outward form. Boehme's world, both cosmology and biblical, convulses with category errors, melting and modalized, continually changing. Nothing is itself.

One other facet of Boehme's exegetical practice that has often been noted is how frequently he lambasts the pridefulness of "wiselings." But the Bible is a text built to resist the cunning of the self-interested reader. Throughout his writings, Boehme preempts and incorporates objections to his own spiritual readings. In *Aurora*, this is often against the "high masters," the professors, and those who traduce the simple and the unlearned. In *Mysterium Magnum*, however, the anticipation of objections is more often couched as what "Reason saith."[94] In the second epigraph to this chapter, I quote one of Boehme's most beguiling, but deadly serious, hermeneutic statements, explaining how he knows what he cannot know:

> Albeit *selfe-Reason* might heere cavill at us, and say, we were not by, when this was done: yet we say that we in a *Magicall manner* according to the Right of Eternity, were really there, and saw this: but not I, who am I, have seen it; for I was not *as yet* a Creature; but we have seene it in the *Essence* of the Soule which God breathed into *Adam*.[95]

Describing the "Fall of Lucifer with his Legions," Boehme concedes the "event" to be shrouded in its impenetrable past ("we were not by, when this was done"), except for the fact that we still tingle with the matterless animation of Eternity, smoking within us, a bodiless atom of the divine "breathed into Adam."[96] This knowledge is not singular to mere Boehme ("but not I, who am I"), but is kaleidoscopically knowable, for God "manifesteth himselfe in his own mirror," which shard exists still in the soul, such that God might or one might look "back through the Essence of the Soule, into the *beginning* of all Beeings."[97] Properly examined, we are time machines, back to the seething abyss. Attending as they do to the terrain of a fraught theodicy, the chapters on the fall of Lucifer and those on the fall of Adam and Eve are thick with the caveats and cavils of reason—"Thou askest; what was that which did cause it in himselfe?"[98] This practice of dynamic knowing, however, is not confined to things out of time, to the palpably unknowable prehistory of creation. The same seething is intrinsic to the acrobatics of reading scripture (which is reading the world) from start to finish. Scripture is mud to the learned, to "the *Selfish* wiselings of outward Reason."[99] Anything worth knowing has to be known through the crystal and Christology of the spirit: "The words of *Moses* concerning the Creation are exceeding clear; yet unapprehensive to reason"—which, as I noted earlier, is Boehme's comment on the opening lines of Genesis.[100]

Again and again, we meet with this dynamic, a quintessential logic of enthusiasm, of knowledge by swarm and volatile poetics. "*I have read* the Writings of very high Masters, hoping to find therein the ground and true depth," he writes in *Aurora*, "but I have found nothing, but a *half dead* Spirit, which in anxiety travelleth [travaileth]."[101] Knowledge must gush and is understood in its texture and movement. Boehme is generally undaunted by imagining the peevish objections of others, but he will on occasion anticipate complaints. In writing "Of the Paradisicall State, shewing how it should have been if *Adam* had not fallen," he insists, as with his account of the fall of Lucifer, that yes, it may be impossible to know in historical/bodily/literal terms, not having been there in body, but alongside this, that the terrestrial unknowable is only one pulse of knowing. There are other kinds of memory and certainty:

> I Know the Sophister will heere cavill at me; and cry it down as a thing *impossible* for me to know; being I was not there, and saw it my selfe: To him I say, that I in the Essence of my Soul, and body, when I was not as yet I, but when I was in *Adams Essence,* was there, and did *my selfe* foole away my Glory in *Adam*; but being Christ hath restored it againe unto me, I see in the Spirit of *Christ,* what I was in *Paradise*; and what I am now in *Sin,* and what I shall be againe: and therefore let none cry it out as a thing un-knowable; for although *I Indeed* know it not; yet the Spirit of Christ knoweth it *in me*; from which knowledge I shall write.[102]

The argument here is yet more elaborate than the earlier example: not only that Adam's essence still retains its ghostly pulse and godly mirror in him, but that though he, himself, is empty of any such knowledge, "the Spirit of Christ knoweth it *in me*." In this opposite of kenotic action, Christ re-inhabits the body so wholly as to re-instill the spark of the eternal and overflows into the writing Boehme.

Reading Boehme in Radical England

The early modern English radicals who admired Boehme can similarly be characterized by their disdain for the pedantic and the elaborate learning of the universities; in looking at Anna Trapnel, in chapter 5, we will find the same rhetorical dynamic. Sufficient for such readers was that the Christ inside would dictate what was worth knowing—plain and true—and all the rest was empty. But Boehme is not plain, by any stretch of the imagination. His immensely complex cosmology and modalities of the divine, his distortions of the temporal and the "modalization" of the eternal into existence, into levels, properties, and impulses is hardly the clarion Word of a Christ-of-the-simple. It is true, particularly of *Aurora*, that he rails against the theologically baroque and the learned. But it remains the case that Boehme's Genesis is a cornucopia of explanatory mechanisms, more complex than the Ptolemaic universe and its ellipses. A recent return by Nigel Smith to Boehme's writings is entitled, "Did Anyone Understand Boehme?" and notes the defensive, evasive, and sometimes baffled prefatory statements by his translators.[103] That he was "hard" was a given. He was, as one of his early modern translators, John Elliston, put it, an author who dealt in "the Science of the Nothing, Something and All things . . . the deepest, darkest, and hardest Questions, and *Quaere's*, that can arise within the minde of man."[104] But we should not imagine, I think, that his radical readers are necessarily troubled by his difficulty. If his natural philosophy was strange and idiosyncratic, it may be that the theopoetics of his text appeared less so. Boehme's inside-out reality, prophetic with the eternal pulsing in the temporal, was a hermeneutic model that was not entirely unfamiliar. When, in and around the English civil war, radicals, women in particular, produced their quasi-prophetic writing, they were wholly attuned to the notion of a pneumatic inner pulse modulating into outward manifestation, or finding Christ in the Old Testament.

The cast list of English Behmenists (or in one case *Bethmenists* and another *Beemists*) is large, as noted in brief earlier.[105] John and Samuel Pordage, father and son, are evidently indebted to Boehme, while figures including Morgan Llwyd, TheaurauJohn Tany, and John Webster have been variously and convincingly linked.[106] The community that developed after Pordage's death around Jane Lead and the Philadelphian society has long been noted as Behmenist.[107] An impressively full cast of other early modern radicals have been linked to Boehme, if sometimes in speculative fashion, including William Dell, John Saltmarsh, Gerrard Winstanley, Lodowicke Muggleton, and Henry Vane.[108] As much might be gleaned from those who attack the followers of Boehme. Richard Baxter and others can be found abhorring their dangerous incoherence, and he numbers Boehme's admirers (particularly "Dr. *Pordage* and his Family") in taxonomies of radical sects, characterizing him as an *ignis fatuus* for his impressionable followers.[109] Gerardus Croese, in his *General history of the Quakers*, writes of Boehme as "a Man, who if he was not stark Mad, was yet highly disturbed in his Mind and Understanding"; his followers put forth a Theology too "gastly, and even terrible to be uttered."[110] As was the case with Boehme's *bête noire* in Görlitz, the pastor Gregor Richter, the problem was not necessarily any heretical specifics, but rather a class animus that a shoemaker should meddle with theology. Alongside this was also a converse phenomenon, of writers impressed that someone of unlearned upbringing, "being brought up at first a Cow-keeper or Herdsman, and after a Shoe-maker and Cobler in a Village," could produce such "inestimable Works." The anonymous writer goes on: "for what deep Mystery, what great *Arcanum* is there in Natural, and Moral, and Divine Philosophy, which he hath not been perfectly acquainted with, without the study of Books?"[111] Perhaps closest to later opinion about Boehme, however, in its somewhat warmer condescension, is Henry More's comment in a letter to Anne Conway, that "Honest Jacob is wholsome at bottom though a philosopher but at randome."[112] More has some admiration for Boehme's sincerity, and he is in many respects open to what he (mis)understands as Boehme's nascent, homemade Platonism.[113]

For all that Boehme's cosmogony is spectacular, its reception, in early modern England at least, was less concerned with the sublime landscapes of the uncreated, than impressed by his hermeneutic agility. While his attention to the motile, elemental enkindling of life no doubt impressed some readers, of a Paracelsan bent, it was his model of the surging inner spirit, producing immanent religious knowledge, that endeared him to his radical English and Dutch readers.[114] Boehme mattered because, as Nigel Smith notes, he was understood as writing within a prophetic hermeneutic.[115] The wild and unkempt illogic that brought its raging elements together was part of the appeal. Here was a writer who could pleat and overlay scriptural, symbolic, and esoteric languages together, with a very particular poetic of chaos and the unknowable. It is the nature of this prophetic poetic that is at the core of this chapter: its continual refiguration of Genesis, as hexameron, as narrative of the Fall, and on into the cold annals of weary humanity. This is a quite different figure from the Boehme of the philosophers, but is closer, I think, to how early modern readers encountered him. No biblical story, we find, is merely its own ethical or theological entity. Each and every one crackles with the energy of the universe and a fiery inner physics, discernible to the Spirit, its essence numinous to the prophet and listless, bare, to those, as Boehme's translator, John Ellistone, puts it, "who are *meerely* trained up, and skilled in the litterall and Historicall Schoole of this World."[116] Boehme's theopoetics consist largely in his stretching of logic to replicate an experience of divine immanence beyond words, beyond categories, and which makes a mockery of orderly cognition. It is a poetic of things that are there and then not there, a world in which reality is a fleeting affair.

In his *Perfection Proclaimed,* Smith cites John Perrot, writing in 1661, in a slightly baffling passage seeming to link Boehme to Thomas Browne, pairing them as writers illuminating the mysterious nature of God:

> I might say unto you, how that in the dayes of *Luther,* GOD moved in the *Darkness* upon the *face* of the *deeps* thereof; but they which made *him* [Luther?] their *Rest* are *confounded,* and their *head* is *broken* as Clay. He [God] appeared *brighter* by *Behman* and *Brown;* but they which built their *Travels* as *Towers,* the LORD *confounded* with many *Languages,* and even running up to the height, *Baptists, Seekers* and *Ranters.*[117]

Boehme and Browne are unlikely bedfellows. Browne is generally averse to schism. He is sober, if mystical, and would not generally be understood as an enthusiast. Perhaps this could be a different Browne whom Perrot has in mind, but I think Smith is correct, and that they belong in a seventeenth-century taxonomy of the unknowable, in a manner that belies political affiliation. Browne's *The Garden of Cyrus*, the subject of the next chapter, is, in many respects, as skittish as Boehme, no mean feat at all.

CHAPTER 3

Thomas Browne's Poetics of the Unspeakable

DENYS TURNER'S *The Darkness of God*, his brilliant account of the medieval and neo-Platonic apophatic tradition, opens by describing it as a "philosophical history of some theological metaphors"—interiority, ascent, light and dark—noting how, with overuse, they become tired. We cannot suppose that any formulation of God has captured some essence of the divine, because metaphor fails, and language that hurled us once into ecstasy becomes crass, thick, and lifeless. Better to imagine God drunk and hungover, cursing and swearing or sleeping it off—the metaphors are from Dionysius the Areopagite—because God imagined as light or sun or king no longer jolts; the analogies are exhausted. Outrageous comparisons "have greater power to shock us into a sense of the divine transcendence by the magnitude of the metaphorical deficiency." We need new names. We need new metaphors, the odder the better.[1] The poetics of the apophatic constitute the experience. They are not a helpful description of an experience that takes place in some other (nonpoetic) mode. They work their crafty effects on the inattentive mind, and in sudden, skewed insight transport the self. Early modern Protestantism, though frequently keen on the idea of unpremeditated prayer, eschewing the dead forms of ritual language, would perhaps find it distasteful to suggest that there is a *rhetoric* to addressing God, implying as it does shrewd and wily prayer that works its crafty effects, to wheedle one's way into an experience of the divine. But the era was very much aware of the distinctly rhetorical character of the scriptures, and of that quality of metaphor, that it loses its luster, that it has a short half-life (atomically speaking) before its energy decays. The apophatic is ravenous, and constantly needs to be fed with fresh scraps, new metaphors, a cataphatic hunger. The same might be said of early modern natural philosophy, in its state of Baconian ecstasy, its gluttonous accrual of fact upon fact. Science too was hungry, prone to inattention and never able to rest. In most writers, these might be quite distinct kinds of intellectual or spiritual avarice. But sometimes, in the seventeenth century, they could coincide.

"We behold him but asquint upon reflex or shadow," writes Thomas Browne of the elusive, too-bright God, "our understanding is dimmer than Moses' eye, we are ignorant of the backparts, or lower side of his divinity."[2] When we are faced with what cannot be looked at directly, because it is either too immense or too intense, strategy is required. To glimpse the sheen of Yahweh ("thy glory"), Moses in Exodus was placed in the cleft of a rock with God's hand in front of his eyes until, whipped away as he passed by, Moses was permitted to see God's enigmatic "back parts"—a holy peekaboo. In a not dissimilar Ovidian scenario, Semele, the mother of Bacchus, was tricked by jealous Hera into tricking Zeus to show himself, and was burned to a cinder for it.[3] The transcendent needed to be approached askew or glimpsed in rapid movement, and in the apophatic tradition, there was a poetics and a rhetoric to this, less to describe what by its nature is indescribable, than to suggest the experience of not quite managing to. Though it was something other than the unmediated Mosaic encounter with the rump of God, mere human thought about the world needed its maneuvers too, veiled, crooked, or metaphoric habits of thinking, approaching its mysteries aslant.

Thomas Browne, whose considerable early modern reputation was established with *Religio Medici* (1643) and *Pseudodoxia Epidemica* (1646), was a writer of such variety and so elusive a quality that neither contemporaries nor posterity knew entirely where to place him. His theological, speculative, and passingly philosophical prose was admired; the royalist and Arminian political sympathies threaded through his work were palpable enough, but not such that he obviously engaged controversy. He was encyclopedic in range, melding the classical, biblical, pictorial, and historical into what can seem strange amalgams of knowledge, and he seems little inclined to compartmentalize his humanist and theological learning away from the natural philosophy and the medical that was his home disciplinary turf, so to speak. Browne saw the world through the lens of his medical training, and its botanical, biological components. His experimentation was careful and wide-ranging, and was admired by numerous figures from the nascent Royal Society and the august Royal College of Physicians. Robert Boyle, Walter Charleton, John Evelyn, John Ray, Nehemiah Grew are some few of the many who comment on the acumen of his early publications. His 1658 works were quite different again in temper: *Hydriotaphia or Urne-Buriall*, published as the companion piece to *The Garden of Cyrus*, was an antiquarian and meditative threnody, while *Cyrus* was an evasive collage of speculative knowledge. There is every possibility, as Claire Preston has shown, that in among the Platonic dazzle of *Cyrus*, there is substantial scientific content in its precision of observation and its carefully differentiated understanding of growth and structure in the natural world. The generation of plants, their growth and physiology proves spectacular, and Browne attends in minute detail to the unpodding of seeds and unfolding of leaves, in an encyclopedia of natural process.[4]

Browne's *The Garden of Cyrus* (1658) might be the strangest text of the seventeenth century, or at least it might compete with Boehme for the laurel. It is learned, humanist, and scientific, and it is also capricious, puckish, and uncharacterizable. It treats the domino-five shape of the quincunx as the animating pattern of the world, in garden and planting design, in art and artifice, in furniture, in warfare, in nature. In fact, *The Garden of Cyrus* can hardly be described at all except by list, elaborating on how diffuse its objects of attention are, a very particular delirium and plenitude. From its discovery of pattern in the material and natural world, it moves to describe increasingly intangible cross-hatching, found wherever one looks or in whatever one thinks. Browne discovers deep-set pattern and design in the world, finding the chiastic as a principle of art and architecture, nature and society—he sees quincunxes everywhere, how trees are planted and bricks are laid, in Persian botany and Egyptian symbology, in crucifixes and pineapples, the sprouting of seeds and the scales of fishes, in Euclidean theory and in birds' wings, how our legs swing and how light enters the eyes. It is a delirium across "the whole volume of nature." And to what end might any of this be? This most knowledgeable of texts seems intent on putting its learning to purposelessness. *Cyrus* contains an undecidable, malleable, and quite possibly flippant epistemology. Is it a leg-pulling treatise, of infinite frivolity? The suspicion runs deep, from Johnson to Coleridge and beyond, and yet tonally it does not seem so. It would be hard to detect any satiric crescendo; on the contrary, it moves to a somewhat solemn, spiritual denouement. Such humor as exists in the profuse excess of earlier chapters gives way first to the scientific precision of the central book, and by its fourth and fifth chapters, its dynamic is something entirely different, more austere, more holy.

Among its trickiest of quincunxes is that of shade and light, which, abandoning shape, proves decussive (or X-shaped) across time: "Darknesse and light hold interchangeable dominions, and alternately rule the seminall state of things. Light unto Pluto is darknesse unto Jupiter." This mystical chiasmus, in which even the slow roll of seasonal time with dormant then generative seeds proves quincuncial, culminates in a glancing decussation of God and the world: "Light that makes things seen, makes some things invisible . . . The sunne it self is but the dark simulachrum and light but the shadow of God."[5] The divine flicker, on and off, is some kind of shadow experience of a reality that stretches from the minute observation of nature to the glimmer of a God, always passing by. The prevailing critical intuition about these latter parts of *The Garden of Cyrus* is that in their turn to quincuncial theology, they constitute a version of the Platonic, in which the visible, whether sun or seed, provides only an earthly echo of eternity.

This chapter makes the case that the *Garden of Cyrus*, a work premised on the profuse regularity of the world, on its geometric order and the pathological discovery of pattern, has its crescendo in the unknowable; or rather, a very particular variety of the unknowable—which consists in the unsustainable glimpse and always only ineffable experience. The vertiginous motion of *Cyrus*, its quick-fire cornucopia of artificial, artistic, and natural decussation, may be a dazzling collation of scholarly content and may be partly mischievous, but it also replicates an experience of an ungraspable, always tenuous knowledge; the argument here is that *Cyrus* should be seen as a work of scientific apophasis, that mode of thought that articulates the failure of words and unspeakability of God; but also that it suggests a feverish analogical cast of thought that is, after a fashion, a shared habit of scientific and theological ways of thinking.

CHAPTER 3

Browne's quincunx, traced in its protean, volatile, and kaleidoscopic shifts, endlessly reiterated, always changing—its latent shape tucked into every wall and crevice and flower pod—is less a sign of good order in the world than a mimicking of its absence or only brief presence. *Cyrus* might well be a work of poetic physico-theology, in which the deep pattern of the world displays the after-throbs of God's part in them, or a work in which the natural world exists as the exemplary configuration for thought and art. But the agitated pulse of the text, in which any instance of order can only be represented in the flit and flicker of changeability—the center of the quincunx never discoverable, never stable—is a characteristically theological and apophatic maneuver. It is also, not incidentally, a strange philosophical-theological facet of Plutarch's *The Ei at Delphi,* the text that comes closest to being a source in this most unsourceable of texts. In arguing for this philosophical-theological lineage of *Cyrus,* the chapter will trace both the relatively sparse presence of the apophatic within early modern Protestant cultures, and also the longer lineage of the mystically unsayable whose roots in Catholic mysticism are well-established. This is less, however, to offer any confessional or doctrinal affiliation for a text as idiosyncratic as *Cyrus* than to suggest that for Browne, and for the era more broadly, the resources of the apophatic were increasingly turned toward the natural world.

Nothing about Browne's thought, it might be said, is wholly divorced from his style, his rhetoric.[6] Very often, it is a trick of pace and rhythm: *Cyrus,* no less than *Hydriotaphia,* is stately and serene of movement, on one metronomic measure at least, even while its propulsive, obsessive changes are rapid and manic. Browne's prefatory comment in *Pseudodoxia* is pertinent here, when he describes the two "great and exemplary wheeles of heaven . . . whirled on by the swindge and rapt of the one" while maintaining "a naturall and proper course, in the slow and sober wheele of the other."[7] The clockwork skies both reel round in their diurnal spin and, at a different pace, in their annual turn.

Cyrus likewise is a work with two pulses. This is not just a point about prosody or texture, but is as much a theological matter, in a work that builds to its oblique mis-vision of the divine. Pace, in *Cyrus,* is a complex issue. The subject of the text is never really any individual quincunx, whether orchard or orchid, but rather the mystical structure that can incorporate all history, artifice, and the natural world in one quasi-animate design. It is divine plan and design that is the real quincuncial subject, in its sublimely fitting the things of the world to its stable and serene pattern. And yet the quincunx, as well as providing tranquil pattern, is also viral, if not virulent, in its infecting and inflecting of all and every object with a discursive energy, or entropy, quite at odds with this well-composed serenity, demanding its *copia* and an endless, voracious reproduction of fresh exemplarity, presupposing always an only fleeting unity. This dynamic—endless similitude, always approximating, never exactly capturing its object of attention—is a strategy of the apophatic. Taking its cue from *Cyrus* in all its indirection, this chapter begins with a quite hefty digression into the rhetoric of the apophatic, from its post-Reformation guises back to a lineage in patristic antiquity, looking at a theology and poetics of failed thought and muddled longing.

The Post-Reformation Apophatic

The post-Reformation centuries, I noted in the introduction, might be considered an era that did not much countenance, even while it might concede, the unknowability of God. Though it remained a theological commonplace that God existed in incalculable mystery and that the best one could hope for was to approach him via *remotion* or the negative theology of saying what he was not, the supposition ran deep in the seventeenth century that the sufficiency and simplicity of the scriptures would provide and, where it did not, then the book of nature would supplement.[8] The long Reformation produced a profusion of doctrinal subtlety, multistory theology, deep-layered exegesis, and phenomenal biblical scholarship. Hard unbendable Truths do not always lend themselves to thinking in the inexpressible register of the apophatic; seventeenth-century English doctrinal thought has been aptly characterized by Noam Reisner as beset by an "implicit fear of semiotic nihilism." But that was not, of course, wholly the case. The ineffable proved necessary, even while its runaway nature, its "solipsistic spirituality," was, for many, what Protestantism sought to rectify.[9]

Among the contemporary works that are apophatic in temper are the quasi-Laudian and quite Brownian writings of Thomas Jackson, whose *Treatise of the divine essence and attributes* (1628) was part of a multi-volume commentary on the Apostles' Creed published over a number of years. This particular volume attracted the ire of William Twisse over its equivocal stance on predestination.[10] There were countless works that dealt with the "divine essence and attributes," lamenting the inadequacy of our understanding. Jackson's work bears particular examination, however, in that it produces a poetics of linguistic failure, a sense that the repertoire of metaphoric thought both misses the mark and ossifies over time. The darkness or the hyper-light or the drunken love of God, as metaphors that sought to capture our conception of the inconceivable deity, could themselves atrophy and become platitude. The treatise devotes substantial attention to the difficulties of articulating anything about the unsearchable: "How farre wee may seeke to expresse" any aspect of the Divine, his "incomprehensible Essence, or his Attributes." That God is beyond what can be thought, beyond any plausible comparison ("whereunto shall wee liken him?"), produces, for Jackson, the compromise not that we represent him as best we can, but that we "illustrate this truth, that he cannot be represented" (representing unrepresentability), or that we produce in ourselves, by reference to the pluriform world, a heightened bafflement: "By variety of such resemblances as his works afford, may our admiration of his incomprehensiblenesse bee raised."[11] Metaphor and similitude, however, are built to fail and to represent only in part. Any one comparison will, intrinsically, be inadequate. In the face of this truth, that language turns stale, an accumulation of inexact likeness will go some way toward mitigating the deficit in our powers of comprehension and intuition of God:

> the more right resemblances we make to our selves of any thing, the greater will be the symptomaticall impression of the latent truth; some part or shadow whereof appeareth in every thing, whereto it can truly be compared.[12]

This need for "varietie" emerges from the insufficiency and partiality of any single comparison. We must, of necessity, continually reformulate our similes, to reinvigorate our always flagging emotions. Every definition demands another to correct its insufficiency. We should aim, he suggests, "to erect our thoughts, by varietie of resemblances (made with due observance of *decorum*) unto an horizon more ample then ordinary."[13]

The problem for Jackson in large part devolves on the problem of oneness and multiplicity, that God encompasses and embodies unfathomable and infinite variety without forfeiting his unity. Jackson, whose initial set of reflections on the divine essence deals with a troubling profusion of infinities, has Parmenides, Plato, and Aristotle tumble on a truth of multiplicity, which he paraphrases: "Multitude of things visible, is but the multiplied shadow of invisible independent unitie."[14] Everything we see as differentiated is so only insofar as we cannot discern its modality of the divine. Philosophical variety in polyphonic concert with theological oneness drives Jackson's discussion—indeed, he laments that Aristotle, in his "extraordinary talent of wit," wasted his energies in attending to particulars, to the many vagaries that constitute the scattering of scientific variety, rather than unity.

These conundra of apophatic thought have their quite direct echo in the manic similitude so characteristic of *Cyrus* and in its profusion of examples, all about the same thing, the single and the multiple, in an apparent tug-of-war. Each quincunx seems like a similitude for or an instance of something that remains beyond definition. Browne was, quite probably, familiar with Jackson. Reid Barbour notes a set of Pembroke connections via Thomas Lushington, Browne's tutor, and they share at least some habits of phraseology and ecclesiological inclination.[15] Jackson, in elaborating on the apophatic, and its delirium, deploys among his many examples the very Brownian, albeit commonplace, trope ascribed to Trismegistus of God as a sphere whose center is everywhere and circumference nowhere, his gnomic use of which annoys Twisse thoroughly.[16] Indeed, the sphere metaphor, borrowed from Cusa and before that Hermes Trismegistus, was a calling card of the long and loose tradition of mystical theology.

Before returning to Browne, it is worth digressing further into how an apophatic lineage had dealt with the issues that Jackson raises and which are deep-set in mystical thought, the sense of the always only partial, always flawed glimpse of the incomprehensible divine that religious practice could produce, and the suspicion that poetic language becomes stale, that in our growing immunity, we need ever more outrageous, paradoxical conundra to experience the necessary hit (in the druggy sense). Apophatic thought is plentiful and august, and it managed to be both immensely respected and implicitly distrusted within Christian theological tradition, its ecclesiology and devotional orthodoxy. God is, as the *Corpus Hermeticum* puts it, "Omninominabile"—the god of all names, and no name, "You whom we address in silence, the unspeakable, the unsayable."[17] At the patristic root of this trope that focused on the multiform name and nature of God was the fifth- or sixth-century writer, (Pseudo-) Dionysius the Areopagite, whose *Divine Names* recounts how God's baffling profusion of titles could never be encompassed at once. The representation of the divine could only be fleeting, whether as philosophical concept (monad, henad, trinity, cause), as adjectival kaleidoscope (the good, the wise, the eternal), or as the "dynamic energies" applied to the divine—fieriness, anger, anthropomorphized or physical object—all of which presuppose their own insufficiency, that simplicity representing complexity can always only capture one facet.[18] Where in human expression, we can encounter these only sequentially, in scripture, for Dionysius, they are all present at once. Describing the "unified and differentiated Word of God," he writes that all the varied terms of scripture refer to the whole, not to an aspect of God, "regarding the whole, entire, full and complete divinity rather than any part of it, and that they all refer indivisibly, absolutely, unreservedly and totally to God in his entirety."[19] The point of this is scripture's privileged, impalpable poetic rightness, which transcends anything the non-scriptural can muster, or indeed those same names or metaphors used outside of the scriptural tapestry. Each individual similitude is both insufficient and entirely apt. He uses an analogy to describe how this paradox works: 'In a house the light from all the lamps is completely interpenetrating, yet each is clearly distinct. There is distinction in unity and there is unity in distinction,' the divine 'dispensing itself . . . to multiplicity.'[20]

I noted in the introduction the deep-set suspicion of Dionysius as a purveyor of nonsense, a suspicion voiced by Casaubon, Stillingfleet, and others, and that his work was rendered still more dubious by the textual controversy in which his antiquity, his purported or implied contemporaneity with Paul (the Areopagus was the council that met on the rock in Acts 17.34), was disproved. If he was a fraud in his historicity, the accusation went, then might he not be equally fraudulent in his opaque theology, a mountebank in his snake-oil mysticism as well? While he was demonstrably a pre-scholastic patriarch of the church, with commentaries on his corpus by Hugh of St. Victor, Robert Grosseteste, Albert, Aquinas, and others, it was also the case that he could seem alien to Protestant sensibilities. His *Celestial Hierarchy*, with its profusion of angels like a roll call of saints, his effusive liturgical musicality, might well be seen as a quintessentially Catholic cloud of verbal incense.[21] It was perhaps always only a grudging respect that he was accorded in the Protestant world, but his distinct thought had its value.

Pseudo-Dionysius's *Divine Names* was a book of paradox on the compatibility of profusion and singularity, endless difference integrated into seamless oneness. The naming of God in the apophatic tradition is never about naming in the way that one might guess the name of Rumpelstiltskin; there is no answer, no final veil beyond which is only luminosity, or at least not for anyone but Moses. Nor is the thing at issue the accumulation of jigsaw pieces toward the whole, such that each name (Holy of Holies, King of Kings, the Good, the One) contributes to the diligent assemblage of knowledge and the encyclopedia of deity. Just as each name of God in scripture is pitch perfect and indivisibly whole, each name in its own insufficiency is also entirely wrong. Any affirmative thing we can posit of God is bound up with God's containing all opposites, so that it is not true at the same time as it is true. This is the paradox, articulated by Johannes Scotus and others in the traditions of negative theology, that makes apophatic thought so dangerous. It can say wonderfully misconstruable things like "existence is not an attribute of God," so God, a wayward reader might infer, does not exist.[22]

If this constitutes a canon or a tradition, it is diffuse and unsteady. One strand given to such paradoxes was German mystical thought— Meister Eckhart, Sebastian Franck, Daniel Czepko, and, as explored in chapter 2, Jacob Boehme—adept at rousing impossibilities, to stir the slumbering mind awake.[23] Browne's contemporary Angelus Silesius (Johann Scheffler), wrote an expansive series of aphoristic paradoxes, in his 1657 work, known as *The Cherubinic Wanderer*, which, after the manner of Eckhart, have Silesius prone to imagining a parity with the divine. In one couplet God dethrones himself, "leaping from His high throne" to place Silesius upon it. If anyone doubts his, Silesius's, perfection, then he has no belief in God. "I am God's child and son, and yet my child is he"; "I am God's other self."[24] There is in such writing an expectation that the reader knows how to interpret the epigrammatic, the paradoxical, and para-reasonable. This is not, by any means, theology rendered into couplets. Rather, the aphorisms respond to the slow dying and banality of once vibrant religious language and serve to jolt the reader out of their stupor, to demand that we decode the positive true nonsense that may be contained in the aphorisms.[25]

A quite distinct parallel strand in the canon of mystical thinkers (of some importance to the Brownian style of mysticism) might be exemplified by Nicolas of Cusa, the fifteenth-century German cardinal and political thinker, who produced a dazzling set of variations on apophatic thought, on ignorance and the ineffable, and the character of vision. In his *De Deo Abscondito* (1444), the *Dialogue on the Hidden God*, he crystallizes the idea that what can be apprehended, either physically in the natural world or conceptually, is at best a metaphor for or semblance of what really is, an always insufficient quotient of reality.[26] Cusa's most notable addition to the lexicon of the incomprehensible, in his *De Docta Ignorantia* (*On Learned Ignorance*, 1440), was to mathematize the apophatic, finding paradoxes in geometry that characterize something about God, that for instance "as a circle expands, the curvature of its circumference diminishes and at infinity, would become a straight line," and similarly with the flattening of a triangle, such that Cusa showed, as William Franke puts it, "how mutually exclusive geometric shapes coincide at infinity . . . how all contraries coincide in the divine nature."[27] That there might be a mathematics to our nescience, our ignorance, is in itself a dazzling coincidence of opposites. At times, the apophatic could come close to skepticism and the Pyrrhonist, in works such as Franciso Sanches's anti-Aristotelian *Quod Nihil Scitur* (*That Nothing is Known*,

1581), and Sanches was placed (with Cusa) on the Index.[28] The scope of the apophatic might be philosophical and very often was an adjunct to the poetic and theological renunciation of language, the "prolix speechlessness" by which a failure of words stood in for the inexpressible experience of the divine.[29]

Fidget Thinking

But the unthinkable changed in the seventeenth century and was put to new purposes, other than the relentless one-upmanship of apophatic unknowing, in which each mystic claimed more thoroughgoing ignorance. It changed in ways that relate to Browne and my sense that his reiteration of fivefoldedness in creation should be deemed apophatic. *The Garden of Cyrus* is not about God in the way that texts by Dionysius, Cusa, or Jackson are. Neither is Browne a Thomas à Kempis for his times—his is an accomplished pedantry and often a painstaking scientific frame of reference. Negative theology, as it emerged in the long, slow traditions of Catholic mysticism, tended toward inwardness, to the self's relationship to knowledge and God. It was a mode of the personal and spiritual pilgrimage to unknowing, or at least in some of the sixteenth-century mystics, John of the Cross or Teresa of Ávila, that is very much how it is presented, even while a part of the Christian mystic tradition, from Dionysius to Eckhart, was less concerned with the devotional or experiential.[30] The early modern apophatic, to generalize, tended to emphasize less the individual's spiritual longing than what might broadly be called an epistemological apophatic that theorized the edges of the knowable world as symptomatic or reminiscent of the edges of divine knowability. Its apophatic—and this, I think, is where Browne comes in—addressed frequently the inscrutable in nature and what its partial glimpse might reveal. The apophatic returns in strange seventeenth-century guises, such that writers and scientists encountering epistemological barriers, to knowing God or knowing the world, were not always looking for a definitive solution (it's Rumplestilskin!), so much as a way to incorporate our constitutional ignorance of at least certain things into our understanding of the world. It would not be right to say that the apophatic was secularized, but it was turned to the natural world. There is, I think, a not-well-recognized, counterintuitive sense that early modern natural philosophy, far from blazing always in its empirical light, attends as much to the texture of the impenetrable in nature.

The second reason for thinking that *Cyrus* borrows from this apophatic tradition emerges from the form of the text, the manner in which it lays out its hunting for similitude. God in apophatic thought, like the quincunx in *Cyrus*, is glimpseable primarily in the high-velocity relations between things, the startling palimpsests by which its brief manifestations hurtle into view and away. In the face of the unknowable, the mere darting glimpse must suffice, the back parts of God being as much as we get to see. As Jackson, quoted earlier, has it, in responding to God's unrepresentable, unthinkable nature, we are forced upon mere quantity: "the more right resemblances we make to our selves of any thing, the greater will be the symptomaticall impression of the latent truth"; a brief rightness is as good as it gets, "some part or shadow whereof appeareth in every thing, whereto it can truly be compared."[31]

In this respect, it is worth noting that the "negative" in "negative theology" is never entirely a list of all the things God isn't, but rather a list of what God is nearly, when there is a fleeting possibility of resemblance, which turns out to have been wrong or merely partial.[32] Indeed, one of God's many elusive attributes was his similitude to everything. Edward Evans's *Verba dierum* (1615), discussing Thomist "two fold Divinity . . . Affirmative & Negative," writes of divine metaphoricity, "The Essence of God conteineth the Similitude of al things." This God of the apophatic either is never more than impishly present or is pervasively unmissable, producing "Excellent and Superexcellent Negations, taken from things visible and within our reach . . . raysing in our viewe the sparkles, and the spangles of his Glory."[33] Nathanael Culverwel, sometimes grouped with the Cambridge Platonists, proposes, in his *Spiritual Opticks* (1652), a style to correlate with the impalpable nature of the truth it cannot capture. He will include no preface, he explains, because "The work is weaved of Sunne-beams, to hang any thing before it, were but to obscure it." Speaking of the divine enigma, he writes that the enfolded riddle of God "is properly *obscura allegoria,* an allegory with a mask on; it is a borrowed speech and a cloudy speech. A knotty intricate speech sealed up and lockt from vulgar appehensions . . . First, by way of removall or negation, when we take away all such things as are inconsistent with a Deity. And thus the Scripture riddles him forth."[34] How we fail to grasp the divine becomes the prize of the apophatic search.

One further instance of early modern natural philosophy struggling with language at the edge of the sayable is warranted. The idiosyncratic Norfolk medical colleague of Browne, the physician Nathanael Fairfax, writing in his *A treatise of the bulk and selvedge of the world* (1674), spoke of the divine riddle, and the unthinkable character of eternity as a manifest problem of our embodied state of being. In a work that is an impressively strange combination of the colloquial and the poetic and a philosophical language that attempted to purge itself of scholastic Latinisms, he notes how our ponderous material bulk and intrusive "thingsomeness" necessitates a thinking in material analogies, whose spiritual referent can barely be discerned, and that we must "uncloath . . . all those answerings or analogies, that do arise to them upon the account of our animalities or beghosted bodyhood."[35] Philosophical and Latinate abstraction, it seems, removes language from "the whole bulky throng of the world." Fairfax returns repeatedly to the insubstantiality of thought and word in attempting to picture the eternity of God; language being inextricably bound to things and the world's enmeshment in time ("successive or jogging on and on"), it produces its inchoate notion of God's "cleaveless or indivisible *now*." Entertaining the divine shatters grammar, and we are as word-bound as we are body-bound in the four-walled world, "little squared to unboundedness." We can no more speak of God in eternity than "Logick and Philosophy" can be uttered "by the neighing of Horses, the barking and howling of Dogs, the hissing and gagling of Geese."[36] The aim of this philosophical language reform ("allfillingness" in place of "ubiquity," "thingsomeness" for "reality"), for all that it seems to have a certain rusticity if not comedy about it, is not a withdrawal from the philosophical questions of his time, however. Fairfax engages in philosophical dispute on the hotly debated matter of Absolute Time, with Henry More, Pierre Gassendi, Walter Charleton, and Samuel Parker, among others, on whether God has his entity wholly outside time and space, and whether time exists, independently of motion and extension.[37]

CHAPTER 3

The divine muddles thought in the way that a strong magnet skews an electrical device. One cannot approach it with a right mind, because it befuddles. In one sense, this is the core of the apophatic, and its theological lineage is long. But there is something distinct in its deployment in the seventeenth century, in that it is so implicated in natural philosophy. Fairfax shares with Thomas Browne a taste for plunging into the unfathomable and the maelstrom of God's tempestuous being within and beyond the thinkable. Thinking, in this kind of encounter with the ineffable, is not syllogistic. God could not be worked out. Rather, the thing at issue, be it infinity or divine pattern, was always only the subject of a glimpsed insight, a truncated and fleeting thing resembling a thought.

Browne's quincunx at speed involves just this kind of rapid coming into brief being, when he notes, for example, Christ at the lattice window in the Canticles (typologically speaking): "which ours hath rendered, he looketh forth at the windows, shewing himself through the lattesse; that is, partly seen and unseen, according to the visible and invisible side of his nature" (562), which flicker enfolds two decussations together, the patterned diamond of the lattice and the other, the strobe light of Christ, there and then not, in the manner of a ghostly figure passing by behind, Browne having by this point rendered a madness in the reader such that all patterned and textured opposites constitute quincunciality.

While Browne's work may be singular in many respects, it is worth recalling Francis Bacon, who most dramatically insists on and deploys a "restless" knowledge, an aphoristic, fragmented form, that aimed to preempt and disrupt our disposition to wholeness. Whereas knowledge, traditionally, tends to preen, and boast about its "magnificence and memorie," Bacon's broken knowledge will aim at "progression and proficience." Natural philosophy, given to *sententiae* and magisterial summation, needed to reform its expression not in the cause of clarity and certainty, but to craft itself in "scattered sentences not restrained by rhetorical method," that would stir and provoke, its discoveries contingent, constitutionally unfinished, provisional. "*Aphorismes*, representing a knowledge broken, doe invite men to enquire further; whereas *Methodes* carrying the shewe of a Totall, doe secure men; as if they were at furthest."[38] For all that he was a totemic figure of the era's scientific ambition, Bacon's fidget epistemology, as it appears in *The Advancement of Learning* and *Novum Organum,* was not much imitated by those in the Royal Society or Henry Oldenburg's *Philosophical Transactions,* who liked to think of themselves as Baconian acolytes, but it may have a correlate in *The Garden of Cyrus,* perhaps the ultimate example of restless knowledge.

The High-Velocity *Cyrus*

Any single page of *The Garden of Cyrus* heaves and tumbles with examples of the quincunx replicated. A passage from the central chapter, for instance, minutely observes and scientifically expands on the morphology of plants, the miserliness of nature, always acting with maximum economy, in play with its profusion, finding pattern everywhere:

> The white umbrella or medicall bush of elder, is an epitome of this order: arising from five main stemms quincuncially disposed, and tollerably maintained in their subdivisions . . . A like ordination there is in the favaginous sockets, and lozenge seeds of the noble flower of the sunne. Wherein in lozenge figured boxes nature shuts up the seeds, and balsame which is about them . . . The like so often occurreth to the curiosity of observers, especially in spicated seeds and flowers, that we shall not need to take in the single quincunx of fuchsius in the grouth of the masle fearn . . . For even in very many round stalk plants, the leaves are set after a quintuple ordination, the first leaf answering the fifth, in laterall disposition. Wherein the leaves successively rounding the stalke, in foure at the furthest the compass is absolved, and the fifth leafe or sprout, returns to the position of the other fift before it.[39]

Though for long stretches, the text draws upon Browne's considerable knowledge of and minutely observed attention to plants, it would not be right to suggest that the work is *about* plants or gardens or the natural world. At whichever decussive object we enter the text, whether cocked scissors, reticulate spider, or the planted orchard itself, we find ourselves apparently surrounded on all sides by cognate shapes, the sheer generative profusion of a work that discovers its pattern with such ubiquity, enmeshing itself in a tangleweed of all things. Browne's quincunx exists in a state of restlessness, its epistemological itch and unsettled formlessness driving forward furiously like a scholarly berserker. The reader encounters the world, natural or artificial, from the cultivated garden, to the "language of . . . fingers" (561) crossed numerically, from the foliate leaves of architectural design, to the battle formation of the Romans, or the leafy lateral disposition of shoots on a spiral or helical stem, each in turn, but all in momentary glimpse only.

The objects of *Cyrus* suggest, demand even, that they should be understood to convey deep pattern, figuring divine care and design by providence, and they suggest also that in their beauty and utility they are heuristic. The world is there to teach us about the unspeakable nature of God. The limits of physico-theology are plain, however, in this respect. The things of the world convey only obliquely any facet of God. We see though a flower darkly. Any one object, once the expression of awe at its intricacy has been uttered, becomes again mere opaque object rather than a conduit through which to view the divine.[40] The very nature of wonder is that it is unsustainable and needs fresh meat continually (wonder is a carnivore), a new first glimpse of that which bears some echo of, some similitude to God.[41] Each object of *Cyrus* doesn't quite resemble the pristine quincunx; each in decussive turn is elaborated differently, attenuated, stretched, such that the very nature of resemblance, of similitude, comes to be the thing at issue. If divine stasis and unchangeabilty is one of God's characteristics, and orderly structure is the mundane reflection of that placid and rested God, *The Garden of Cyrus* represents less a mimicry of that stasis than an imitation of human restlessness, perceptual and perpetual fidgetry, a need for constant obsessive variety.[42] This is a very particular kind of plural—not the multiplicity of an encyclopedia, but the profusion of a single thing, a practice of infinite resemblance, each one of which is not entirely sufficient. It is the plural of the Dionysian names of God, each one of which is both perfect and partial.

Browne's quincuncial legerdemain creeps stealthily and grows steadily across the text. The opening garden quincunx, the embodiment of good rustic order, is pleasingly physical and solidly classical. There were quincunxes in Eden, in Babylon, from Xenophon or Varro, whose *De Re Rustica* describes

> rows and orders so handsomely disposed; or five trees so set together, that a regular angularity, and through prospect, was left on every side, owing this name not only unto the quintuple number of trees, but the figure declaring that number, which being doubled at the angle, makes up the letter χ, that is the emphaticall decussation, or fundamentall figure. (557)[43]

The history of agriculture, it seems, serves as a long meditative lesson in pattern. Likewise, the numerous "Artificiall contrivances" (561) of the second part, discovered with such ferocious invention, are palpable objects—pleated leaf sculptures, diadems, beds, stonework, nets, chess-boards, nutcrackers, or battle formations, all within a few pages—and some extended quotation is warranted, to give the flavor of Browne's elegant discontinuity:

> The beds of the antients were corded somewhat after this fashion: that is not directly, as ours at present, but obliquely, from side to side, and after the manner of network; whereby they strengthened the spondæ or bedsides, and spent less cord in the work . . . The same is not forgot by lapidaries while they cut their gemms pyramidally, or by æquicrural triangles. Perspective picturers, in their base, horison, and lines of distances, cannot escape these rhomboidall decussations. Sculptors in their strongest shadows, after this order do draw their double haches. . . . In chesse-boards and tables we yet finde pyramids and squares, I wish we had their true and ancient description, farre different from ours, or the chet mat of the Persians . . . Physicians are not without the use of this decussation in severall operations, in ligatures and union of dissolved continuities. Mechanicks make use hereof in forcipall organs, and instruments of incision. (562–63)

After this collation of material things, however, the quincunx becomes ever more pliable and frequently meta-quincuncial, prompting Samuel Johnson's comment "that a reader, not watchful against the power of his infusions, would imagine that decussation was the great business of the world and that nature and art had no other purpose than to exemplify and imitate a Quincunx."[44]

The botanical central chapter, the longest and most detailed in its horticultural cacophony, is formidable in its sleight of hand, not only describing how seeds and roots and stems and pods are quincuncial, but also presenting a profusion of plant-shapes hardly decussive at all. It attends with scrupulous scientific exactitude to the generation of plant seeds, the structural unfolding of stalks and leaves, and the seminal principles that impel the plant to life, and it is certainly the case that early readers seem to have understood the text through a horticultural lens, though it produces also its precision quincuncial observation of bones and skin, the lungs of fish or the texture of snakes. The chapter not only describes but, as Claire Preston has it, "effulgently enacts the theme of germination," changing so rapidly that the logic of their inclusion—similitude to the plain quincunx—is outpaced by the cascade of new instances.[45] Christopher D'Addario writes of Browne's close-up gaze upon the objects of his attention producing the kind of distortion his era was becoming used to in the warp of the microscope.[46] Everything, to Browne, starts to look chiastic.

Though he follows his vertiginous logic of decussive figuration, he also bends and indeed distorts his own quincuncial thinking: it comes to include spherical bodies; it ropes in the "sexangular cels in the honeycombs of bees" (576) and the "sphærical rounds of onyons" that mirror the "planetical orbes." The "irregularity of roundnesse in most plants" (586) proves no bar to their inclusion: "The cylindrical figure of trees is virtually contained and latent in this order" (589), that is, the quincuncial regularity of the world. If Browne cheats in shape, with increasingly tenuous resemblances to the Platonic crisscross, he does not stint to cheat likewise in number; the suspicion emerges that the mystical five that animates garden and art might itself be arbitrary. The octopus in its eightness, though initially an affront to Browne, can nevertheless be encompassed in the quincuncial pattern. The arbitrary in this, its "abstrusities of no ready resolution" (597), is palpable. Six might do as well for the mystical number, and indeed one writer cited by Browne in *Cyrus*,

Jacques Gaffarel, records a Hebraic riffing on the number six, alongside Kepler's snowflake "figured like a Star, having perfectly Six Angles, of an Exact Proportion."[47]

The final two chapters feature an increasingly wraithlike memory of the animating shape—the mere mirage of quincunx, whose brief and spectral presence is formed of the perspiration of trees, the diffusion of "effluviums perceptible from odours" (584) from the roots and treetops, the very smell of the world on the effluvial winds, all of which form a kind of X. Quincunxes discovered in the spiral twine of plants, in the "inward circles" (586) of tree rings, or in the tapering cones of tree trunks, become so inculcated a manner of seeing that the discovery of irregularity, something that is actually not quincuncial, causes a gasp. Browne notes trees made knotted and gnarly by "piercing windes . . . which hindreth oftimes the beauty and roundness of trees," whose very irregularity is mystical, whose lack of symmetry prompts wonder (586). If this account of the providence of nature is nearly mathematical in its description of the rhomboidal forest-disposition of trees or their conical shapes, if it is in some sense a meticulously observed botany, nonetheless it is scientific only in the most elusive of modes. The geometry of plants comes to echo architectural space and increasingly produces experience inside out: the negative space between things, the "proportion of intercolumniations" (589) between trees. The text rises across its five chapters to an impalpability, in a not dissimilar way to Raphael's well-known monist flower in *Paradise Lost*, that begins rooty and ascends through an increasingly insubstantial greenery to its airy and rare bloom, all in metaphoric resemblance to the promised metamorphosis of life for Adam and Eve, increasingly disembodied, as they hurl their moral way towards angelhood.[48]

Impalpably, the negative space of *Cyrus* moves on to negative light, and color in its quincuncial disposition, the light of forests providing a synesthesic moment when the hollowing hand that protects the eye from sharp light "maketh a quiet vision":

> and therefore in diffused and open aspects, men hollow their hand above their eye, and make an artificiall brow, whereby they direct the

dispersed rayes of sight, and by this shade preserve a moderate light in the chamber of the eye; keeping the pupilla plump and fair, and not contracted or shrunk as in light and vagrant vision. And therefore providence hath arched and paved the great house of the world, with colours of mediocrity, that is, blew and green, above and below the sight, moderately terminating the acies of the eye. (590)

That there is blue above and green below conforms to all the world's quincunxes. Browne describes the pulpy darkness of forests in which both we and nature are providentially secluded and the calicular enclosures in which seeds are carefully protected and enfolded against too searing a blaze, in the apophatic lines quoted in briefer form earlier:

Light that makes things seen, makes some things invisible . . . The greatest mystery of religion is expressed by adumbration . . . life it self is but the shadow of death, and souls departed but the shadows of the living: all things fall under this name. The sunne it self is but the dark simulachrum, and light but the shadow of God. (590–91)

Light produces only negative vision and the shadow of something else, something not quite like God. This hopscotch of semblance, things of momentary likeness, produces ultimately only dissimilitude, hardly decussive at all. This is both the wit of the text and its quasi-theological point, a world whose perfect patterned order can only be viewed aslant and obliquely.

If at this point, in the apophatic culmination of the unseeable divine and shadow of God, the quincunx has all but disappeared, Browne returns to it in startling fashion, explaining that light in rays, striking upon the "retina or hinder coat" and inverted on "the optick or visual nerves in the brain," produces its clinching ubiquity, in the observation that "all things are seen quincuncially" (591–92), that light in lines makes a quincunx of everything. We can, it seems, never escape the presence of chiastic form, as he moves on to the decussation of voice and echo, engrossing all our senses, even if the "mathematicks of some brains" (592) may be too irregular to perceive this; hallucination, even madness, may arise from want of quincuncial, multisensory perception, alert with a single purpose to everything, able to discern even "the ghost of a rose" (598).

The Protean Plutarch and *Cyrus* in Flux

Browne's apophatic and shape-shifting mathematics produces the very particular rhetorical dynamic of *Cyrus,* where the thing at issue, the thing that these comparisons refer to with such manic similitude, becomes increasingly elusive (the tenor is lost to the variety of vehicles, to use the language of New Criticism). No one thing, we might suppose, could suffer such a cornucopia of objects that resemble it—without its key characteristic being not stability but changeability. This is taken still further in Browne's final, numerological chapter with its quite different delirium, its collation of "decussated number" (594), in which any pattern of five produces its quick-fire echo of the quincuncial. Browne's sacral five has its source in Plutarch's *The Ei at Delphi* (the "Ei," or "E," the "Thou art" above the entrance). If *The Garden of Cyrus* has any forebear or presiding spirit, this is it, a text that has at least the ghost of a quincunx within it. Plutarch is cited by Browne as an authority on the number five's containing all things, "how antiquity named this the conjugall or wedding number," how male and female were figured as the numbers "two and three"; "inexcusable pythagorisme" (594–95) it may be, but it nevertheless constitutes fleeting quincunciality.[49] Whether the "quintuple section of a cone" (594), musical proportion, mystical and scriptural fives, the five-act structure of classical drama, or Platonic shape and divisions of the soul, five proves a number as ubiquitous as the quincunx.

However, the importance for *Cyrus* of *The Ei at Delphi* goes beyond number, and the latter's curious argument is worth dwelling on, as a source of at least a kind of apophatic thought, albeit from the classical pantheon of pagan gods. Plutarch's account of the oracular city attends also to the vertiginous and unstable divine presence over the oracle: "That this concerneth not *Apollo* alone, but *Bacchus* also, who hath no lesse to do with the city of *Delphos,* nor is of lesse authority there, than *Apollo* himselfe." He notes (pagan) theologians saying, "That this god being of his owne nature incorruptible and immortall," yet "he is transmuted and changed in many sorts."⁵⁰ This paradoxical characterization of God, incorporating both immutability and oneness together with ceaseless change, is very much the skittish dynamic of *Cyrus*.

One understanding of the quincunx might be that it represents some kind of the Platonic Form, by which the world is patterned, in which it participates. Or, it might be the celestial template by which physico-theology works, finding the trace of divine pattern in nature and, it might seem, in artifice; that the design of things reiterates in choral fashion the well-intuited Form. However, *Cyrus* might as easily be said to illustrate something very different, something that will not stay still, a shape-shifting, logic-defying Proteus of thought. Here is Plutarch on the nature of the Delphic divine (in Philemon Holland's 1603 translation):

> Sometime he is all on a light fire, and causeth all things to be of the same nature, and like unto all things: otherwhiles most variable, in all maner of formes, passions & puissances all different, and becommeth (as now he is) the World.⁵¹

This bi-divinity (Apollo and Bacchus) oscillates between "a constancy uniforme and evermore the same, a regular order, a serious and syncere gravity" and, alongside this, a figure animated by "games, wantonnesse and insolency." The Plutarchian flicker we find here, is very much the tonal mutability of *Cyrus*, which so oscillates between the serious and the puckish, and in which wholly diverse objects and ideas insist on their congruity. If the bacchanalian seems a long way from any form of apophatic theology, it is worth noting that Ficino's edition of Dionysius, according to Michael Allen, advocated the "Dionysian style not as dialectical but as dithyrambic, as the utterance of a poetic frenzy that resembles a festive incantatory drunkenness."⁵² This is a far cry from the spiritual stillness we might expect of the apophatic.

But there is a further Plutarchian trick to this disturbing divine inconstancy whereby the inherent multiplicity of the divine pretends to be all unity. The God who rules being dangerously inconstant, a trick is needed "to conceale and keepe these secrets hidden from common people," who must not know that the lordly Apollo, in his role as presiding Delphic divinity, lacks stability. Plutarch explains that the "sages and wiser sort," to cover up this scandal, practice a deception. They, in a tremendous act of epistemological duplicity, "name this mutation & change of his into fire, *Apollo;* signifying thereby, a kinde of sole unity whereunto it reduceth all things, and negation of plurality."[53] To allay the unbecoming spectacle of a god who cannot remain solid, one names that very process of protean change something solid and quotidian. But this is not just a trick to be played upon the vulgar. The truth of the divine, such as it is, is intrinsically fleeting:

> And if paradventure you bend your minde and cogitation for to comprehend a substance and essence thereof, you shal doe as much good as if you would cluch water in your hand with a bent fist; for the more you seeme to gripe and presse together that which of the [sic] owne nature is fluid and runneth out, so much the more shall you leese of that which you will claspe and hold.[54]

The mind that can adequately understand flowing water can nevertheless not clutch it to study, but in gripping at it, it disappears; the more one's attention aims to capture in thought the essence of this divinity, who is also the world, and who embodies mutability, the more elusive the divine becomes. This flit and trick is somewhere between an epistemological and a theological tragic fact, that "reason seeking for a reall subsistence is deceived, as not able to apprehend any thing subsistant in trueth and permanent."[55] This could be the leitmotif of *The Garden of Cyrus*, whose spirit of inconstancy figures in its torrent of brief learning, experienced in the manner of the apophatic, what is unspeakable, ungraspable, and momentary only. The fleeting shape of the absent God, the subject of a long strand of mysticism, becomes, in Browne, but also more widely in the seventeenth century, the model for a very particular kind of scientific concession: that nature itself poses its irreducible puzzles, susceptible only to its flood of unanswerable questions and briefly conceivable truths.

Plutarch's Delphic texts—the *Ei at Delphi* being one of several—have a varied afterlife, and he was much valued both for his sheer miscellaneous nature and for his matchless depictions of the moral, theological, and intellectual life of Greek and Roman antiquity. But he would rarely be seen today as a Jobean kind of writer. It is, then, curious to find Philemon Holland's introduction to *The Ei at Delphi* referring the text to and contrasting it with the Book of Job, the most apophatic of biblical texts. In explaining how "[t]he judgements of God are unsearchable," Holland comments on the quasi-Jobean unfathomability of the things of God, that "they have neither bottom nor brink; the riches of his wisdom and knowledge are inscrutable and beyond all computation: his waies are hidden and impossible to be found out."[56]

Browne has quite regularly been seen as a writer with a bent toward the numinous, imbricated in a mysticism that he discovers in the natural world or which emerges in the skew of his prose. One correlate of recognizing the apophatic in *Cyrus* is how it reinforces the elusive pairing of the work with *Hydriotaphia or Urne-Buriall*. That the two are entwined, in structure or in tone, has long been presumed, but not that they share a theological mode of inquiry and nescience. The conclusion of *Urne-Buriall*, with its breathtaking disavowals of knowledge, its threnody for the oblivion that "blindely scattereth her poppy," is perhaps Browne's most engaging statement of negative theology and of the poetics of unknowing.[57] Like *Cyrus*, *Urne-Buriall* moves simultaneously at both funereal, stately pace and in a kind of scholarly machine-gun fire, fact upon fact passing quickly to obscurity, swept away in the current of its prose. The elaborate monuments to the dead, traced over the first four chapters, produce as conclusion a lament on the vanity and futility of funereal remembrance ("man is a noble animal, splendid in ashes and pompous in the grave"). Perpetuity, Browne concludes, is unknowable, and even immortality, in its "handsome anticipation of Heaven," involves the wholesale destruction of the self: "annihilation, extasis, exolution, liquefaction, transformation, the kisse of the spouse, gustation of God and ingression into the divine shadow."[58] Both *The Garden of Cyrus* and *Hydriotaphia* pursue their immense learning on the presumption that it is but a frippery in the longer scheme of divine time that exists beyond words and into which knowledge will tumble.

CHAPTER 4

The Bewildering Surface from Boyle to Cavendish

BOEHME, BURNET, THE BOOK OF JOB and Thomas Browne, though they may be great writing, are not generally considered great science. One of the key claims of this book is that seventeenth-century natural philosophy considered the unknowable and its borderlands as fertile, that it was good to think with, as the phrase goes.[1] In the introduction, I noted Robert Boyle's dialogue on *"Priviledg'd Things,"* facets of the world that lay just beyond reason, that were "supra-intellectual," intuitable but beyond the thinkable. Boyle's hyperlogical and hyperpolite characters, in exemplary nonfractious dialogue, begin by wondering if the "subject of our Discourses is not Chimerical." They conclude, however, that there is every reason to press on with their attention to what they distinguish as the Incomprehensible, the Inexplicable, and the Unsociable—the last of these implying a truth that is incompatible with other truths.[2] The context of this was an amorphous set of heterodoxies around Socinian and deist thought on the role of reason in religion, and an older set of debates over whether truths of philosophy could be or needed to be reconciled with truths of religion.[3] For Boyle, there was traction in the voluntarist argument that God sometimes suspended the natural order of things in miraculous action—such as the virgin birth or the figures cast into the fire by Nebuchadnezzar who emerged unscathed—but this did not, by any means, preclude the inexplicable in the ordinary course of things. Some attempts to fathom the world just stupefy the mind—the examples he recurs to being both theological, the compatibility of free will and God's foreknowledge, and mathematical, the "divisibility of Quantity *in infinitum.*"[4] Things transcend reason, Boyle avers, in the way that things elude the senses. Bloodhounds can smell what we are constitutionally unable to, and things invisible to the senses—atoms, effluvia—can nevertheless be accepted as true, deductions proper to the evidence we have. "I see no necessity, That Intelligibility to a *humane Understanding*, should be necessary to the Truth or Existence of a thing."[5] This might be a statement we would expect of a religious or hermetic enthusiast, but Boyle's scientific and philosophical speaker is cautious and reasonable. He insists there are clear limits here—we cannot claim just anything to fall into this category, nor can we permit manifest absurdities, such as a "triangular square" or a "sunshiny night," but for all this, we can, we must, believe "that some things *are,* and so have general and dark *Ideas* of them, when at the same time we are at a loss to conceive *how they can be* such . . . that one may have some kind of *Idea* of a thing incomprehensible."[6]

Just as God could only be intuited in glimpses, refracted through the metaphorical, the paradoxical, and the partial, so too, aspects of the natural world might have to be known fractured, incomplete, as conundra. Boyle, when he is wearing his philosopher's apron, measuring the spring of the air experimentally, might seem the most methodical and august member of the Royal Society, optimistically probing the mechanics of nature. However, he insisted across his works—as did seventeenth-century thought more broadly—that any natural philosophy worth its salt had to contend with the ineffable, with the eternal, with the interim lightning flash of other realities that we might encounter, the quality of knowledge that was natural to angels, the mutability and partial character of logic in the world.[7] Both Boyle and Browne, writes Claire Preston, were writers "attuned to the incomplete character of natural knowledge" and who sought in complex generic form to express this. Boyle's remarkable suggestion that we could have an "*Idea* of a thing incomprehensible" is only a philosophical starting point, because one still needed to communicate this idea. It is never meant, in the dialogue, to represent a private experience, its irrationalism to be guarded away among one's personal paradoxes. On the contrary, the debate has the air of an academy, in its probing of difficult questions, such that the incomprehensible has to be incorporated into some version of natural philosophy. To do this required a poetics, not as embellishment, but as the investigatory strategy itself: language and rhetoric were constituent elements of how one could make sense of the natural world.[8] This was a pressing matter, not at the speculative edges but at the very center of early modern science.

Catherine Wilson's *The Invisible World* describes how, in the seventeenth century, ostensibly smooth, composite, uninterrupted matter turned out, under the gaze of amplificatory technology, to be a treacherous, gnarly landscape, pocked and intricate, not only permeable, but in a state of continual streaming with effluvia and an oozy unsolidity. The microscope offered a long series of encounters, both textual and visual, with the minimal, as counterintuitive as quantum physics proved to be to the twentieth century. "Science," Wilson points out, or at least science in the process of discovering new things, "is *improbable*."[9] Here were surfaces so utterly unlike anything the unaided senses could discern, that they could not but bewilder: they demanded both that the augmented senses be trusted as the conduit of knowledge of nature and that we concede those senses were deceived in the first place. Microscopy was deployed to support a resurgent corpuscularity, albeit there was skepticism about what exactly was being seen. As Christoph Meinel has noted, the imaginative work of producing atoms from what could be seen through the lens was considerable.[10] The coordinates by which one could map the surface to the inner structure of things became ever more complex, not least in the response of Margaret Cavendish to early microscopic publications, which was to elaborate on the relationship between exterior and interior knowledge, not in regard to what the observer knew, but to how surfaces themselves knew, surfaces that were vital and after a fashion perceptive, and which responded to their surroundings. It was by no means clear, in the early modern world, that microscopy was more than a distorting toy, like a kaleidoscope.

Early modern surfaces, scientifically and atomically speaking, were discovered to be a hilly, steamy rind of reality, characterized less by a common-sense solidity of objects than by their poor borders, leaky in all directions. Robert Boyle was far from alone in being troubled by sweat: "the great plenty of matter that is daily carried off by Sweat, and insensible Transpiration," as he put it in his *Experiments and considerations about the porosity of bodies* (1684).[11] Effluvia and extramissive qualities by which objects gave off their atomic exfoliations meant that few or no surfaces could be deemed solid, deep down (so to speak). Solidity was a matter of scale and a failure of attention to the minute. Porosity and permeability, the openness of bodies to the external, came to seem a fact about matter that was startlingly new. Innovative and strange as it might be, and dependent upon a microscopy whose epistemological corruption was still up for debate, the sciences of augmented reality were for Boyle a quintessentially Baconian mode of unknotting nature's intricate structures: "I scarce doubt, but if such little things had not escaped the sight of our Illustrious *Verulam*, he would have afforded a good Porology (if I may so call it) a place, (and perhaps not the lowest neither,) among his *Desiderata*."[12] Boyle's imaginary Bacon would have produced a science of neglected surface, a "Porology" to map the topographical terrain of the only apparently smooth. Bacon's expansive wishlist of things missing from the purview of human knowledge, his *Desiderata*, was a repeated reference point in the early modern rejuvenation of science, placing special heuristic value on the anomalous in nature (the "prerogative instances" in *Novum Organum*), and for Boyle, the microscope revealed a majestic strangeness and profusion of new discoveries in need of explanation.[13] Microscopy would discern the secret conduits and "perforations that pass quite through the leather" of the skin, the disturbing correlates of which include Boyle's presumably offhand comment that "when a mans skin is tanned it is of a greater thickness then one would expect."[14] The permeability of objects, their lack of borders, was not only a matter of anatomical curiosity, however. It produced, in early modern writers a sense of a new, near-sublime texture to things.

Whether fluid or firm, the stuff of nature might intuitively be deemed continuous. Surfaces kept the in in and the out out. There could of course be objects whose characteristics included the perforated and porous, but matter could nevertheless be thought of for practical (and even scientific) purposes as uninterrupted. An Aristotelian legacy firmly opposed to atomic speculation, and presuming the continuous nature of matter, albeit under qualified circumstances, was part of the furniture of philosophical learning.[15] Beneath the threshold of the senses, as Boyle phrases an interim "objection" to his speculations, "the body must appear an uninterrupted or continu'd one." However, Boyle was not prepared to concede much ground to this merely common-sense idea, when he addressed the subject in his *History of Fluidity and Firmness*, published in *Certain physiological essays* (1669).[16] His corpuscularity, chemical as much as mechanical, had little time for an illusory continuity.[17] Boyle's sense of omnidirectional porosity depicts the surfaces of things as never more than contingent and temporary:

> A Body then seems to be Fluid, chiefly upon this account, That it consists of Corpuscles that touching one another in some parts only of their Surfaces (and so being incontiguous in the rest) and separately Agitated to and fro, can by reason of the numerous pores or spaces necessarily left betwixt their incontiguous parts, easily glide along each others superficies.[18]

Fluids are in this sense illustrative of the motile reality in which, atomically speaking, constant motion is the very nature of things. Spherical corpuscles "conduce to their easie rouling upon one another," a continual turning upside-down and a churning of apparent surface. Discussing how "Salt-Petre" in gunfire "emulates a fluid body," he wonders whether this fusion involves "the Ingress and transcursions of the atoms of fire themselves" into the niter, and concludes that the "pervasion of a foreign body" is the most plausible explanation, not in the relatively gross manner of liquid diffusing into liquid, but a "more thin and subtil" invasion and interpenetration.[19] Natural philosophy sought, in such a formulation, an account of the forces that governed the "unloosable mobility of Atoms" and the interatomic "cement to unite them." The task of natural philosophy, faced with these corpuscularian dilemmas, was to theorize why things remained together.[20] To assert the boundedness of things, the simple integrity of objects, was not enough.

The emergence of scientific modernity is often still viewed as a sad but necessary putting aside of the poetic, a coming into rationality that is almost a narrative of the Fall. Whether via the disenchantment of the world, as Max Weber and others have posited, or via the Foucauldian epistemic shift away from an analogical "world view," a loss of the metaphoric capacity of reality was part and parcel of this epochal shift.[21] Liz Oakley-Brown notes Bruno Latour in similarly elegiac mode for the epistemological fullness of a time before the shrinkage and tautening of the cold seventeenth century, and this is perhaps not too distant from Michel de Certeau's account of the atrophy and gradual implausibility of mysticism, through the sixteenth and seventeenth centuries.[22] Joseph Amato, in his *Surfaces: A History*, describes just such a denuding of the poetics of the world that pits Da Vinci against Descartes. The medieval was engrossed in its "immanence and transcendence of every surface," embodied in the cathedral's lithic, luminous being, whose hulking blocks of stone could nevertheless orchestrate light and color, an experience of immense if not impossible geometry inside the stony lung of the outsized church. He tells the tale of this soaring, spatial encounter with the ineffable, which in the seventeenth century came up against an "antithetical way of reading surfaces," the Cartesian calculus, which could map the curve in astringent mathematics and a precision rationality that "washed the surfaces of the visible world clean of their sensuality and textures," along with the cosmological flight and ontological acrobatics of the medieval.[23] If ever there was a Fall, this was it, science and philosophy hand in hand with wandering steps and slow, making their way into the scrubby featureless earth of the everyday: "gone too were the whorls and shells of analogies, metaphors and symbols that had enwrapped entire peoples."[24]

Microscopy has similarly been crafted into a narrative of pigeon-stepped empirical progress, hubristic and cack-handed occasionally, a story inhabited by cartoonlike *virtuosi*, but in essence marching to the drum of rationalism and technological progress, ousting the idea of occult qualities and inching, by degrees, toward a more coherent understanding of forces.[25] There is no doubt some accuracy in this, and yet it remains the case that the intellectual *terra incognita* of the surface, newly available to the minuscule gaze of the seventeenth century, provided an epistemological jolt, a counterintuitive texture of reality that mesmerized natural philosophers: "well into the eighteenth century," notes Christiane Frey, "microscopists all note that the look through the microscope initially overwhelms all faculty of comprehension."[26] This experience of the tiny sublime, its bottomless abyss, was all the more daunting in that this strangeness could be wrought on the plainest of ordinary objects, a pin or a drop of water. Surfaces, those least metaphorical, most literal of things—the opposite of deep—became objects of untrustable paradox. This was experienced in writer after writer as an almost mystical buckling of reality: the definitively dull and paradigmatically ordinary-superficial had become mysterious.

That many things were beyond the ken of mere fallen humans, cosmologies too immense, or creation too intricate to fathom was a given of early modern thought.[27] But microscopy presented something different, and this chapter traces the amazement of early modern natural philosophy in the face of the newly unknowable, when the apparently smooth and continuous surface of the real proved calloused, inscrutable, and inconstant. This is a tale neither of the triumph of rationalism over a poetics of seeing, nor the reverse, but rather of their enfoldedness. The frequently florid rhetoric of early microscopy, in figures such as Henry Power and Robert Hooke, was less an ornamental addition to empirical description than a tactical poetics; a rhetorical mode that inoculated their descriptions of microreality from the harsh strictures of plain description that Restoration science prided itself on. Close observers of the busy phenomena under the microscope were not so much weighed down by the kind of "theory laden" observation that Thomas Kuhn or Paul Feyerabend warned about, as baffled by the experience.[28] What they were seeing rendered the thing they were looking at not just uncertain, but unfeasible. Ofer Gal and Raz Chen-Morris, in their *Baroque Science*, open with attention to painters' use of anamorphosis, the distended depiction of objects that make no visual sense. However, seen from a particular vantage point, the foolable mind corrects its skewed perspective, as a model of "*both* correct and distorted representation." Experiment that played in any such paradoxical gap, yielding apparently empirical or mathematical information, had something of the same distortion about it.[29] Microscopy suggested incommensurable realities: what was ordinarily seen with the senses alone, and what was seen with the senses augmented. Perhaps one of those ways of seeing was simply false. Or perhaps incommensurable realities could coexist. If that was not an acceptable proposition, and on the whole it was not, then a manner of describing, of negotiating their difference was necessary. The problem of what could not be seen—what lay beneath the next level of magnification—was hardly less serious than the problem of what could be seen but hardly believed. And more disorientating still was when the nominally unproblematic, that which barely presented natural philosophy with any significant difficulty, turned out to be riddled with surprises. The origins of microscopy involved a kind of shock, such that scientists came to think reality had been cheating on them, living a lascivious second life. Pepys's diary written in code, describing his sexual affairs, was not half as shocking as the revelation that the surface of the world concealed a dark and seething underside.

In its central part, this chapter will suggest that writers of the era found in Lucretius a model and a language for addressing the apparent irreality of scale and texture they encountered in microscopy. Lucretius was not considered a particularly serious scientific thinker, for all that corpuscularian and atomic thought might acknowledge him in their lineage; Walter Charleton opens his *Physiologia Epicuro-Gassendo-Charltoniana* (1654) with a quotation from Fernel on how laughable ancient atomists seemed.[30] But the Roman atomist, cited so frequently in the era, did provide a provocative *poetic* for thinking through the relation between the infinitesimal and the quotidian. The challenge that all of this presented is vehemently illustrated in the most strange and brilliant responses to microscopy of Margaret Cavendish, whose attention to surface, to the discontinuities of inner and outer, exemplifies the scope of the philosophical puzzle that the seventeenth century found itself faced with. However, the seriousness of her response has often been underplayed via her satirical writing on microscopy, in *The Blazing World*, whereas it is her *Philosophical Letters,* together with the *Observations upon Experimental Philosophy*, that most fully develop an alternative vision of the scientific apophatic.

Rugosities and Protuberances—Microscopic Disorientation

Early modern natural philosophers describe, with some excitement and some vertigo, the disorientating experience of the small, and the shifting scales of reference by which the straight line came to seem pocked, the smooth surface became jagged and the barely perceptible fleck of an insect proved intricate beyond any imagining. The complex response to such discovery involved, in the first instance, and in the first publications, a recourse to the poetic. Merely to communicate the strange sights, the dazzling order and bewildering disorder, the earliest accounts of microscopic vision sound at times like travel marvels, and elsewhere as though they need to coin a labyrinthine vocabulary to convey the remarkable world of the tiny: a nettle appeared to Henry Power like a "Sword-Cutler's Shop, full of glittering drawn Swords, Tucks, and Daggers." Describing a "line drawn upon paper," he notes how it "appears all ragged, indented, and discontinued by the rugosities and seeming protuberances of the paper."[31] Writing about "the Edge of a Razor," Robert Hooke notes that this most exact of objects, with its "affinity to the sharpest Point in Physics, as a line hath to a point in Mathematicks," seems so only "till more closely viewed by the Microscope, and there we may observe its very Edge to be of all kind of shape, except what it should be," a jagged "roughness of those surfaces," such that one "may find reason to think there is scarce a surface *in rerum naturâ* perfectly smooth."[32] Microscopy's discovery in the period was the outlandish irregularity of things, the illusion of plain surface, and its findings took Restoration London by storm.[33]

Power, a writer who, secluded in Halifax, remained peripheral to the tumult of Royal Society and Hartlibian science, was one of the earliest enthusiasts for microscopic exactitude.[34] Where Hooke, publishing a year later, commissioned and made his intricate, beautiful, monstrous, and outsized pictures of fleas, gnats, or the eye of a grey-drone fly, all swollen to the size of a football, Power's *Experimental philosophy* depends upon intricately wrought prose for its effect, depicting the world from its immensity to its most minute in a state of constant motion, such that there is no "absolute quiescence," neither in the pulsating heavens nor in the infinitesimally small. He argued, citing Bacon, that natural philosophy had for too long been held hostage to mere sight, in all its limitations, while its task ought more properly to be discerning the intricate surface of matter, by augmenting lenses as well as by deductive inference: "whatsoever is invisible, either in respect of the fineness of the Body it self, or the smalness of the parts, or of the subtlety of its motion, is little enquired."[35] Power's Faustian ambition was to discern the previously indescribable streaming of bodies, both celestial and effluvial:

> and as for the Opace [opaque] and Planetary Bodies of the Universe, they are all porous, and the aetherial Matter is continually streaming through them, their internal fire and heat constantly subliming Atoms out of them, the Magnetical Atoms continually playing about them . . . is it not, I say, more than probable that rest and quiescency is a mere Peripatetical notion and that the supreme Being (who is Activity it self) never made any thing inactive or utterly devoid of Motion?[36]

Not only did matter subsist in motion and mutability, a ceaseless subliming of itself, but God himself consisted in theological seething and insurgence, the raw principle of activity. *Ebullitio*, the boiling of God into creation, though now most often associated with Meister Eckhart, had a longer lineage and in early modernity, gained some scientific currency.[37]

Magnification, Power argued, did not distort as much as did ordinary sight, which was doomed to the intractably flat, a surface no closer to reality than a painted, perspectival stage set. The quotidian gaze was an epistemological trick, and any honest natural philosophy demanded that it be rectified by a technology to circumvent our planate human habits of perception: "without some such Mechanical assistance, our best Philosophers will but prove empty Conjecturalists, and their profoundest Speculations herein, but gloss'd outside Fallacies; like our Stage-scenes, or Perspectives, that shew things inwards, when they are but superficial paintings."[38] The theater of the world had been exposed, its illusory set being no longer believable. Power noted the decay of sensory powers as a facet of the long, slow Fall of the senses, asking whether the "Aged world stands now in need of Spectacles" and whether our "Primitive father Adam might be more quick & perspicacious in Apprehension," a passage we might suppose to be itself quite porous and absorbent of Joseph Glanvill's wonderful claim that "Adam needed no Spectacles. The acuteness of his natural Opticks (if conjecture may have credit) shew'd him much of the Coelestial magnificence and bravery without a Galilaeo's tube."[39]

Power's optimism in this "mechanical assistance" was thoroughgoing and uncompromising in its call for whatever might bring us closer to the reality of the miniature, to atoms in their oscillation and the secret motions of microscopic being. Indeed, he suggested that the sight of and insight into effluvia itself was not far off:

> we might hope, ere long, to see the Magnetical Effluviums of the Loadstone, the Solary Atoms of light (or globuli aetherei of the renowned Des-Cartes) the springy particles of Air, the constant and tumultuary motion of the Atoms of all fluid Bodies, and those infinite, insensible Corpuscles.[40]

Later in the body of the text he seems to backtrack on any imminent prospect of understanding how effluxions function, suggesting, in a phrase taken from Thomas Browne, with whom he corresponded, that it is "[a] part of Philosophy but yet in discovery; and will, I fear, prove the last Leaf to be turned over in the Book of Nature."[41] This uncertainty of scale—how much further humans would need to go to sound the bottom of physical reality, and what additional unsettling paradoxes one might meet in probing down—was not just a question of technological boundaries.[42] It presented also a serious epistemological problem. If atoms remained beyond the visible, what kind of demonstration was philosophically sufficient to make assertions about their nature? Did the rules of reason change as one approached absolute smallness or absolute magnitude?

Seventeenth-century theorization of atoms, from Gassendi, through Sennert, to Power and Charleton, was deeply invested in analogical models from the visible world, motes in the sun or clouds on mountaintops whose solidity proved illusory.[43] In the absence of any empirical demonstration of atoms, natural philosophers had to make do with extrapolation and metaphor, and early modern science was adept, in this respect. "I have more than once taken pleasure to look upon an heap of swarming Bees," wrote Boyle, "for though they make not up a liquid but coherent body, which may be turn'd upside down without losing its coherence . . . yet these motions of the particular Bees destroy not the coherency of the heap."[44] The era's stock of analogies was not, however, all of its own making.

Implexions and Entanglements: Lucretius and the Language of Texture

Microscopy "takes away the privilege of a surface," writes Catherine Wilson. The closer one looked, the more it became evident that the mere similarity, and microcosmic correspondences based on it, could tell us very little. Surfaces were open to their own interiors in the sheer knotty complexity of fibers and pores, and "in the interior of things there is no resemblance," Wilson continues.[45] The surface that looped in on itself, that dipped into its own involuted interior, revealed just enough of itself to demonstrate its unfathomable nature: "Implexions and Entanglements. . . Omnifarious Particles, jumbling together with infinite variety of Motions," as Ralph Cudworth wrote, not kindly, of neo-Lucretian atomic speculation.[46] But the era's perplexed engagement with nonobvious surfaces, which might churn into new layered realities before one's very (prosthetic) eyes, demanded not just more thorough empirical recording, but a language to correspond to this apparently metamorphic reality: "The division between inner and outer is just a tactic," writes Steven Connor, in his history of skin. Its exchanges are chronic and intrinsic and as unmappable as smoke: "a column of smoke possesses no simple inside or outside, but the supposition of interiority and exteriority, repeatedly insurgent and abandoned."[47] To speak of a "tactic" of reality might seem, initially at least, at odds with the Restoration desire for plain language in its science. But much early modern natural philosophy would be wholly at home with Connor's formulation of a turbulent inner and outer. Early modern writers were positively effusive and irredeemably poetic about the epistemological involutions, the baffling irreality that microscopy suggested. The surface of things was pocked; there were scaly rinds where things would be presumed smooth; there were shadow valleys dipping ever inward on the exterior of things, labyrinths folding in on themselves. To explain such epistemological chaos, writers turned frequently to the poetic, which provided some perhaps surprising, ready-made resources.

Natural philosophy in the second half of the seventeenth century saw a surge of interest in Lucretius, the "faithful Disciple and paraphrast" of Epicurus.[48] He is quoted in early modern philosophical writing out of all proportion to his "scientific" worth. His atoms were slightly preposterous by most seventeenth-century corpuscularian standards.[49] His fantasies of omni-explanatory philosophical breadth—that what explains the first grass also explains the weather and sex and feeling plaguey—were wholly beyond the philosophical pale. They were the opposite of Baconian sobriety, or Cartesian precision, or even the theophysics of those who would attempt a biblical mechanics of creation. He denied and indeed mocked divine providence and the immortality of the soul, and was frequently seen as straightforwardly atheist, albeit occasionally Christianized.[50] He was derided for the tale, apparently originating in Jerome, that he had fallen victim to a love philter, given to him by his wife, which drove him to suicide.[51] Any one of these things might have precluded his being taken seriously, and yet early modernity could not stop thinking about Lucretius.[52] Some worried that he was too good, with the seductive elegance of his poetry, "by the extraordinary Goodness of the Verse, the Badness of this Epicurean's Notions is (I fear) unhappily instilled into the Minds of young Gentlemen."[53]

Lucretius mattered to the natural philosophy of the era, however, not because he provided any particularly convincing demonstrations of atomism that would meet the exacting (or perhaps speculative), standards of early modern scientists, but for reasons more tangential: first, because of his poetics of *scale*, and second, because he spoke so impressively about *texture*. The disorientation of microscopic scale, by which continuity of surface proved only illusory, has its direct correlate in *De Rerum Natura*, which produces similar perspectival shifts that defy or mock the senses. Explaining how atoms in fervent motion could be constitutive of objects that were or seemed entirely placid ("motions which to us more obvious be, / At a farre distant space seeme to stand still"), Lucretius makes sense of their elusive motion below the range of the senses by reference to two scenes, one of pastoral stillness and serenity and the other, a ferocious melee. Both of these scenes, from a lofty enough stance, seem to be nothing like their close-up reality: when the "white-fleec'd sheepe, feeding on a greene hill / . . . the fresh tufts crop / And thus fed, skip about." From a distance, however, this hill is only as motionless a hill as any other: "farre of[f] seene, / Appeare only white heaps, on mountains greene." Or, in his second image, Lucretius has us imagine this hillside thronging with the maneuvers of soldiers in training: "when the armed legions exercise / And battells represent . . . And as they grapple, their guilt armors shine, / Whose glittering in the vaulted skie beheld." But from a height, the wheeling of horses and flashing of armor means nothing, a blaze of light only "from some farre mountaine view, / Where 'twould but like a standing brightnesse shew."[54] An apparent stillness of surface tells us only so much about its real, vibrant life. Just as the tumult of atomic activity passes below the range of any human scrutiny, so too scale renders emotion insignificant: the slow lovely pastoral or the intense tumult of battle are, from some lofty perspective, negligible, indistinguishable. From the distance of the gods, who will not be gazing down, from the perspective of the indifferent universe, or from our mere human perspective on a hill opposite, nothing significant has changed; the surface is placid, the world unruffled. *De Rerum Natura* makes divine indifference key to haughtily neutral matter; atoms have no design on or care for human welfare.

But the reader's disorientation, in quick-fire flight between scenes, does matter. Lucretius produces endlessly reframed analogies for how atoms move or are combined, and the reader has to adjust the scale of reference with some agility; they are, by turns, like motes in the sun in chaotic battle; like the flotsam of a wrecked flotilla of ships, "Plancks, rudders, sayle-yards, decks, masts, floating oares, / And all the tackling cast on severall shores"; like racehorses let loose with coiled energy; like the delirious unreplicable individuality of animals ostensibly all made from the same atomic matter.[55] Any one of these analogies is just model and metaphor, but in their consistent rapid reconfiguring of images, they produce their perplexing, but far from innocent, effects. I have been citing here from Lucy Hutchinson's rendering of the poem, the first full translation in English, from the 1650s, which large-scale work of, presumably, many years she was to repudiate in the preface of her epic, *Order and Disorder,* as a work "blasphemously against God, and brutishly below the reason of a man."[56] Many ostensibly agreed. And yet the poetic logic of Lucretius remained beguiling.

It is not just that atoms are "like'"these things, but that they in fact become them; the tiny anarchic atom produces the anarchy of the sea. John Evelyn, who translated the first book of *De Rerum Natura,* wrote in his animadversions on the manner in which the apparently invisible, unobservable atoms could manifest themselves though their cumulative effects:

> . . . which though they consist indeed of *Atomes* altogether inconspicuous to our weak organs, yet do their monstrous effects (which he there compares to that of precipitating Rivers and Cataracts, which have violated their banks, and spoil'd the adjacent places) prove them to be bodies.[57]

The Lucretian poetic embodies the stochastic, the scattered event, the infraction of the normal course of things, the *clinamen* whose almost undetectable deviation from its flow produces its cataclysm and butterfly effect of variety.[58] And this ability to replicate life at large on the scale of the infinitesimal proved an attractive quality both in the poetic and the proto-scientific deployment of Lucretius.

Thomas Creech, in the notes following his translation of Lucretius, attacks his author on many fronts, including his atheism and "endeavour to disgrace Religion," but is also concerned throughout with his scientific (im)plausibility, in the course of which Creech makes reference to the "many experiments of the Honorable Boyl," and other early modern natural philosophers, on for instance the nature of air, fluidity and continuum, and on the Epicurean ascription of weight to atoms, with the corresponding implications for their motion, "resilition" (rebound) and declination.[59] Boyle, in the preface or "Advertisement" to the *History of Fluidity and Firmness,* explained that he was only eclectically Epicurean: "The Authors Explicating things chiefly according to the Atomical Principles will not be thought strange, nor be lookt upon as a sure Argument of his being wedded to the particular opinions wherein the Atomists differ from other modern Naturalists." Indeed, he notes the merely strategic explanatory value of Lucretius, and that he himself is quite content to dispute or augment, when necessary, "especially since he has on some occasions plainly enough intimated the contrary, by proposing, together with the Atomical ways of resolving a thing, another Explication more agreeable to the Cartesian, or some other modern Hypothesis."[60] This claim to a productively strategic use of *De Rerum Natura* should, I think, be taken at face value, rather than supposing a nervousness about appearing too Lucretian—Lucretius answered a very particular set of seventeenth-century needs in natural philosophy, one of which was the Latin poet's conception of scale and solidity, that could be easily cordoned off from his theological indifference.

Another, not unrelated use of Lucretius was his phenomenal imagining of texture and touch, the knottedness and entanglement of matter up close, the atomic variety of texture explaining the diversity of things. This had its correlate in the early modern experience with the intricate (if synaesthetic) tactility of the microscope, revealing the knobbed, rugged, and fibrous surface of things. Boyle deploys Lucretius in both parts of his *History of Fluidity and Firmness*, first to illustrate the "gliding of the Corpuscles" and the "easy rouling" of their spherical form, and then to demonstrate their knitty and gnarly complexity. Atoms are, he asserts, constructed in intricate protrusions, "some like buttons, others like loops, some like male, others like female screws."[61] They snag with hooks or "slender twigs." Quoting from the Lucretian account of touch—"*tactus enim, tactus, pro divum numina sancta*"; "This touch, this touch! O sacred deities," as rendered by Lucy Hutchinson—Boyle extols how their design, albeit for Lucretius chance design, produces superlative strength from minimal components.[62] He gives among his examples "of the power of the bare Texture of many small Bodies" how slender threads produce "Ropes and Cables; where only by twisting together and wreathing the slender and flexible threds the Cable is made up of, they are so well as it were wedg'd in between and fasten'd to one another." They can hold fast a ship violently driven by storms, in their intricate corpuscular strength, of which he notes: "This figuration of the Corpuscles that make up consistent Bodies, seems to have been the chief if not only cause of their consistence in the Judgment of the antient Atomists, this being the account that is given of it by *Lucretius*."[63]

Atoms, continually re-forming in their *ars combinatoria* out of which everything constructed itself, produce what Michel Serres, in *The Birth of Physics*, calls the "voluptuous knowledge" of *De Rerum Natura*, its coordinating of multifaceted godless life, scientific, mythic, emotional, and all-encompassing, the "physics of Aphrodite," voluptuous of theme, and sensual in its epistemology, a world abrasive, alive, emerging "like Aphrodite from a flux of elements . . . complex, twined, twisting its long thick hair."[64] Touch, not vision, is the coordinating sense, and even vision, in the work's extramissive sight theory, in which frail simulacra produce a universe of phantoms in continual exfoliation from every surface, is tactile. Walter Charleton, citing Lucretius, concludes that "all Sensation is a kind of Touching."[65] The crush that natural philosophers had on Lucretius in the second half of the seventeenth century derived, at least in part, from the seductive, dangerous nature of this tactility, that "most exquisite and delicate sense of Touching," as Charleton comments, before shifting from natural philosophy to temptation, "the titillation whereof transports a man beyond the severity of his reason, and charmes him to the act of Carnality."[66]

De Rerum Natura provided a poetics of *texture* for describing the physical world, which anticipated the counterintuitive ruggedness of things at a material level. This preceded, but was augmented by, the discovery of microscopic roughness, and the newfound technical ability to penetrate the surface-illusion of uninterrupted, erugatory form. Atoms were unresting. Charleton, narrating the history of Epicurean-Lucretian atoms, recounts their perpetual warring motion, his sheer adjectival bombardment in imitative atomic action: "on all sides crowding, impelling, and justling each other . . . a long, long afflux, reflux, conflux, elevation, depression, coagmentation and other various and successive agitations and molitions of these Atoms."[67] The boundedness of objects made of vigorous atoms was, for early modern scientists, a thing of wonder, that elements so motile could nevertheless through sheer texture prove so solid. Atoms existed in a ceaseless and delirious movement, the "circumvolution, gyration, or vertiginous eddy of them . . . [an] immense vortex, wedged in each other into the form of an integument or cortex," and yet, at the level of everyday things, they constituted all that was solid, their thick texture producing an illusion of surface that was whole and calm.[68]

Lucretius provided a model of perception as perpetual wrong-footedness and disorientation of scale, in a work that is by turns intricate, then vast, an immensity of the tiny that replicated the conceptual vertigo of the microscopic. Those who speculated on the new experience of the miniature in the seventeenth century were all too well aware of perceptual distortion, and of the speculative nature of any atomism. The gambit of truth by which atoms might just approximate to reality was very much Lucretian, a poetics of natural philosophy that was uniquely able to enfold a plain and complex "involution" of truth: "Parabolical and Poetical Fictions conduce *tam ad lumen & illustrationem, quàm ad involucrum & velum*, as well to the illustration of darker, as the involution of more evident peices [sic] of Truth."[69] Elegance of poetry did not of course imply a thing to be true—according to Henry More, Lucretius produced "mere poeticall Smoke or Fume, that vanishes in the very uttering of it"—but the widespread incorporation of Lucretius into natural philosophy spoke to a pressing need for a language, a rhetorical toolkit, for the subvisible.[70] If the infinitesimal was to remain beyond human perception, truth might have to be glimpsed rather than laid out in full splendor.

Margaret Cavendish and the Knowing Object

Microscopy provoked a number of antagonistic responses, some philosophical, some medical, and some just itchy. A 1668 text on the profoundly uncomfortable experience of small life spoke of "several species of wormes macerating and direfully cruciating every part of the bodies of mankind."[71] Gideon Harvey wrote against the College of Physicians in an aspersive account of "their intrigues, frauds, plots against their patients," ridiculing their microscopic practices and the self-publicizing chicanery in which they collected "whatever false appearances are glanced into their eyes, these to obtrude to the World in Print, to no other end, than to beget a belief in people, that they who have so profoundly dived into the bottomless pores of the parts, must undeniably be skilled in curing their distempers."[72] If Boyle could extol the idea of a Porology, for Harvey, any such claims to have plumbed the unfathomable pores of objects were mere mountebank rhetoric and self-inflation.

But there were also more substantial philosophical arguments against microscopy, among which those of Margaret Cavendish, Duchess of Newcastle, are most intriguing. Having repudiated her early interest in atomism, by the mid-1660s she was challenging both the theories of perception that were the premise of microscopy and the framework of matter theory, into which any understanding of surface and undersurface should be figured.[73] Her extensive philosophical writings of this period return frequently to the discontinuity between "interior and exterior," and the nature of self-knowledgeable matter, surface that was aware of its own superficiality. Cavendish's *Observations upon Experimental Philosophy* (1666) has some scathing comments on the epistemological value of microscopy and the overenthusiasm of Hooke and Power for the nascent technology in their recently published works, arguing that the science "is not able to discover the interior natural motions of any part or creature of nature; nay the question is, whether it can represent yet the exterior shapes and motions, so exactly, as naturally they are."[74] In the early part of the work, Cavendish's concerns center on perception, how the artifice (art) of microscopy deforms and misshapes the very objects it purports to "see," failing to acknowledge or understand where sight gave way to conjecture, "interposing and intermixing parts, forms and positions, as the truth of an object will hardly be known." Such technology skewed what one saw, producing "hermaphroditical" knowledge, "mixt figures, partly artificial, partly natural," and Cavendish was perplexed that it had "intoxicated so many men's brains" into attending only to the nature of surface and exterior, such that they valorized "superficial wonders, as I may call them." Indeed, in calling for a more utile science, she urged, with fine-tuned condescension, that natural philosophers should properly adopt the mantle of Bacon, and not act "as boys that play with watery bubbles or fling dust into each other's eyes, or make a hobby horse of snow."⁷⁵ Cavendish no longer needs any substantial introduction. A growing body of writing that treats her as a significant philosopher has developed alongside her familiarity as a literary figure, most recently in monographs by Deborah Boyle and David Cunning, as well as the essays in Emily Thomas's collection on women's writings on metaphysics.⁷⁶ The cacophonous jazz of *The Blazing World*, however, with its imperious dismissal of microscopy and other natural philosophies as though by edict, can obscure quite how subtle and strange were her counter-theories.⁷⁷

Cavendish's opposition to microscopy was more thoroughgoing (and more interesting) than merely exposing its ineptitude in what it claimed and aimed to do. When she writes of exterior knowledge and interior knowledge, she does not mean what *we* can know from the outside and what we might like to know about the inside. Rather, she means what the exterior of an object *knows* and the different knowledge of the interior. Cavendish's world is vitalist; its matter is alive, aware, and perceptive, even while that world is quite some distance, tonally and philosophically, from any kind of mysticism we might associate with vitalist thought. It is not infused with the divine, and if formally it constitutes panpsychism, it nevertheless has little sense of an *anima mundi* or a world electric with god. This makes for a curious reading experience that is the converse of the microscopists. Where Power, Hooke, and Charleton produce baroque and elegiac prose, awe-struck empiricism at the intricacy of the universe, whose wonder borders on psalmlike prayer, Cavendish might be said to be at the nitpicking and pedantic end of the spectrum of philosophical rhetoric. At times, she repeats her ideas into the ground, and yet in themselves, they are exquisitely strange and original. "I am of opinion," she says, "that nature is a self-moving, and consequently a self-living and self-knowing infinite body," the correlate of which was a world never at rest: "I do not mean exteriorly moving . . . but interiorly, so that all the motions that are in nature, are within herself."⁷⁸

Cavendish's matter is triune; it is on the one hand inanimate, but it is, without exception, imbued and suffused with animate qualities of both the sensitive, in that it perceives, and the rational, in that it "knows" how to respond to contiguous matter. This tripartite "commixture" of qualities is the constituent and universally present nature of matter. As Karen Detlefsen writes: "no portion of material nature, regardless of how small it is, lacks any of the three aspects, and so every portion of material nature is self-moving, sensitive, and rational as well as limited in its abilities," its inanimate portion acting as a fetter on its ability to self-move: "For there is such a commixture of animate and inanimate matter," Cavendish writes, "that no particle in Nature can be conceived or imagined, which is not composed of animate matter as well as of inanimate."[79] Matter *senses* other matter and knows how to react. The proximity of other bodies prompts things to respond accordingly, not in any purely mechanistic interaction, but with a degree of free will on the part of the matter. It is less that cause produces effect than that one object is the "occasion" of an interaction to which the matter responds, knowingly.[80] Cavendish explicitly and frequently refuses to allow the reader to misconstrue what she is saying as merely a distinction between mineral or animal, that the latter is animate and the former inanimate. Indeed she refuses to distinguish between the knowledge of matter *in general* (how the whole body of nature "knows"), and the capacities of its individual, but not entirely distinct parts, matter already preformed into discrete figures, whether pebbles, flowers, or humans: "such composed figures, as, for distinctions sake, we call finite wholes; as for example, an Animal, a Tree, a Stone."[81] What is important and what unites these is a thing's dynamic knowledge of its own being, how matter knows.

In explicating and differentiating between "exterior knowledge" and "interior knowledge," Cavendish is less interested in an observer's putative knowledge of the outside of a thing (produced by "patterning out" an always imperfect copy, in their own mind), than in how matter "knows" how to respond to the world.[82] Remarkably, a thing knows in different ways on its surface and in its interior. Outside and inside respond to different impulses and kinds of potential motion simultaneously. This is not exactly a spatial distinction between inner and outer, in so far as the "interior knowledge" describes something like the inner properties of a thing. If, Deborah Boyle explains, we were to dice an object smaller, the observer would always encounter the exterior motion, rather than the inherent nature of the object.[83] At the same time, the spatial character of Cavendish's vocabulary, and her attention to the integral motion of matter, is thorough-going. There is the "figurative motion," by which the object's "outward figure or shape" reacts, but there is also action athwart this, a "retentive motion," by which an object produces its own longevity, the "preservation and continuance" of itself: "By which we may plainly see that one figure lies within another, one corporeal figurative motion is within another, and that the interior and exterior parts or figures of Creatures, are different in their actions."[84] Matter dances to several tunes at one and the same time, and the example she gives returns us to Boyle's interest in fluidity: "the ebbing and flowing, or the ascending and descending motions of water, are quite different from those interior figurative motions that make it water."[85] The complex plunge of water as it falls, whose state is intricately distinct from moment to moment, produces its shapely reaction to any contiguous surface, be it air or solid, that it "senses." Its gush "knows" and responds to the "occasion" of any surrounding and proximate object. In one sense, this is like Lucretian smoke, its continual reformulation of itself, its involutions resembling Connor's contingent tactics of inner and outer. But Cavendish's matter is purposeful. It wills how to act insofar as it knows how to act, both at its external edges and in its interior being, its "retentive motions," by which it moves and remains the same, "those interior figurative motions that make it water." We might recall too the occasion in Plutarch, mentioned in chapter 3, in which gushing water was the paradigmatic instance of what we could not know, our attempt to clutch it doomed to frustration.[86] Cavendish, by contrast, understands water as embodying, or at least as being an excellent analogy for, the quasi-mappable dynamics of object-will.[87]

Cavendish remains adamant that merely mechanical action, proceeding in linear cause-and-effect fashion, is an insufficient explanatory model. When a hand encounters a ball, there are, she insists, two acts of self-motion, the ball not less decisively part of the action than the hand:

> Therefore when a man moves a string, or tosses a Ball; the string or ball is no more sensible of the motion of the hand, then the hand is of the motion of the string or ball, but the hand is onely an occasion that the string or ball moves thus or thus.[88]

Kourken Michaelian notes of the passage the extent to which Cavendish embraces the seemingly outrageous implications of this: "she holds that the hand is not necessary for the motion of the ball on the specific ground that the ball moves itself, so that it could have moved as it does even had the hand not been present—the actual cause of a thing's motion is always the thing itself."[89] Not only is the ball perceptually aware of the hand, but its movement in a particular trajectory is a matter of its own knowledge (of how it should move) and decision (that it will move):

> I will not say, but that it may have some perception of the hand, according to the nature of its own figure; but it does not move by the hand's motion, but by its own: for, there can be no motion imparted, without matter or substance.[90]

A parallel passage in Cavendish's *Philosophical Letters* (1664) develops the example with a bowl instead of a ball ("When I throw a bowl, or strike a ball with my hand"), which may, I suppose, imply a bowling game or some kind of early modern frisbee, or which might involve a dramatic moment in the kitchen. The argument in both cases is premised on what Cavendish views as the incoherence of concussive, mechanical theory, based on the transfer of motion without a loss of matter, which fails to account for diminution in material substance.[91] For Cavendish, matter is wholly aware of what is contiguous. It knows not only itself (in interior fashion) but also what it comes into contact with, such that its surface perceives other surfaces: "the infinite parts of Nature have not onely interior self-knowledg, but also exterior perceptions of other figures or parts, and their actions; by reason there is a perpetual commerce and entercourse between parts and parts."[92] While the perceiver may know an object, the object, it seems, knows back.

Matter knows to act both when it is considered in undifferentiated, theoretical ur-form and primal clump, and when it is composed into discrete figures. At the same time, however, nature's perceptive qualities are curtailed in composite figures by the inability of one part to know another, an "ignorance of forreign parts, figures or actions, although they be parts of one composed figure."[93] This idea is threaded through the *Observations*, as the faultline in perception, that sight does not understand touch ("It is known that man has five senses and every sense is ignorant of the other"), and even that one touch cannot quite make sense of another ("one of his hands knows not the sense and perception of his other hand; nay, one part of his hand knows not the perception of another part of the same hand"). This radical discontinuity of the "sensitive" parts is mitigated by the rational, which can coordinate and rectify its insufficiencies ("Whatsoever the sensitive perception is either defective in, or ignorant of, the rational perception supplies"), but Cavendish creates in her human condition of nescience and partiality a state in which the perceiving surface is, after a fashion, more cognizant that the perceiver.[94]

What kind of unknowable is all of this? Cavendish is not a writer immediately associated with the apophatic, and microscopy is not usually seen in concert with the mystical and the sublime. Nor, indeed, is her purpose in any explicit way to create an opposition between sentient matter and nescient observer. But surfaces, newly opened with a disputed technology, presented to the seventeenth century a new kind of ignorance. Natural philosophy of the post-Restoration era returned repeatedly to the idea that surfaces were discontinuous and vibrant. Continually and in a streaming litany of matter, bodies exude, and the occluded stuff of nature was emitted and absorbed. The omnidirectional pulse of matter that is present in Boyle or Power has its correlate in the perceiving matter of Cavendish, quite different in many respects, but sharing an attention to the nonobvious, nonquotidian nature of body. Prompting something akin to vertigo, the surface imagined up close became monstrous, in the shifting scale by which the atomic and human-sized became conflated. Imaginative shrinkage produced for early modern writers a perceptual disequilibrium. The early modern microscopist was something of a Gulliver, startled in Brobdingnag to discover at close quarters things terrifying to his sensibilities, whether outsized bees, or the Maids of Honour who use him as a sexual toy, and whose nakedness and magnified smells so horrify him. Up close, the natural philosopher fumbled through the blasted landscape of magnified textures, in a state of both shock and awe. Early modern surfaces were anything but straightforward. They might produce involutions such that outer and inner became perplexingly similar, like a Möbius strip whose surface has only one side, and they might, in Cavendish's case, have their own perceptual powers. Cavendish's ideas of animate, of thinking matter, substance whose interior and exterior might have different notions of how they want to react to stimuli, is among the most intriguing of responses to the philosophical vertigo of microscopy.

Cavendish was, for a long time, easy to exclude from the "real" business of early modern scientific thought, in its conversations about the character of empiricism, and a culture of the nascent Royal Society marking out its Baconian territory. Not a small amount of misogyny might likewise have gone into cordoning her off from the intellectual mainstream, with the frequently told tales of her outlandish and mockable appearances at Royal Society meetings. Perhaps it might be said that, even while she responds to her contemporaries in intricate fashion and several genres, she does not join the philosophical conversation on its own terms. This is, I think, what recent scholarship on Cavendish has done a great deal to show. The very idea that she was or was not part of *the* conversation presupposes that we know what that was, whose trajectory, after all the false turns, led to where science ended up. But in the conversation on the limits of reason and knowledge and the ways we engage that dim realm of the unknowable, Cavendish produces her own, very particular terms of reference. Matter knows. There is a poetics to this, a plunging shock of what the word "knowledge" might mean, when it is not just humans, or angels, who get to know, but that the qualities of knowledge are distributed in the very texture of things.

CHAPTER 5

Anna Trapnel's Aesthetics of Incoherence

AFTER TWELVE DAYS of hard prophecy and public spectacle like no other, Anna Trapnel, exhausted and exhilarated, described the breaking of language, how it ceases to mean, how even the Bible can empty itself, becoming a mere bloated corpse of scripture. The words can carry on being uttered, by a Cromwell or the addled Council of State, but it is only "dead men, dead things" speaking. Cromwell's words infect and undo him, even as he speaks them: "Does not he confound himself in his own language?" Trapnel's prophecy, in the winter of 1654, was remarkable for many reasons. Begun in the precincts of Westminster, attracting large crowds, it was an event of vehement prophetic impropriety ("They will say the spirit of madness and distraction is upon her, and that it is immodesty") and another cacophonous fortnight in the country's political-spiritual perma-crisis ("This is the saddest day that ever poor England had"). Taken down in shorthand, as near a record of prophecy as we are likely to find, it is also a text that is exuberant about its own plunging into the unspeakable.[1]

Prophets are unseemly because what they have to say is incommunicable. In one sense, of course, that is not the case; their message of iniquity and impending doom is all too clear, but at the same time, the prophet's ventriloquizing of God has much in common with any other report of what God said, the transcription of theophany: a need to recount a message that is unearthly, a white noise of God that fugs the mind, like and unlike a whirlwind or a burning bush that does not consume itself. It is too loud, hurling its imprecations at the suddenly puny, exposed arrogance of humans and kings. It is not enough that a straightforward message be delivered by the prophet—that Israel or London is teetering on the precipice again. He or she must shake the befuddled listener to the core, make briefly present not only their imminent peril, but also the sheer terror of God. So he—God, that is—instructs the prophets to cook with human dung, to go naked, to marry "a wife of whoredoms," to burn their lips with live coals.[2] Or he has them lie down in Westminster Hall, and cajole the miscreant nation. No one would want to be a prophet—God hounds them, then kings hound them, and they themselves hound and shock the recalcitrant people in turn. They hover close to madness, their language and actions densely symbolic and opaque.

There is a poetics of prophecy that, at first sight, is little like the generic practices of negative theology. It is raucous in its pummeling of recalcitrant kings, in its attention-seeking theatrics, where mysticism, we might presume, has some transcendent quality about it. But they share habits of thought in which language fails and derangement takes over—what in Trapnel is, more or less, an aesthetics of incoherence. Before coming in more detail to her spectacular performance, however, it is worth elaborating on quite how fraught a thing prophecy was, as a channel to and from God. This chapter will recall, after a fashion, the antics of Jacob Boehme, who so appealed to the down-at-heel radical milieu of Trapnel, but it is also in some respects an anomaly in the book in that, unlike most of the other chapters, it attends not to early modern natural philosophy, but to its politics. The prophetic was, however, central to the character of the unknowable in the era and, hence, to the character of knowledge. To narrate the era's reforging of the mystical without attention to its more pugnacious forms of prophecy would be to miss something essential about it.

At the more sober end of early modern exegesis, preachers and annotators typically aimed to explain what God meant and what, in turn, the prophet intended with their bracing impropriety; they sought to domesticate and encapsulate the meaning of the Bible's wild words, and in the process they generally, even self-consciously, drained them of their toxicity. The two child prostitutes raped in Ezekiel 23, Aholah and Aholobah, were metaphorical representations of Samaria and Jerusalem—in the strong sense that the Book of Ezekiel says so, not just as a facet of interpretation. But early modern commentators vary between insisting that this is only analogy, not a real but a "metaphorical whoredome," and slipping into a defense of the vicious punishments meted out to them as wholly deserved, "God being very angry with these two women for their lewdnesse and abominations."[3] The idea, in commentary of this stripe, was this: once you have taken out the message from its envelope, the nut from its husk, the radium from its canister, you can dispose of the shell—you have understood the point. But there is something intrinsically wrong with this. The carcinogens linger, the theo-rape does not disappear. Metaphor works through its connotative excess, the residue of associations once the logic of the comparison is understood. The scriptural prophets blaspheme and are politically unbiddable. They are also theatrical and operate with a poetics of disgust—they aim to offend, and we are meant to be repelled by the endemic intertwining of, as Yvonne Sherwood puts it, scatology and eschatology. Hugh Pyper points to this as a constituent biblical lilt to the lurid and the stomach churning, that we read with our gut and a hermeneutic of recoil in the face of the unspeakable.[4] Such a reading, though in one sense very much a modern and postmodern approach to the Bible's emotional dynamics, is nevertheless one that early modern readers of the scriptures would understand. The Bible can make you retch. Rowan Williams comments, with the story of Aholah and Aholobah in mind (together with the parable of the unjust steward), that among our stock metaphors for God, we should not only have shepherd, or king, but "magistrate who ought to be struck off."[5]

Seventeenth-century commentators on prophetic language tend to presume that the books are explicable, but they are also aware of how wayward the writing can seem, how its "imagery," if that is what it is, can be revolting. In any case, the unhusking of any single metaphor is hardly the major issue in reading the prophets. It is how they roll from one to the next outrage, each on a different scale, cosmic one instance, interested in their own shit the next;[6] the lurch from one to another magnitude, the plunge through layers of reality, all uncalibrated to anything except one's own iniquity, disorientates. This is language that provokes at the level of both logic and propriety. Henry More, discussing "Why *Prophecies* are wrapt up in some considerable Obscurity," distinguishes between what he calls the "externall *Cortex* of Prophecies" and their pulsing inward sense.[7] William Day, in his account of Isaiah, insists that quadrigal interpretation is insufficient to the prophets and that there exists a further "Mysticall, or Sublime Sense," a language of things.[8] Few exegetes remain sober across any extended contact with the prophets, albeit they frequently insist that biblical prophecy is less unbalanced than its pagan equivalent. Thomas Barlow, in "A *Letter* Answering a *Question* about the *Temper* of the *Prophets,* when they *Prophesied*," insisted that they were "of a sedate, calm and quiet temper; and not troubled with defective fits of anger and overflowing passion."[9] They were not, commented Lambert Daneau, "like unto the prophets of the Heathen, taken with a madde phrensie, when as they prophesied . . . neither were they ougly in visage, neither ignorant, or not knowing what they saide or did."[10]

But the early modern *practical* prophet—Quakers, Ranters, Baptists, Fifth Monarchists, and some preachers—was quite different from the sober exegete who unfolded the biblical, verse by verse, downplaying its vertiginous quality. From the viewpoint of their antagonists, and from their own perspective, the mid-seventeenth-century prophetic mode, borrowing a stylistic repertoire from biblical forebears, was altogether wilder. They rant and rail, delivering political damnations to self-interested governors. Their language, their leaps of logic and subject are demented and bedlamesque, because that is proper to the fury of the divine. They cross-hatch their speech with a frenzy of reference, with enormous mood swings from the apocalyptic to the celebratory, the merciful to the wrathful, because that is how prophets unhinge. It is generic. Prophetic speech—and we can find versions of it in the hopscotch of Fast Sermon, as well as the fringe politics of uncompromising Fifth Monarchists—mirrors the anger of God in the disorientating lash of the prophet's tongue.[11]

But a caveat is needed to this: God's moods are not like human moods, because God is "impassible"—does not suffer the ravages of emotion—and to imply that he does is anthropomorphism and slips swiftly into idolatry. There is, of course, a venerable hermeneutic toolkit, to explain the merely figurative nature of such humanized language, how it is accommodated to our perception and language. Nevertheless, it remains an insoluble puzzle that the immutable, impassible, unruffleable

God needs to be represented in terms of human agitation.[12] Whatever modality of the divine it is that seems to be represented in the Bible's designation of God's emotional volatility has be qualified. It is an unutterable thing, both like and unlike fury; it is a God-event that can only be registered with the seismometer of the apophatic, and a poetics to circumvent that unutterable state. This, I think, matters for how prophets speak. Prophecy, it was common to note, is an unfolding and interpretation of the present: "The primary notion of a prophet," wrote Edward Stillingfleet, "does not lie in foretelling future events, but in declaring and interpreting to the world the mind of God which he receives by immediate revelation from himself."[13] But neither does this quite capture what is required of the prophet, who needs to touch on the unfathomable über-modality of the divine wrath.

This ventriloquism of the unknowable will of the divine is not the same as the inability to grasp God's inscrutable essence, some hypercategory of beyond-beyondness. One aspect of a prophet's message is relatively mundane, albeit urgent. Desist, O Israel, from thy truculence, may be the instruction, but the prophetic dispatch is never only a court order, delivered into the hand of king or Cromwell or the city aldermen. It has emotional work to do, to register a pain that is massy and uncontainable in God's twisted entrails, metaphorically speaking, but quite literally how Jeremiah expresses suffering, "My bowels, my bowels."[14] While it is the case that the prophet's message is nothing as unmanageable as trying to think through God's essence, nevertheless, the prophetic voice must translate a thing that is like, but is not, anger into human, political-moral terms. But what kind of equivalence can they achieve? When like a jack-in-the-box they rage in their wild symbolic maelstrom, they are presumably not suggesting that God is kicking the dog in heaven in his uncontainable fury, or that he, like Milton's Satan, sits "disfigured . . . his gestures fierce" railing with "mad demeanour."[15] Certainly, we could suggest that prophets convey the message they are given and that is all, that it arrives already in the envelope—that the thing-like-emotion that God will have conveyed has already passed through the mill of translation. The prophet, after all, has been coopted, if not coerced: in the words of Leonard Cohen, "he only has permission / To do my instant bidding / Which is to say what I have told him / To repeat."¹⁶ But prophets in mid-seventeenth-century England hardly seem straitjacketed into the role of humble postman. They are required to be theatrical, unpredictable, unbuckled, with disequilibrium as their signature poetic. John Oldham writes of their coltish exuberance, "The rage young Prophets feel, / When they with holy Frenzy reel / Drunk with the Spirits of infus'd Divinity." George Fox, the Quaker, writes of ranting, canting enthusiasts, as the *"Phanatick* . . . full of Fury & Rage." Neither intends their description to flatter.¹⁷ And yet they did impress their listeners. They did convey enough wild authority such that they might just be genuine.

The Unspeakable in 1654

The English republic, such as it was, did not last long. By late 1653, the religiously uncompromising Barebone's Parliament had been dissolved, the revolution rolled back, and Cromwell's de facto monarchical assumption of power as Lord Protector led to a widespread disillusionment among the radical godly. No taxonomy, it seems, can impose much order on the varied political-religious groups, emerging, disappearing, and reformulating in this tumultuous period, the motley radicals with their discordant, sophisticated sense of reality, and a discursive mode to match. Following the arrest of her fellow radical, Vavasor Powell, in January 1654, the Fifth Monarchist Anna Trapnel (to resume the story) sat in the Palace at Whitehall for news of his fate. While she waited, she fell into a trance and ecstasy, in which she began to prophesy, alternately in song and in prose, in a scriptural weave and fierce social commentary, which continued for eleven or twelve days, and became a much talked-about public spectacle, with a large and political crowd, including members of the Council of State, ejected MPs, and prominent London ministers, as well as the spy and pamphleteer, Marchamont Needham, who reported with some disdain back to Cromwell.¹⁸

Once it became clear that this was an ongoing marvel, a "Relator" began to take down, presumably in shorthand, Trapnel's words, and the text, *The Cry of a Stone,* emerged—incomplete, but more extensive than any equivalent report—somewhere between performance, prophecy, and exegesis. "[O]f the four first days no account can be given," the relator explains, "there being none that noted down what was spoken" (2 [4–5]). At times, the crowd was too great, her voice too weak, or the relator not sufficiently indefatigable, but the text accrued, with the relator taking down ad-libbed hymns, a scriptural hopscotch of prose, both apocalyptic and contemporary in scope. What subsequent revision and reconstruction took place, how far it was filtered through the relator's ears, and the extent to which Trapnel might have overseen or been involved in readying the transcription for publication remains elusive, but plainly she did attend, in some respects, to its final form. Occasionally the relator clarifies whom she is referring to, bracketing his comments in the text, with the implication that the words are otherwise hers.

The text might properly be linked to other vehement para-biblical writings by lower-class women; Trapnel herself was the daughter of a shipwright. But *The Cry of a Stone* is unique in its fullness, as a record of a prophetic event, narrated "live," as opposed to a report of visions, or a conversion experience, retrospectively reported. Such "prophetic" writing or transcription is not generally considered to be stylistically conscious, caught up as it is in the winds of prophecy. But Trapnel's *The Cry of a Stone*, through be-tranced, has about it a style that is at once exegetically precise and typologically tempestuous, involving a class-conscious hermeneutic that lambasts the obfuscation of "university learning," which wilfully obscures the limpid scriptures—or at least limpid after a fashion.[19] Though the scriptures, understood in a torrent of enthused spirit, might be all clarity, it was also the case that prophecy, with its thick-knitted scriptural webs of reference and its continual swivel of subject matter, presupposed its own opacity. There was nothing to be clear about. Speaking of her eschatological times as themselves corrosive of meaning, Trapnel understood herself to be living in a time not only of political fracture and fragmentation, but of a more thoroughgoing crisis: "many are infected, their language is infected, it was sweet before, but now it is confused, it had an harmony, but now it hath no relish" (37 [39]). Scripture, for the uncompromising civil war prophet, needed to pulse dangerously close to incoherence before it might become suddenly interpretable, in a dazzle of political revelation.

The crisis of this winter moment was multifaceted—at one moment, the politics of the city was at issue, and at the next, the imminent eschaton and Cromwell's part in it —but the focus of this chapter is the cacophonous language of a prophecy that wholly embraced and crafted its turbulent style as the proper, necessary response to a deeply unstable spiritual-political ontology, in a world whose fragility had been repeatedly exposed, by civil war, regicide, and the fast-moving events of the Republic and Protectorate. It will make the case that Trapnel and, by extension, women prophets of the revolution more generally understood themselves to be working within a scriptural poetic that could properly be termed *experimental*, in the literary sense, that they were consciously aiming to disrupt the parameters of language and coherence, and that the nature of this cracked language was tied to their crafting an authority to speak. Closely connected with this was the fact that prophecy involved outlandish performance—bodily and unbodied, unearthly and gutsy. The Word was a wind through the prophet, body and soul: "thy Spirit takes the Scripture all along, and sets the soul a swimming therein" (67 [71]). The soul immersed, drown-swimming in the near-incomprehensible Word, is a characteristic state for prophetic women writers, channeling or channeled by the divine. This was a speech that was barely voluntary, and there was little a prophet could do about it when it seized them, whether Trapnel in Whitehall, Hosea "whoring" in Samaria, or Isaiah naked in Judah. All respond to an ontological instability with answerable style, with delirium and fabulous theatrics.

To argue thus for Trapnel, however, demands that we square apparently incompatible positions: first, that her performance is crafted and generically astute, exegetically subtle in its weaving of the biblical and the political, as well as alert to and guileful in response to patriarchal, as much as political, context; alongside this, we need to suppose that she is genuine in her religiously infused stupor, that the spirit's rending her body, her language, and her soul is how she and how the times construed reality, and how they construed the biblical, if sometime incoherent surge in her. To imagine that Trapnel is not wholly, rigorously certain that the divine was bellowing through her body is, I take it, to misunderstand the era, and the seriousness of religion. If these seem initially irreconcilable—that it might be a ruse and resolutely cannot be a ruse, that she can be both conscious of her exegetical maneuvers and be genuinely be-tranced—they converge in the early modern understanding of prophecy. The prophet is gripped and powerless, but also a fearless voice of political truth, which speaks outside the ordinary temporal fabric, such that the scriptural past is manifested in the eschatological and political present.

Prophetic writing, since it first came to serious scholarly attention, in the work of Hilary Hinds, Phyllis Mack, and others, has not been neglected, but its alienating biblical idiom has remained at least slightly baffling, and for many unappealing, in its temporal tangles of the thickly biblical-apocalyptic and the immediately political. Hinds, in *God's Englishwomen*, comments on writings that are audacious, in political-religious as well as literary terms; that are rhetorically sophisticated, playful, and that frequently brought down mockery, poverty, and imprisonment upon the early modern prophets. She asks why they have so failed to make it into the literary canon.[20] Though a great deal has changed since her 1996 work in terms of the canon of women writers, it remains the case that women prophets are often a hard sell compared with what Teresa Feroli calls women writing in the "Tory cause," an aristocratic poetry of friendship, well-educated allusion, and a politics of privilege, although neither the prophetic mode nor its apocalyptic fireworks is intrinsically radical—Lady Eleanor Davies is similarly turbulent, to quite different ends.[21] The issue is very probably the abrasive, biblical medium of this style of early modern thought. Phyllis Mack's work made the case that prophecy has almost invariably been secularized, if not pathologized, as emotional excess and catharsis, as psychological instability, not *thinking* as such, but being soaked in theology. "Did the female prophet have a mind?" she asks, rhetorically and in response to these women's abrogation of any authorship as such, their adopting a role as merely and vehemently the vessel for God's political wrath.[22] Even reading it as a sublimated radical politics in which women appropriate a traditionally male discursive and social space (though in some ways this is clearly the case) cannot escape the crude effects of a secularization that tries to make the religious idiom more palatable.

Anna Trapnel is more readily accessible than many other early modern female prophets, given Hilary Hind's excellent edition of *The Cry of a Stone* (2000) and, subsequently, the quasi- martyrological and autobiographical *Report and Plea* (2016), telling of her travels, trials, and arrest following her public prophecy in Whitehall against Cromwell. Some impressive scholarly writing on Trapnel has done a good deal to contextualize and make sense of her— for example, work on the pathology and performativity of the fasting female body and the dynamics of the prophetic and gender.[23] Sue Wiseman writes of the unlocatable nature of the prophetic female voice channeling an irredeemably male God-voice, and of the predicament of feminist response to this ventriloquizing role.[24] James Holstun sets Trapnel in a political context, writing on how she "strategically explores the gaps and contradictions inside the patriarchal theology of the spirit," and he goes on to suggest that her fasting has a political edge to it, in the manner of a Gandhi or an IRA hunger strike.[25] Other critics have incorporated Trapnel into larger cultural-political arguments about the politics of the period, its pamphleteering, or its religious discourse, so it is far from the case that she has been neglected.[26] With a few important exceptions, however, it is also the case that criticism on Trapnel's prophecy has gone quiet in recent years.[27]

Trapnel in Whitehall

Trapnel wrote in a number of genres, from the martyrological and prison narrative of *Report and Plea* (1654), to the autobiographical confessional experience in *A legacy for saints* (1654).[28] She produced a printed collection of poem-hymns, *A voice for the king of saints and nations* (1657), many of which are reproduced in the vast single printed copy of a title-less work in the Bodleian.[29] A brief report, *Strange and wonderful newes from White-Hall* (1654), describes the same events that occupy her major and most famous prophetic experience, *The Cry of a Stone* (1654). Other of her prophetic and lower-class compatriots were more directly political—Elizabeth Poole's role in the Army Council deliberations over the regicide and Mary Cary's Fifth Monarchist political program are both bracing—but there is little to equal Trapnel's flair for the dramatic and her agility with the biblical.[30]

The preliminaries to the prophecy itself are quite extensive, including a biographical account, which pre- or postdates it. That this is separate from the trance-prophecy itself matters; it is a different kind of narration, more carefully crafted. It attests, certainly, to her good character, and shows a degree of concern for social propriety, but is far from meek. It includes details of Trapnel's spiritual battles, her fasting herself into hallucinatory vision states, her being buffeted by a suicide-inducing Satan, her prophetic induction in her mother's dying words, her series of wild visions and prognostications of war, from the late 1640s and 1650s, each provoking in her an epiphany of a biblical verse, dazzlingly apt, suffused with the current military-political emergency, in Scotland or Holland. Again and again, events in the present disappear into the holes in scripture, subsumed and reconstituted in it, made real in its omnitemporal illumination. As the narrative approaches the "present," Cromwell increasingly becomes the subject of her typologically infused visions, his betrayal of the godly cause cast in terms of biblical apostasy and apocalyptic chaos. She sees a vision of a bull, whose "Countenance was perfectly like unto *Oliver Cromwels*," which runs furiously at her, "neer with his horn to my breast" and thence to the saints in his violent rage "scratching them with his horn, and driving them into several houses, he ran still along, till at length there was a great silence, and suddenly there broke forth in the Earth great fury coming from the Clouds" (13 [15]). This is fervent and spectacular, but it is not live prophecy as such, in its reportage of scripturally infused phantasms; it is, rather a remembrance of visions past. The prophecy within *The Cry of a Stone*, by contrast, has no real visionary element. It is less hallucination than hermeneutics.

Prophecy is an awkward, if not an embarrassing category for the modern historian or literary historian. Even when hedged with the proper caveats—that it is less soothsaying and prognostication than interpretation and appropriation of a biblical form, that its ventriloquizing the fury of the divine provided a conduit for political speech—even when slyly secularized, when it is understood as holy delirium brought on by excessive fasting, or a ruse to wriggle out of clearly real class and gender constraints or an expression of separatist religiosity, it remains hard to credit and, what's worse, repetitive. In verse, the accusation goes, it is doggerel and in prose, it is a tissue of biblical rags. Whatever we make of it, it is hard to make literature of it. Despite this, it is a *genre*. It has its shared stylistic habits, its rhetorical modes, and its typical subject matter—admonition, exhortation, and dire warning, all referred to the tremor of the explosive biblical Word, the angry God recalled, reanimated in the volatile exegetical tradition of reading Revelation, Isaiah, and Ezekiel.

Could we say that, in the 1650s, it was an *experimental* genre? That it was a little *avant-garde*? That Anna Trapnel was a radicalized Virginia Woolf, a kind of H.D. for her times? If this is preposterous (where's the *chaise-longue*?), it remains the case that this writing was *formally* shocking (in the literary sense), and that the surge of the prophetic form was a conscious and dramatic rejection of religious propriety. Certainly, we can trace a history of the vagrant prophet-radical back through Elizabethan times and beyond, but after the regicide, the storm-gates burst open, with what M. H. Abrams terms a practice of "internalized apocalypse," the transposition of the cosmic theater of events into the quaking, flailing self.[31] The unprecedented biblical literacy, up and down the social scale, and a discovery of the Bible's own bracing lack of propriety are the main facilitating circumstances. And the most potent consequence was, undoubtedly, the political convulsions of the country. But it had a not-unconnected set of effects in how people thought, in their styles of thinking and their styles of poetic reckoning, what Sue Wiseman calls "women's use of poetic vocabularies in political struggle."[32] Can we think of the radical movements—Fifth Monarchists and so on—as coming into being around new "literary" forms as much as new(ish) theological-eschatalogical ideas? For all its potential anachronism, there is something both appealing and off-kilter in understanding prophecy as, for example, an *écriture féminine* in that its riot of eschatological thought is so consciously disruptive, wild, and ranting, an *écriture prophétique* at least.[33]

CHAPTER 5

Ranting with Trapnel

Trapnel has a capacious knowledge of the Bible, and her prose is an intricate weave (or a thick sludge, depending on one's perspective) of quotations bearing on the present calamities, a temporal knot of ancient Israel, the contemporary, and the eschatological. But she rejects with some vehemence the specious chicanery of the learned and their distortions of scripture, "what disputing, what reasoning . . . vaine conceits, vaine speculations, and high notions" (38 [40]). This disdain for "university learning" runs deep in the text, and indeed across radical prose of the era. It is not necessarily the case that writing which styles itself as enthusiastic, from Ranter to Quaker literature, is in any sense primitive, or less adept at producing the tumble of precise biblical reference characteristic of the era. Something other than mere density of learning is at play, for Trapnel, because the same holy Word can poison or can nourish: "they say these waters are very clear and sweet that come from men, but at length they make the Soule very muddy" (35 [38]). This oozy capacity to taint even the scriptures ("many are infected, their language is infected") is a product of blighted times and self-interested sophistry. One can say complex things that mean nothing at all. Such are universities. But nor is this garble new. Citing Isaiah 33.19, where the Assyrians issue commands in a wilfully obscure tongue, she warns the learned ("all you Disputants, Monarchs, Scribes, and Rabbies of the world"), with their tricksy impenetrable language, that their day is done, that they cannot oppose the spirit of prophecy:

> because thine are of a stammering speech, and of stuttering tongue, but thou hast promised that the time shall come that there shall not be a people of a deeper speech then thy people, and they shall not be of a stammering tongue." (37–38 [40])

There are two kinds of deeper speech here: the obfuscatory and alien, that of the Assyrian, of the learned university-churchmen, or latterly of Cromwell, and the promised new prophetic fog, a deeper deep, "a people of a deeper speech" whose prophetic language passes through incoherence—the stammering speech and stuttering tongue associated with reluctant biblical prophets, Moses, Isaiah, Jonah, and Jeremiah—into its preternatural clarity, where all the scriptures cohere. But that time has not yet come.

If then we can allow some design in her prophecy, an aesthetic even, Trapnel's is one that courts incoherence. *The Cry of a Stone* is dazzlingly atonal. It is generically amorphous, breaking into hymns, threats, self-exculpatory digressions, exhortation, and jeremiad; it is a complex tapestry of palimpsestic times and rhetorical modes. It is capacious in its political, class, and apocalyptic concerns. It is breathtakingly rude, aggressive, and threatening. But above all, it revels in its wild state and its unpredictable sea-changes. For both biblical and early modern political prophets, the fragmented form of the text, its rapid shifts, its broken logic, is a correlate to deranged times. It expresses a madness of what is beyond expression. It hurls itself at the impenetrable, insisting on its access to the mysterious: "go into the Marrow, what matters it for the bone." While Trapnel has some aphoristic gems of this kind, however (though they may at times be common property), the rhetorical effect of her prophecy is only experienced in the more extended twists and zigzag of her prose:

> Oh, But who is he or she that admires the Lord Jesus through all, in all, and above all; He is all in nothing-Creatures, the Creature is nothing, but thou hast said, thou dost great things through nothing: Oh, that thine were taken with Truth for Truths sake, that they would seek into the bottome, and goe into the golden Mine, and not onely gather up the shavings thereof, let them not take up the sparks but the fire it selfe. That a poor Creature should subsist without sustenance, what a gazing is there at this poor thing, while you forget the glory that is in it, go into the Marrow, what matters it for the bone, let them have the Spirits, it is no matter for any thing else. (38 [40])

Trapnel rants. Trapnel is also keen to dissociate herself from Ranting, but notes too how, at points, she had been intrigued and tempted by its resources—albeit that was Satan tempting her in the midst of her periodic spiritual buffeting, prior to the Whitehall events, when "he [Satan] endeavoured to bring me into those Familistical ranting Tenents, that I had almost spent my lungs in pleading against" (10 [12], also 57 [62]). No doubt Trapnel understood Ranters at least in part through the lens of heresiographers such as Edwards's *Gangraena*, or she may of course have known those underground groups who may not have existed, but whose many pamphlets have come to be grouped as Ranter texts.[34] As far as we know, there was little formal association with the Fifth Monarchist visionaries of a quite different bent, but there was very possibly a rhetorical association, in their shared rejection of the dry diet of university language, their shared sense of the wild "whisperings of the spirit" (50 [54]), what Nigel Smith calls radical "cultures of Illumination."[35] Clement Hawes speaks of Enthusiasm as a mode of speech that managed to encompass both a mystic annihilation and a sense of manic omnipotence, enunciation bordering on the sublime, a language at once purgative and apophatic in its conscious irrationality, as well as class-conscious.[36] Trapnel's sense of the prophetic is not incidentally incoherent, but is so at the level of structure—the text's rapid-fire shifts of genre—and indeed at the level of the sentence and in its local misdirection.

Sometimes, it is true, a Renaissance sentence (and a text more broadly) has an intricately rhetorical structure, architectural in its balanced clauses and curlicues. But at other times, with no less design, it is a swarm of bees.[37] The desired effect of the sentence is one of calculated disorientation, all its parts askew, working according to a mysterious pattern. The early modern sermon, for example, while it may have its formal rhetorical staging—exordium, peroration, and so on—can seem in any individual sentence mad as a box of frogs, hopping between scriptural example and its typological valence. This scriptural steeplechase is in some respects a thoroughly domesticated form of writing, in a culture that routinely collated texts and commonplaced its ideas. However, in the case of the era's most radical syntactical thinkers, whether a Nashe or a Browne, the prophets or the Ranters, the polyphonic motion of the thought and the fate of the sentence was often precariously balanced between sense and nonsense. That this is by design rather than accident is evident insofar as a figure like Trapnel so often comments on the practice.

Trapnel produces meta-prophetic commentary on her own state of bodily and scriptural incoherence, reporting on her audience's rationalistic and quasi-medical diagnosis: "They say these are convulsion fits and Sickness, and diseases that make thy handmaid to be in weakness." This, she suggests, both is and is not the case: it matters that the prophet is a woman, and a starving one at that, in a state of hallucinatory fasting and self-mortification. But the holy anorexia and its paroxysms are not the real issue. Trapnel has one and one only explanation of what is happening: "But oh they know not the pouring forth of thy Spirit, for that makes the body to crumble, and weakens nature" (29 [29]). She is, so to speak, beside herself, outside of her own control, beset by the spirit, possessed of an enthusiasm that has seized her rationality, the divine throb of dissatisfaction coursing through her. "[T]hy Servant is made a voyce, a sound, it is a voyce within a voyce, anothers voyce, even thy voyce through her" (42 [45]). This is a convulsion poetics, in its pauselessness, its surge beyond the powers of the relator to take down, as the Word torrents through her, and as extempore verse flows into expository prose, here political, there exegetical, a hodgepodge at the edge of coherence. This godly ventriloquism demands that the listener—the august audience cramming into her room—and the reader not only follow the logic, but accept the disorientation, the illogic. The spirit veers drunkenly, and not only does the individual sentence swarm with its garble of scriptural quotations, but the form of the prophecy across its eleven or so days is likewise turbulent, reeling in the unbidden spasms of prophetic woe.

The title, *The Cry of a Stone*, seems to come from Luke 19.40, when at the point of Jesus's entry into Jerusalem, the crowds raise a cacophony of praise, and the Pharisees tell Jesus to rebuke them, to which he responds: "I tell you, that if these should holde their peace, the stones would immediatly cry out." That this is the source has been pointed out via a late seventeenth-century (possibly Scottish) reader-annotator of Trapnel.[38] The title has also been plausibly connected to the visions in the Apocalypse of Ezra (2 Esdras or 4 Ezra): "And blood shal drop out of wood, and the stone shall give his voice, and the people shalbe troubled" (2 Esdras 5.5). That the two texts echo in each other, rather than its being a case of choosing one or the other as a source, is very likely.[39] Both "sources" point to something beyond words, beyond the ordinarily expressible, such that a voice is forced into and through the inanimate object, the dead stone. Though Trapnel has little truck with Pauline notions of female reticence, she is at least playing with the idea of a woman forced to speak, unnaturally, in the face of radically unnatural times. Hilary Hinds notes how common a trope it was for female prophets—Mary Cary, Elizabeth Stirredge, Jane Turner, or Katherine Chidley—to insist they were a "contemptible instrument" or a "poor worm."[40] This is at least in part because their message is unearthly, unwelcome, and at one and the same time, supremely complex and startlingly straightforward.

Character of the Prophecy

The Cry of a Stone twists and turns in its fast-paced shifts of idiom, subject matter, and addressee. It includes numerous songs to the soldiers, sergeants, and merchants of the city; it involves extensive typological reformulating of Israelite kingship as English Protectorship; quotidian one moment, eschatological the next, but continually voicing the anguish of the betrayed saints and God, frustrated by the lukewarm English.[41] The insufficiency of university learning is frequently recalled, and she turns again and again to the rank treatment of the poor, the hypocrisy of those ostensibly saintly ex-soldiers who betray the revolution by pandering to the wolfish aristocrats, whom Cromwell has sold out to.[42] I have been suggesting that we attend to the work's exegetical-literary dynamics, its texture and its absorption with the nature of language, dead and alive. How, though, does such a reading fit with the evident political aims of a work so involved in the rough and tumble of its moment, as the brief Republic seemed to crumble?

The infamy of Trapnel's text was grounded on its searing political critique of Cromwell, its fearlessness, pulling no punches and bracingly nondeferent. But its reputation was very much a product of its prophetic performance and the worrying (or heartening) possibility that it was genuine, that it was really God's manifestation, because it is clear that many of its auditors and subsequently its readers believed it, or didn't disbelieve it. That Trapnel was arrested and accused subsequently only added to its credibility. But it was plausible (or it wasn't) insofar as its auditors credited its prophetic character. And this was wholly bound up with its tone and style, its habits of discontinuity, and enthusiastic propulsion. This is where it most evidently generates its "literary" quality or quirks—that it needed to be credible within its discursive, prophetic parameters, that a work whose *raison d'être* was its channeling of scriptural reality to oust worldly self-interest needed to be exegetically plausible.

A prominent motif of this style, alongside and intertwined with its more evidently political comments, was its exposure and lamenting of the pernicious malleability of sacred language, wrought to unholy purposes. Indeed, the millennial cast of *Cry of a Stone* is frequently couched as a battle around pure and corrupt language. She speaks of how Cromwell, formerly capable of godly speech, is now able to utter only a "confounded" bastard language: "And how has thy Servant disputed, declared, remonstrated and appeared in the field against Antichrist, and how is his language now confounded?" (42 [45]). This was New Babel. He, Cromwell, might try to speak, or might indeed be wholly eloquent, but his words were empty and spiritless. This is a recurrent idea for Trapnel, that one must inhabit the scriptural, and body forth an inner meaning of its words, that language, in the world of the civil war prophets, was vital, alive, and shimmered with haunted meaning. Or language, even if it was the very same words, was corpselike, rotten and spiritless. Words must be "tried," in the sense of trying a coin, to see if it was real—they needed to be put to the spirit test. An examination of the mere outward form of words was insufficient.

At the point when the "relator" begins to record things, on the fifth day, Trapnel's prayer-song interweaves the captivity of the Israelites in jeering Babylon with Christological escapology, "Oh but what fastness, what locks, what bolts that could keep in a Jesus," and she sings of his escape from the prison-grave, transposing as she goes to the present: "Thou knowest who are the Babylonians that are now about thine." The "thine" here are the undauntable, endlessly imprisonable speakers of truth to Cromwell, in constant yearning "to understand more of the mystery, and of the entrals of scripture" (17 [17]). The entrails of scripture, its windabout inner workings, are to be traced in their mysterious convolution, back and forth, following impalpable paths, clues that lead from one to another text, accruing and reinterpreting as they go. On cue, a slew of scriptural references records the nature of the gusts and winds from the Bible that are the emboldened spirit speaking in storm—in quick succession, James, Exodus, 2 Peter, Acts, Job, Psalms, Isaiah, and Daniel. The meek and lamblike whisper of Trapnel as "handmaid . . . swift to hear, slow to speak" becomes, via a quick-step of biblical quotes, a storm-voice and rushing wind, a hurricane through scriptural oak trees of Isaiah ("I will make you ashamed in the oaks that you have chosen") and apocalyptic Daniel. The oaks, associated with monarchy in Caroline iconography, and a staple of Trapnel's exegetical repertoire, now give way to a blasted fallow ground of the Cromwellian present: "you shall have no green grass in these gardens . . . we have hankered from mountain to hill, we have said salvation is in this hill and in that" (17 [18]).

The biblical improvisation continues, but "because of the press of people in the chamber," the relator misses the full riff, returning only when Trapnel shifts genre, into song.[43] In a profusion and riot of writing, she invokes both spirit and furious saints to write the regime to destruction: "you shal have great Rols of writ / Concerning Babylons fall" (19 [19]). Penning their crimes for the coming reckoning, Trapnel produces a political taxonomy of those colluding with and corrupting the government, "Come write also that great Powers shall, / From off their thrones be cast," and in a series of anaphoric anathemas, she invokes the reprobate lackeys of the regime: "Oh write that those great Counsellors . . . ," "Come write down how those sparkling ones . . . ," "Oh write also that Colonels / And Captains they shall down . . . ," concluding at the top table of political malice:

> Write how that Protectors shall go,
> And into graves there lye:
> Let pens make known what is said, that,
> They shall expire and die. (19–20 [19])

What most grieves Trapnel, perhaps, is the lower classes falling into line as the "sergeants" and enforcers of the Protectorate: "Poor Serjeants that were honest men / Oh how are you fallen, / Oh how are you now taken with / The vanity of men?" (20). Such singing with intermittent prayer continues "four or five hours together," the somewhat exhausted relator reports, and what we have is the mere snippet, albeit full throttle calumny, quite sufficient to have her arrested, after the fact. The recorder notes her continual singing and the political character of the hymns. As verse, it needs to be understood as psalmic, in a culture attuned to slow rousing Davidic psalmody, a sung-form whose dynamics and rhythms differ from poetry.[44] It is certainly the case that we misread the verse if we imagine it as lyric. Its alternating with and its interaction with the prose-prophecy produces, on the one hand, a quality of the liturgical, and, on the other, a continual wrong-footing, an unpredictable element to the prophecy, as it veers from prose exegesis to verse.

When she resumes, the next day, it was taken down as an extended piece of prose, ostensibly to lament and pity fallen Cromwell: "Must thy Servant that now is upon the Throne, must he now die and go out like a candel? Oh that thy servant could mourn day and night for him!" (22 [21]). And yet the prayer turns out to be a list of his misdemeanors: "Oh that he might be laid in thy bosome, that he might not refuse to come among thy people! Oh that he might hearken to a praying people, rather then to a wicked Counsel, rather then to a Politique crue [crew] about him!" Surrounding himself with "glory and pomp," with "all the great Doctors and Rabbies," his "grave, wise, judicious men," Cromwell had forgotten the purpose of good government, in an eschatological age: "Now is a measuring time," Trapnel reminds him, and he is failing to measure up (22–23 [23]).

If on some days, the subject was a more loosely defined backsliding of the godly nation, on others the relator finds Trapnel in vehemently political mood. In quick-shuffle typology, she takes up Cromwell's favorite Old Testament identity and mantle as Gideon, who in the Book of Judges refused to accept the proffered crown of Israel:

> If he were not (speaking of the Lord *Cromwell*) backsliden, he would be ashamed of his great pomp and revenue, whiles the poore are ready to starve, and art thou providing great Palaces? Oh this was not

> *Gideon* of old, oh why dost thou come to rear up the pillars, the stones which are laid aside? tell him, Lord, thou art come down to have a controversie with him; Oh sin will lay thee flat to the earth; Oh sin will bring down a dark smoke into thy judgement, oh sin will hinder that judgement thou intendest to bring forth in the earth oh *Gideon*, is it thy Statesmen shall carry on the work of the Lord, when they are together in brainwork. (50 [54])

Over the course of several pages, ostensibly still in trance and laid out on her bed, Trapnel produces an intricate mesh of biblical references that touches on more or less every part of the political Bible, in its intricate language of political thought, the calamity of kingship in Samuel and Deuteronomy, the wretched family and national betrayals wrought on David, Samson, and Gideon, again moving into song that promises retribution: "When thou, Lord, pluckest him from thence" (54 [58]). Returning to a theme that occupied the earlier days of her public prophecy, she chastises those who are going along with Cromwell's malign turn, soldiers, sergeants, and advisers: "O poore Souldiers, take heed that you never draw your sword against the Saints; do not smite with your tongue, as they did against *Jeremiah!*" (56 [61]). At times, it can seem to be policy as much as prophecy, the nitty-gritty of government and allegiance, albeit policy with an eschatological tinge, infused with dark warnings, richly amplified with biblical examples of neglectful rulers and their fall: "It is now much, that great Ones do not tremble, that they have such greedy mindes after things here below" (58 [63]) she warns. In tempo, in its analytic mode, in its taut political typologies, this can seem wholly different from the borderline apophasis of the previous days' prophecy, with its attention to the involutions of the spirit, the channeled voice, the deeper speech, and the plumbing of the unutterable. Trapnel seems almost awake, alert, astute, rather than in stupor, transported in vision, and the relator is keen to note "the press and noise of people in the chamber" (56 [61]), the very public nature of the prophecy.

Trapnel's final day of prophecy might prompt us to wonder: does she know the Bible off by heart? It is a quite phenomenal act of collating a political-typological argument. We see such compilations in Fast

Sermons, for instance, but the presumption is that these are the work of long-term commonplacing. Trapnel's extemporizing returns for its electrifying finale both to the apostasy of those who surrender their services to Cromwell, and to the issue of language: language that is dead, and that which is infused with the elusive spirit.

"Oh when the hand-writing is come up in their veins," she warns the reprobate soldiers, "will not their knees smite together?" (62 [67]). The very blood that pulses through the veins carries the handwritten liquid Word that both constitutes them—this is the scriptural stuff of life—and writes in its blood-ink the indictment that condemns them. A stark justice is to come. Noting Ananias and Sapphira in Acts, "who did lie against the Holy Ghost," by their cheating the communist property rules of the early church for which they were struck dead on the spot (Acts 5.1–10), Trapnel prophesies that not only is a wholesale and revolutionary change imminent, but that when it comes, it will be accomplished with such summary justice and accompanied by the breaking of language. No longer will the Word allow itself to be manipulated:

> Up in thy glory and thy Majesty, thou wilt make some to rise that are feeble, poore, low creatures to utter forth against the wise ones of the world: oh they have not thy sap, thy spirit, what ever they pretend. Wilt not thou come forth and confound their language? Oh! thou wilt say, what have you to do to take the name of God in your mouths, when you act for your bellies? (62 [67])

This usurpation of spiritual authority by "feeble, poore, low creatures" is the great threat of Trapnel's prophecy. She is positively enacting the change by which the words of the "wise" are shown to be empty, when God comes to "confound their language," to reduce them to Babel-like babble. Trapnel's account of the change is worth quoting extensively. It is a gendered challenge to the patriarchal morass of Cromwellian rule, and to those who would pathologize her prophetic state, and at the same time, it is an impassioned defense of unlearning, swimming in scripture, and the benefits of being an idiot:

> thy servant was one that was simple, an Ideot, and did not study in such things as these, and must thy servant now float upon the mighty and broad waters? [meaning: of the Spirit] thou saidst indeed that thy servant should declare in *Gath* and publish in *Askelon:* They will say the spirit of madness and distraction is upon her, and that it is immodesty; but thou knowest Lord, that it is thy Spirit; for thou hast cast thy servant where she would not, and hast taken her contrary to all her thoughts; . . . thy servant would not have any take it in without tryal: let them try whether it is from thy Spirit, or from what it is; Oh thy servant knows it is from thy Spirit; let them know that it is so too, by the language of it, by the Rule through which it comes; how is the written Word carried forth in it! thy Spirit takes the Scripture all along, and sets the soul a swimming therein; oh, those things that are concealed are made manifest, when thy Spirit comes forth; oh that they might know what is the true fountain, and what is pudled water. (67 [71])

Such a passage, at the culmination of Trapnel's prophetic trance, embodies the drama of a revolution that is as once social and spiritual. This is the moment when madness reveals itself to be sanity, when the unlearned reveal themselves to be the truly wise. This is the world turned upside-down because language rids itself of fear. When Trapnel is instructed to declare in Gath and publish in Askelon, she is being asked to do what David demanded *not* be done, at the death of Jonathan, "lest the daughters of the Philistines rejoice, lest the daughters of the uncircumcised triumph" (2 Samuel 1.20). This is the moment when language is to be "tried," in the sense of separating out, the true from the false, the ore from the dross. Cromwell's downfall will be his descent into incomprehensibility when, in the coming eschaton, the spiritless, barren language of the kingly is revealed as shallow "pudled water," and the madness, the cacophony of ranting prophecy comes to be sane and full, holy idiocy and boundless flow.

Conclusion

Denys Turner, in *The Darkness of God*, writes of a "theological tradition which consciously *organised* a strategy of disarrangement as a way of life" (8). The prophetic writings of mid-seventeenth-century enthusiasm have something of this about them. Trapnel's *The Cry of a Stone*, is disarranged, awry, and elliptical, because that is how the spirit blows. But this is not to suggest a wholesale lack of control, or that as an oral text, it is not crafted. Trapnel can write a martyrology and can life-write her tale of Satan and Free-Grace, when she so chooses. *The Cry of a Stone*, however, speaks of disorder at the root of things, in language, in the State coming apart at its seams, and Time collapsing in on itself, and its form—literary, prophetic, typological—is a part of that. Poor Cromwell cannot even speak—his spiritless words have become mere gibber. Such is the politico-spiritual nature of language. Such is the decay of England on its knife-edge, with its pampered and self-indulgent Council of State, behaving like courtiers and kings: "you Councel, you think you have done well in this, but surely the passing-Bell shall ring for you," she warns, but to little effect, till revenge is wrought and kingdom come: "this is the saddest day that ever poor *England* had" (67 [71]).

For all that we can speak of scriptural prophecy as a model for the civil war visionary, it is also the case that there are various biblical styles of prophetic rhetoric and performance. Few, barring the Ranters, are prepared to go full Ezekiel, with wild-eyed apocalyptic vision, churning blood and eating dung. Isaiah's searing visions of desolation and cities tumbling, interfolded with its disabled and suffering servant redeemer, was crucial to the typological thought of the era, but few early modern writers attempted to imitate in any conspicuous form its unmatchable poetics. Then there are the fighting political prophet-actors at the court of corrupt kings, Elijah and Elisha. They, certainly, provided the most vehement model of the unwelcome, uncompromising message of the ferocious divine, ready to crush, entrap, and destroy recalcitrant and idolatrous kings. The fervor and fearlessness of Fifth Monarchist rhetoric toward Cromwell is deeply indebted to these as models of political speech. Indeed, Trapnel's description of her mother's deathbed blessing, "Lord! Double thy spirit upon my child," is a direct echo of Elijah's passing of the prophetic mantle: "let a double portion of thy spirit be upon me" (2 Kings 2.9). There are also several female models of scriptural prophecy, from the meek Hannah, thought by onlookers to be drunk in her prayer, to Deborah in Judges, celebrating a military victory wrought by Jael's killing of Sisera, nailing a tent peg through his temple.[45] Such figures frequently underlay how early modern visionary women framed their right to prophesy, against the notorious Pauline injunctions on women's behavior and speech.[46]

For all the importance of these other models of prophecy, however, Trapnel's rhetorical mode shares more closely in the language of the anguished prophets, who know what is coming to the reprobate people and who lament at the terrible knowledge of such visions, as in Jeremiah's laments, "I am pained at my very heart ... Destruction upon destruction is cried; for the whole land is spoiled" (4.19–20), or the fierce and bracingly uncouth writings of Amos and Hosea, who revel in their unhinged performance, even as they lament the coming destruction. Prophecy, it was often noted, had little truck with social propriety, and many noted the lower-class occupations of scriptural writers and characters, "written by the experimental hand of Shepherds, Husbandmen, Fishermen and such inferiour men of the world," as Gerrard Winstanley put it.[47] Thomas Hall, a writer disdainful of sectarians, comments on Amos that "This downright Prophet being not bred at Court, nor coming from the Hall where men use silken works and lofty titles of Honour; but coming from the Stall, according to his blunt and rustic language, he calls a Spade a Spade."[48] Trapnel, who can call a spade a spade, writes of how the simple, plain biblical prophets are wrought into hypercomplex evasions of their plain meaning: "the Universitie learned ones have got these mens writings; and flourishes their plaine language over with their darke interpretation, and glosses, as if it were too hard for ordinary men to understand them." This is a text, a performance, in which a lower-class woman commands center stage in a twelve-day Whitehall drama, and demonstrates a command of that most crucial political language of early modernity, the patterning of the present onto the biblical past, folding events into the eschatological. If it remains alien to us in its scriptural presumptions and obsessions, it is also clear that Trapnel, in literary and in political terms, dazzled in her brief interregnum spectacle.

When Trapnel describes herself as "one that was simple, an Ideot" (67 [71]), it presumably has only a limited affinity with Nicholas of Cusa's *Idiot*, who, having accosted an Orator in a Roman marketplace, dismantles the logic of study and learning as a route to wisdom, but he does it deftly, in the manner of an Erasmian Folly figure or a Platonic dialogue, so that his clever discursive pirouettes never leave any room for doubt about his refined intelligence.[49] His idiocy, in its quick-step dialectic, would never want to be conflated with common idiocy. The enthusiast Trapnel no doubt has more in common with Jacob Boehme, an "Idiot or simple man," according to his earliest and sympathetic English biographer.[50] The two share the idiom of anti-university rhetoric, and both are elegant in their abrasive simplicity. Both are ignorant in a deeply committed fashion, consummate with a world that is skewed, and a humanity that is abject. But neither is Trapnel's guise so far from Cusa and the lineage of august apophatic idiocy. The prophet, in the exorbitance of her reality, its overplus of the political and the eschatological, is a figure ground down in the need to communicate the incommunicable, the whole world blaring in on her. It is in this sense, perhaps, that Job is described as a prophet, in some of the assessments cited in an earlier chapter, the Job who likewise has infinity screaming at him.

CHAPTER 6

Miltonic Vertigo and a Theology of Disorientation

TWICE IN *Paradise Lost,* we witness Satan from afar, and they are both vertiginous experiences. In one, Uriel, angel of the sun, sights him as he stalks toward Eden: "his gestures fierce / He marked and mad demeanour." Only recently fooled by Satan's Cherubic disguise, Uriel, the sharpest-sighted angel, catches a glimpse of the hastily hidden perturbation that ripples across Satan's face, an inner and unangelic turmoil revealed. In the other instance, it is God who "ben[ding] down his eye" sees Satan "Coasting the wall of heaven on this side night / In the dun air sublime" about to step "On the bare outside of this world," meaning the exo-shell of the universe rather than the earth.[1] God too points out how "rage / Transports our adversary," after his long soaring upon the winds of chaos.[2] The vertigo in these sightings is multiform. In both instances, the long-range precision of the sighting is emphasized, and in both, there is a stark shift of moral perspective, in which Satan, viewed from a distance, is laid emotionally bare. The Satan with whom we have traveled from the Stygian depths, and through whose eyes we will see majestic Adam and Eve, is, in a somersault of perspective, revealed and exposed. If we felt him heroic in his defiance and not a little sublime, we see him here grief-stricken and petulant ("O sun, to tell thee how I hate thy beams") and wracked with hell in his belly ("Which way I fly is hell; myself am hell").[3]

God's pinpoint and telescopic gaze has biblical precedent in the Book of Job, albeit there it is Satan rather than the Son who is the divine confidant and super-viewer of minutiae around the universe. *Paradise Lost* shares a good deal with the Book of Job, its shifting between immensity and specificity, all things at once and very personal desolation. Its court of heaven is likewise vertiginous, looking over the banister down to abject humanity, in what is at once an act of omnisurveillance and an apparently casual sighting of things below ("Hast thou considered my servant Job," "Seest thou what rage . . ."), a thing on which you can bet. And like the Book of Job, *Paradise Lost* looks back to the construction of the world out of the chaos and cacophony that was the beginning of time, in a work that recounts creation not once, but three times. The earliest annotator of the epic, P.H., and many since, have heard Jobean echoes in the epic.[4] Such parallels can, however, spill over, and abject Satan, gazed down upon, might just resemble abject, innocent Job. Such is the birdlime of parallels that Milton routinely traps the reader in. Early modernity—as explored in an earlier chapter—viewed the Book of Job not only in relation to its desolate central character, but equally as a work about the intractable dissonance between temporal and eternal logic, and the terrible aporia of Job's simultaneously knowing too much and knowing nothing. This too might be said of *Paradise Lost*.

The long-range, telescopic shifts of perspective that map Satan's trail from the exo-cosmology of the Eternal to the newly birthed temporal world also produce an interpretative vertigo. We must switch from the diabolic to a human scale, from the burning lightless energy of a cavernous hell to the lush green and slow pace of paradise. The melancholy of this is multiform, that we see from Satan's perspective, sat disguised as a cormorant looking in on Adam and Eve and Eden in its terrible perfection, while we like Satan gaze on something irrevocably lost.[5] If, in pointing out the stealthy movement of the spy, trespassing on primordial reality, Milton is allowing us to see Satan right side up—after the all-inverting experience of hell and its epic logic—these instances of Uriel's and God's eagle-eye perception contribute also to a narrative disorientation in its sheer dizzy scale and an epic whose cosmic scenery is, by turns, turbulent, unimaginable, and hyperprecise. Milton's cosmology is variously rendered with a geometrical exactitude and a shape-shifting elasticity in which the insolidity of things is paramount. There is a near-Euclidian precision to the account of Uriel, traveling on a sunbeam to earth and riding the same beam home as it dips below the horizon, the angel gliding the transected circle of the heavens. Adam wonders about proportion in the firmament and the clockwork character of the turning heavens. There may be no resolution to the astronomical dialectics of the epic, in which the apparently exact mathematical character of the cosmos is rendered with a scrawl—the "scribbled o'er" cycles and epicycles—but the poem is full not just of spaceflight, the "strange velocitie" of Angels through immensity, but also the thing beyond immensity, beyond the universe.[6] Here, what is described as space is not really so, just as what seems to be shape—the always contingent form of angels—is, the poem implies, only so for the benefit of human ears.[7]

There is not really any other work of seventeenth-century thought that trades so fully, so brazenly in the unknowable. At one moment, the things of *Paradise Lost* may be susceptible to reason, but then its heady, unreckonable nature, its part in eternity, confounds. Milton's universe oscillates in and out of explicability. The reader is wrong-footed, and Miltonic language distorts, teases, and misleads: the meanings of individual words slip, demanding that they be understood, like angelic shape, as provisional. This insight has long been at the heart of Miltonic criticism, particularly around Satan's magnetic bending of truth, making crooked straight.

The argument in this chapter is that this disorientation is theological in a quite different vein from the theology generally associated with the poem. In an epic describing the indescribable action of eternity, one of Milton's theological modes is akin to the apophatic, where the poem is suspended in the vertigo of its paradoxes that will not resolve. Their contradictions *are* their theology. The poem's "major" systematic theological investments, most prominently in the nature of free will, its "justification" of God and its lapsarian psychology by which we continually veer toward Satan in all his panache, are far from straightforward, but they operate straightforwardly in the terrain of reason. Indeed, the militant exercise of reason, remaining hermeneutically alert, is often understood to be the "lesson" that Adam and Eve fail to take sufficient note of and that the reader, after them, in their fallen straits, is enjoined to heed, according at least to some readings.[8] The vertigo of *Paradise Lost*, however, its state of disequilibrium, is not amenable to well-reasoned correction or interpretative revision of our first fallen responses. If *Par-*

adise Lost was for Samuel Johnson a "thesis-ridden poem," as Victoria Silver characterizes his criticism, if it can seem unequivocal and bullish in its sad theological certainties, it is also the case that the poem's vitality and energy consists in the waywardness of its theological landscape, the "erratic play of . . . perceptions and sympathies" that the poem generates, which she aligns to Theodor Adorno's account of the vertigo we suffer when we come to recognize that reason and analysis, mere "right thinking," cannot encompass or characterize our experience.[9]

That *Paradise Lost*—a work that so trades in action outside of time, in the eternal—might or must have some connection with the ineffable, and that it is a poem in the apophatic mode, has some traction in the long critical history of the epic. But only so much. From one perspective, very little is "unknowable" in *Paradise Lost*, even that which by all rights should be. Where the apophatic tradition can only approach the back parts of God, with eyes averted, as Exodus has it, Milton intrudes in seemingly brazen form in the politics of heaven. The Free Indirect Ubiquity of a narrator who can inhabit the thoughts of God as well as the wiles of Satan produces a universe with all too few *arcana dei*, with all too little mystery. Some readers might suspect the texture of the poem to have little in common with apophatic traditions of "learned ignorance": Milton does not wear his erudition humbly. The epic is voracious and encyclopedic in scope—a work of hyperknowledge, whose cosmology is beyond Faustian, whose monist philosophical framework and embedded natural history are immense and complex. The classical palimpsests, variously Ovidian, Virgilian, or Homeric, that frame the poem, its gazetteer of reference to far-flung imperia, and its political infrastructure seeing the wreckage of the republic and the wounded universe as mirrors of each other, are thoroughgoing, if elusive. This is a noisy and a busy poem.

In any case, many readers of Milton suppose him temperamentally impatient with the ineffable and its all-too-Catholic rhetorical ceremonies of self-abnegation. If the epic tarries now and then with the apophatic and with Dionysian light, this might be no more than a surface resemblance. That Milton is no mystic in any sense that resembles the contemplative medieval tradition can be readily conceded. Even if, in his early poetry, he shows some inclination to dress himself in the vatic, Milton's legal-logical purposes in *Paradise Lost*—to justify the tough ways of God to querulous, carping humanity—do not allow him to draw the curtain of the *mysterium tremendum* around questions that resist straightforward answers. Occasionally critics have allied Milton with the prophetic, that distant noisy cousin of the apophatic: Michael Lieb, for example, argues that Milton may wish to invest things and states—fruit, light, even war—with the "diaphany" of *res sacrae*. There have, however, been relatively few such readings, such that Gordon Teskey notes a characterization of Milton as "the epitome of the classical, the rational, the stable" and "the least mysterious of poets."[10]

Among the most pressing arguments against seeing Milton as a devotee of the apophatic and its incertitude is that he is just too hyperlogical, a thinker who invests a great deal, theologically, in doctrine. The entire theological gambit of the epic—that our possession of free will, the condition of being human, means we are free to fall—is premised on humans' ability to discern, logically, the essential truths that would command obedience. This is at the heart of Raphael's lesson in dialectic reasoning. If humankind was "sufficient to have stood," this sufficiency consisted in those very powers of reason, "discursive or intuitive," that the angel reports as characteristic of humanity and spirits, where discourse "Is oftest yours, the latter most is ours," the lack of certainty in this division between discursive and intuitive knowledge being played out here in the lack of balance in the lines.[11] Throughout, the epic demonstrates a concern with the chicanery and malign logic-chopping by which Satan works, and the need to remain alert to such sleight of hand. The "seduction" gets nowhere, Karen Edwards has astutely shown, when Satan appeals to vanity or self-interest. It is only when Satan twists logic by advocating the pursuit of logic that his arguments succeed, when reason becomes unreasonably the object of idolatry.[12] This is what everything pivots on.

For all this, however, Milton's systematic disorientation, distortion, and the poem's vast scope, with its sweeping sublime, is a work of theological overexposure to what is properly unknowable. The fullness of the epic, with its jostling intellectual frameworks, and its coexistence of such variety, is very much a part of the poem's vertigo, what Gordon Teskey has described as Milton's "*ars poetica* of delirium," a fast-paced disjointedness. The dense texture of every element—the political, the scientific, the humanist, the theological—vies for our attention. The delirium of *Paradise Lost*, according to Teskey, "works by a kind of oscillation, a flickering on and off of hallucinatory moments in rapid succession, driven by some underlying contradiction."[13] The small-scale paradoxes, oxymorons, and verbal illogic of *Paradise Lost*, that hell is "darkness visible," or that Satan upends the meanings of words—"evil be thou my good"—are as nothing to its large, structural derangement.[14]

Noam Reisner's *Milton and the Ineffable*, the most sustained attempt to render the poem in light of the apophatic tradition, notes *Paradise Lost* borrowing various Dionysian hypersuperlatives, God "above all height . . . past utterance" and "Dark with excessive bright."[15] He explores its synesthetic experience, its "sinewy, often luxuriantly tactile concreteness" substituting for the unrepresentable presence of the divine. The epic does not aim to reproduce the experience of the numinous, but rather describes "the literary process which allows Milton to pretend to say the unsayable." God's very words exude ambrosial fragrance—they are sensory as well as intellectual.[16] Reisner's fullest attention in regard to *Paradise Lost* is devoted to "accommodation," how truths and events to which human words are inadequate must be communicated obliquely. What happens in heaven must be understood as true only in a contingent ineffable sense. A good deal has been written tracing Milton's ideas of biblical accommodation, from *De Doctrina Christiana*, in which scripture is superbly fitted to human capacity, on to Raphael's mostly nonbiblical description of heaven, the eternal with its wars, creation and angelic sex, what is outside time and beyond human words. I will not retrace this ground, except to note this: Raphael's accommodation is twice removed from its equivalent in *De Doctrina Christiana*, first, in that the special warrant we accord scripture's accommodated depiction of God does not extend to Milton's poetic reenactment; and second, that where accommodation theory relates to how we render God in human language, Raphael's "process of speech" encompasses a good deal besides (heaven as realm, its wars and sex, and the angels who inhabit the world of the Eternal). It is, writes N. G. Sugimura, "an epistemological parody of sorts" in which its clarifying angel "does not really render things more intelligible."[17] Theories of accommodation in Milton have, as far as I know, attended mainly to heaven, and more obliquely to God, but hell and chaos are equally a part of the eternal: they lie outside the universe, beyond human capacity to imagine, even if a certain homiletic tradition revels in imagining its fiendish tortures. Milton's hell, in its vertigo and paradoxes, might be thought of as accommodated, in the sense that, like heaven, it is a world unthinkable and unstable. That its landscape is described by a mere narrator, and not by a narrating angel, hardly changes the ruses of Milton's accommodation strategy.

The case for a Milton of the unknowable and ineffable does not proceed on strictly theological grounds; his irresolution permeates the poem's every crevice. Peter Herman depicts a poet who, from his syntax to his similes to his allusive habits, has indecision be the "deep structure" of *Paradise Lost,* which emerges as a work of almost constitutive irresolution. He demonstrates the kind of grammatical indeterminacy he finds in a phrase such as "May I express thee unblamed," in the invocation to book 3, noting that the final word can modify either "I" or "thee," that whether God or he himself is "unblamed" must remain unsettled.[18] This sense of a Miltonic syntactical quiver, where the meaning cannot finally be determined, has its correlate in the larger-scale irresolution of the text. In such a reading, we cannot "solve" the political and theological conundrums that the poem constructs, any more than the so characteristic syntactical ambiguities that Milton allows to sit for a moment as possible constructions of a given phrase. Many of Herman's readings seem not out of kilter with the scholarly tradition he sets his face against, in which a theologically didactic Milton can coexist with a poetically liquid writer. Christopher Ricks, who would not (intuitively) be easily aligned with Herman's reading, has a bucketful of such moments, of which he says: "Like a skilful advocate, Milton says something that would be impossibly far-fetched and then has it struck from the record. But his skill has lodged it in our minds and feelings."[19] If there is a dispute (and there is always dispute in Miltonic scholarship), it comes in weighing the character of his poetic incertitude against his intellectual certainties.

In what follows, I argue that the poem's incongruities, its dissonances and contradictions, are structural, load-bearing facets of Milton's theology: we cannot reason our way beyond them. It is true that the poem contains its theojudicial reckoning, its justification of the ways of God—Milton at his most orthodox, give or take a member of the trinity—and also that the poem produces its hermeneutic labors, where the very essence of being human involves its ceaseless interpretative work, its natural theology, but these elements do not exhaust the theological character of the poem. There is an intractable remainder that emerges from Milton's setting his tale in and out of Eternity. We are made to gaze upon what we know is impossible to see. Analogy and language there, in eternity, are continually in a state of failure. I look, first, at some instances of dizzy scale and disproportion in a poem that so relentlessly attends to its geospatial reckoning of the Eternal. Milton's concern in producing an always contingent cosmology, not only of the universe, but also of the beyond where space and time are knotted and confused, is central to the poem's architecture. The chapter will explore the theological character of this vastness, not so much in its hints about ontology—its prime matter, its monist construction—but rather in its crafted indecipherability, first in its cosmology and then in hell and chaos. The manifest universe, that which can be measured and numbered, is tangled up with this rich, unimaginable condition—of hell as well as heaven—whose character must be rendered in analogy that, the poem insists, is woefully inexact. I will suggest that the Miltonic cosmogony and cosmopoetics can usefully be understood as akin to the Behmenist Eternity, explored in chapter 2—in its shuttling back and forth from eternity into the manifest world, and its creation apophatics—even if Milton, writing from his humanist heights, would have little time for Boehme's obscurity and his concocted hermeneutics of the Eternal.

Scale and Disproportion

The sublime—that most elusive of ideas and most Miltonic state—is intimately connected with the vertigo of flight and immensity, transport and *ekstasis*, or the rare ability to mimic or reproduce these giddy states in one's poetics: Milton's loping, tumbling syntax exemplifying what may elude definition.[20] David Norbrook, in *Writing the English Republic*, considers the mid-seventeenth-century sense that it was an era living through a kind of political sublime, with the abyssal moment of the regicide. In a related piece on the Lucretian sublime, he addresses "one of the most remarkable moments in classical poetry" when "the walls of the universe, *moenia mundi / discedunt*, disappear or open out, and the poet sees the movement of things throughout the void, *inane*."[21] Milton, for Norbrook, is likewise at the center of such a poetic-cosmogenic vortex, the mind-wrenching opening of the universe on all sides, things "taking place underneath his feet, *sub pedibus*," beneath the Lucretian surface, and differently underfoot in the crafted imbalance of Milton's poetic meter. The sublime, once so prominent a notion in relation to *Paradise Lost* ("I am sick of hearing of the sublimity of Milton," wrote Mary Wollstonecraft), has not had too much traction in Miltonic criticism for a long time, no doubt seeming overly grandiose.[22] But the experience of vertigo and outsized scale, of terrible beauty, is one of the essential characteristics of the poem.

The intricate cogwork of *Paradise Lost* by which the tiny and the vast interact, the human scale of lunch with an angel in Eden coexisting with the unthinkably vast panorama of the universe, is one kind of disproportion, among several, in the poem. It puts the tempo of humanity, leisured and contemplative, into play with the seething maelstrom of eternity and the surging of its wars. The narrative hurtles from one to another perspective; the whole of creation in its hexamera and the expulsion of the toxic angelic throng out of heaven are boxed inside Raphael's amiable narration. William Kerrigan speaks of the dense interconnectedness of the poem, the hermeneutic work of adjusting the part to the whole, as "the enfolded sublime" of the epic, the perplexing similarity of disproportionate things, and he considers Raphael to revel in this, as the conversation shifts from lunch to the cosmos, an angel who "reshuffles these immensities . . . giddy with the plasticity of huge meaning."[23]

It is never straightforwardly mere vastness that disorientates, however, so much as its indeterminacy, that one has nothing to measure against. Tumbling Satan, having made his way across chaos, in whose adirectionality there is neither up nor down, approaches "This pendent world, in bigness as a star / Of smallest magnitude close by the Moon."[24] The "world" in this, as noted, is not the earth but the entire universe gazed upon from outside, on which "shell" he is about to land.[25] On the one hand, this conveys mere enormity. The annotator, P.H., brings in Gassendi on the magnitude of stars, reckoned 108 times the size of the earth. But the scale of things, here, reels and needs almost word-by-word recalibrating: the "bigness" of a star of "smallest Magnitude" (ought we to be attending to its largeness or tininess?) is set beside a moon that outshines it and renders it insignificant, demanding we readjust our sense of scale and brightness with each clause. Satan and the reader, buffeted in Chaos, arrive at a "pinprick universe that now (barely) greets our eyes," as John Leonard puts it, tracing a critical history mired in a wrongly framed question of the physical shape of the universe.[26] Satan's coming in to land recalls, it has been suggested, the uncertain footing of Milton's Leviathan simile, whose every clarification of size and solidity obscures further.[27] That this insolidity has its ubiquitous effect in the poem is noted by Regina Schwartz, who characterizes the indeterminate "pendent world" hovering in its void, as analogous to the way that Milton "poises his fictive world" in chaos, malevolent, unknowable, abortive.[28] The poem's habit of unmooring its reader, in its political and its theological misdirection, has its correlate in an impossible cosmography. What kind of relationship exists in the poem between the two realms, inside and beyond the measurable universe? That this is insoluble, dependent as we are on our degraded, postlapsarian equipment for thinking and on a language corrupt and unstable, that we can have no purchase on the eternal that is its terrain, is the disabling paradox of the poem. Vertigo, a "swimming in the head" in a contemporary definition, is the condition of *Paradise Lost*, not just in its ungraspable cosmology, shifting and whirling in the eternal, but in the vertiginous poetics of the fallen.[29]

Arriving on the outer crust of the universe, its "firm opacous globe," Satan seeks an entry into its forbidding solidity, on some coast where everything is blown about in the blustery cleric-baiting Paradise of Fools. Perhaps these are the mere shore gusts of windy chaos, the adirectionality a little more localized. Here, stormy particles are not embryon atoms, but abortive snippets of the future, disarranged religiosity, so wild that the abstract and the tangible are indistinct, where the trappings of Catholicism ("Cowles, hoods and habits . . . reliques, beads, / Indulgences . . .") are ripped to shreds.[30] This deranged generic moment, with its fleeting suggestion of the Ptolemaic outer sphere, the *primum mobile*, has been of some importance in reckoning and refuting Milton's cosmological allegiances, but as Catherine Gimelli Martin and others have noted, this needs to be considered as "cosmological spoof," its polemic addressing an quasi-scholastic Catholic world view.[31] If there is an underlying geocosmology—and if here we have the rudiments of the Ptolemaic multisphere universe—it has to be understood within the algebra of Milton's sudden allegorical-satirical mode. The carefully constructed immensity and sublime of the cosmos-beyond-the-cosmos gives way to a Bedlamesque cacophony of Limbo, with its Luther-like scatology on the flatulent "backside of the World." What at times borders on the cosmological then swivels to typology, in the sight of Jacob's retractable ladder, mysteriously meant, reaching up to heaven, but also down to "the sudden view / Of all this World at once," the belly of the dizzy universe.[32]

How far does *Paradise Lost* yield to cosmological cartography, to the logic of the telescope's straight lines, a logic that has at least some angelic warrant in the trigonometrical flight of Uriel? Clearly, there is in the poem an intricate attention to questions that, from a human point of view, are astronomical, and even what happens outside of everything—materially speaking—is caught up in this. There is an august history of mapping the Miltonic heavens, even while Milton's cosmology is rarely understood any longer as, primarily, a straightforward matter of Copernican, Tychonic, or Ptolemaic theories of the well-shaped cosmos (though insofar as it retains its currency as a question, the tide has turned against aligning Milton with the "old science").[33] Schematic diagrams of the universe, swimming in the surround-lake of hell, chaos, and heaven, are familiar aids in Miltonic critical literature, and can perhaps orientate the reader, but they distort as much as they clarify.[34] Dennis Danielson reproduces a diagrammatic "mathematical system of the ancients" from 1614, in which the mappable cosmos swims in an infinite chaos of atoms.[35] We might wonder, gazing at such diagrams, in what sense chaos and hell are not merely more *remote* parts of the one creation, an infinity going on and on. But Milton goes out of his way to disrupt any such supposition of cosmic continuity. The Eternal lacks spatial stability, and its sequentiality is illusory, even while nothing can be said without recourse to sequence. Gross human words are not up to the job of describing the unimaginable ontology of this outerverse; its angels can adopt what shape they choose, and hell or chaos is an elastic space-state.[36] The character of the Eternal can only be represented askew, in atonality, or, differently imagined, in its voluptuous qualities. This goes for hell as much as heaven.

Satan's sight of the centerless universe, "up or down . . . hard to tell," although it has something in common with the chaos he has just traveled through, also bears comparison with the two passages that opened this chapter, the angelic-divine telescopic gaze, with their (almost) flawless scrutiny catching Satan on the hop.[37] Satan too has pinpoint satellite vision. Initially, scouring the zodiac from pole to pole, it is the sun, rather than the "blissful seat of Paradise," that grabs his diabolic attention, and to which he travels, with one of the many allusions to Galileo in which the simultaneous clarity and distortion of the latter's achievements are permitted to coexist, the fiend landing on "a spot like which perhaps / Astronomer in the sun's lucent Orb / Through his glazed optic tube yet never saw."[38] In a phrasal swivel, the sunspot spotting of Galileo's *Siderius Nuncius* (1610) is briefly evoked before that evocation is undermined. This has about it that Miltonic quiver, in which we can never be quite sure about the object or character of doubt; Galileo fails to see the alchemical action of the sun or its dazzling angel—"The same whom John saw" in Revelation 19.17. We are left, I think, to puzzle whether this heightens or diminishes the character of distortion and the poetics of imprecision in relation to the "optic glass," never quite synonymous with the merely physical telescope.[39] Appearing within Milton's seasick similes, the glass seems to emblematize a scrutiny that obscures, or when deployed to characterize angelic-diabolic flight (both Satan's and later Raphael's), it addresses a movement, with "speed almost spiritual" both precise and unimaginable.[40] Satan may imagine his long journey through an epic lens, the poem's imperial, classical, and heroic residue, but he enters in upon scientific forces and rapid shifts of cosmic framework that are, in a fundamental sense, theological. This is Teskey's *"ars poetica* of delirium," where things are there only in flickering fashion.

Galileo's not quite sighting the angel of the apocalypse in the sun imbricates eschatalogical and typic time with the cosmological, a measured and human time, into which Satan intrudes, all vying in the poem's folds.[41] Asequential, proleptic, or allusive, the epic is so layered with temporal disorientation as to suggest that fallen time is fragmented in a way that fluid unfallen, sacred time is not. "It could be argued that there is no time in *Paradise Lost*," writes Amy Boesky, so adirectional or extratemporal it proves.[42] But the "temptation of sequence" is everywhere, and while the lives of angels are lived in the Eternal, Raphael insists on real vicissitude in angelic experience, beyond the mere "process of speech" needed to render things comprehensible for Adam and Eve. Angels, and fallen angels, too, exist in a realm that both has and does not have time, the scholastic *aevum* and the *eviternal*, "a *tertium quid* between eternity and time to describe the domain in which angels exist," writes Ayelet Langer: "The aevum is a formulation, or a kind of logic, that builds durations of the divine and the human into the same structure."[43] That this remains an always abyssal thought, in which we can only get lost, is a facet of what Judith Scherer Herz describes as the poem's "Rubik's cube of time–space."[44]

Satan's approaching the universe, its size ungaugeable, has its more serene correlate in Adam's speculation on calibrating the scale of the turning skies, when he finds himself computing the magnitude of things, and noting that earth is merely "a spot, a grain, / An atom, with the firmament compared." Perplexed by the numbered stars within "spaces incomprehensible" rolling in the heavens, Adam wonders (following Eve, who first framed the question) about geocosmic misshapenness, "How Nature wise and frugal could commit / Such disproportions."[45] Adam, whose Edenic habitus is based on a psalmic natural theology, his spiritualized interpretative encounters with the world, seems to be concerned that this disproportion might be an Unnatural Theology. Raphael's answer, or nonanswer, constitutes the poem's most thorough engagement with astronomy, and indeed with knowledge theory more broadly, albeit built thick with equivocation. One reading of Raphael's astronomical antilecture is that Milton sees astronomy as an indifferent matter, that Adam and Eve ought to direct their intellectual energies to more pressing issues, even if this is slightly out of character with the epic's insistence on the proper and ceaseless pursuit of knowledge.[46] Certainly, Raphael's what-ifery ("What if the sun / Be centre of the world . . ." or the earth a planet, or the sun a star) allows for heliocentric possibilities, without wholly dismissing the geocentric presumptions under scrutiny in Adam's question. Karen Edwards writes that the conversation is "open ended and richly indeterminate . . . structurally unresolvable, designed *not* to meet Adam's demand for a 'solution' to 'resolve' his doubtful reading."[47] Perhaps Raphael is cagey and warns Adam off the question less because there are profound mysteries there than because there are not. The suspended state, where one holds competing knowledge-possibilities in play has, in such a strategy, its own intellectual-spiritual quality. In one or other fashion, however, it seems important, that this astronomy—knowable by angels, if not by Adam—is put into play with the genuine "Spaces incomprehensible" that Satan traverses, that they remain in irreconcilable, structural tension with each other. Satan tumbles toward the hole in the wall of the universe and then down through its immensity, and this is mirrored by Eve's and then Adam's gazing up at the cosmo-balletics of the universe, in all its mysterious clockwork. The geometry that measures the heavens, with compass and telescope, cannot fathom the illogic of the Beyond, the thing like space beyond all space that Satan glides though.[48]

Milton's theocosmology that seems to describe the universe is in one respect closer to Jacob Boehme's surging realities, appearing one way in the eternal and another in the manifest world. There is little evidence that Milton paid Boehme any serious attention, and it might seem likely that Milton was temperamentally averse to the anti-intellectualism of such German, Dutch, and increasingly English mysticism. We could then reasonably suppose he would be only dismissive of that Teutonic cacophony and the illuminist cultures of the 1640s and 1650s that so appreciated Boehme.[49] However (and without supposing the latter to be an unappreciated "source" for *Paradise Lost*), the cosmological scope of Behmenism, with its complex angelology and its sallies into the disorientation of the eternal, shares something important with *Paradise Lost* that cannot be found elsewhere in the era's angelology or cosmology.[50]

The account of Boehme in chapter 2 (to reiterate, for nonsequential readers) recounts the Silesian's description of the manifest world in continual seething exchange with the quasi-industrial, erotic hyperreality of the Eternal. Everything, from the quotidian—a stone, a clod—to the character of emotion, to the figures of scripture, means one thing in the visible world and another in the Eternal: continually they spill into each other, re-forming, emptying themselves in kenotic and deranged fashion, fissile with their uncontainable energy. The Blakean Milton is this one, a Milton who channels Boehme, both of whom suppose relentless, dangerous exchange between the manifest and immanifest.[51] Nobody else in early modernity besides Boehme so readily moves in and out of the Eternal in all its disorientating fullness. Boehme and Milton share a fantastical ambition, to lodge a metacosmology of the Eternal inside matter, inside angels, albeit Boehme's are not anthropomorphized. The one full study of the linkage, by Margaret Lewis Bailey, is more than a century old and aims, rather awkwardly, to understand Boehme's angels, as well as Lucifer and Adam, as they appear in the hexamera of *Mysterium Magnum*, as characters in a narrative akin to Milton's, not as inchoate energies.[52] What Milton shares with Boehme, however, is an impulse, not improperly seen as an apophatic impulse, to disorientation: both describe a kind of pulsing irreality, something that sits outside the real, the created world. Milton's Hell and Boehme's Eternal are constructed of malleable, contingent matter, liable to change its nature, matter that is almost emotional in its ready responsiveness. That it is beyond what can be thought demands that thought itself be sabotaged by illogic and paradox, be *experienced* as insufficient. It is not just that Satan bends words, but that words in relation to the Eternal are by their nature meager.

I suspect Milton knew Boehme's writing, and if so, that he could hold disdain and admiration in a state of suspension, but it is no major part of my argument one way or the other. I draw the link in part because of their shared cosmological sublime, but more particularly to argue that *Paradise Lost*, a work at times stern in the legalism of its doctrine, also utilizes and depends upon a theology of alogical (perhaps multilogical) and nonpropositional perception, with something Dionysian about its embrace of the irrational. That we are wrong-footed and drawn repeatedly into the rabbit-holes of the poem's aporia may be Milton's elaborate metaphysics of fallenness. But it is not necessarily the case that Milton is *constantly* battering the reader with the same single fact, and it may not be the only function of alogic in the poem. *Paradise Lost* stalls us in a manner akin to the paralysis of the apophatic, in which the object of attention can only be darkly known.

At the risk of digression and stretching the Behmenist link to breaking point, it is worth noting that Boehme's thought, though *sui generis* in many respects, arises from a rich Germanic tradition, reaching back to Meister Eckhart (c. 1260–1328) and forward to Milton's contemporary, Angelus Silesius (1624–77), that dislocates reason in other ways. Eckhart says outrageous things that cannot be true, by any theological logic, but in whose pause—while their impossibility is absorbed—something apophatically true emerges. Eckhart inverts categories of God and human, asserts compulsion upon God, and shrinks the divine. He makes claims whose theological nonsense are wild heresy, if they are understood within quotidian categories. Scholastic debate on God's attributes is turned inside out: "And if I say 'God is wise' that is not true. I am wiser than he." Humans command God, who is compelled to pour himself out on the person who has annihilated themselves "or else he is not God."[53] God's existence, and the reality of the world, is predicated on Eckhart himself: "In my birth all things were born and I was the cause of myself and of all things . . . and if I did not exist, 'God' would also not exist . . . There is no need to understand this." Eckhart may very well be God: "God and I, we are one."[54] This is, according to Beryl Smalley, a style of exegesis akin to "an attack of senile dementia."[55] Milton, surely, would tolerate none of it (although his Satan might try such arguments on for size), even after he had decoded its rhetorical purpose. His God, his Satan, may involve all sorts of impropriety, but neither of them is in the same diminished league where Eckhart finds his vaguely drunken

God. "I was the cause of myself," as Eckhart has it, sounds dangerously close to Satan's most malevolent rhetorical fraud in heaven—that angels might be "self-begot, self-raised"—practiced upon the soon-to-be-fallen spirits.[56] In fact, it is even less likely that Milton knew Eckhart than that he paid much attention to Boehme, if we have source-study in mind, but here too, it is the style of vertiginous thinking that I wish to suggest by the comparison: that Milton's hell, in its disorientation, mimics the experience of the ineffable, the Behmenist moment when he pulls us back through the looking-glass.[57] How does one pass through from outside of manifest existence into it? This is a question that Boehme and Milton both have an interest in. In Milton's case, the question can take the guise of cosmology, tumbling through the epic's vast spaces.

Neither Boehme nor Eckhart would presume that what they say needs to be true, literally speaking, but rather that the swimming of the head produced by their cracked writing is a theological state, a theology of vertigo, an apophatic experience. Milton's epic, in its black-hole paradoxes, bears comparison with this vertiginous facet of the Rhineland mystics. It brims with irresolvability, with impossibilities that are true. Some of these can be (relatively) straightforward orthodoxies—that the creation was both instantaneous and sequential, for example. Rosalie L. Colie notes Milton's not having much love for "verbal pyrotechnics of theological wit," those ingrained formulations of faith that the soon-to-be-ejected clergyman Ralph Venning called the Christian "orthodox paradoxes." Milton, as a thinker given to doctrinal certainties, an absoluteness of the moral law, and the ways of God, viewed these, "according to the evidence of *De Doctrina Christiana*," as mere befuddlement, some of which must be tolerated, but not loved.[58] At the same time, Milton continually twists the reader into knots, into moral and temporal labyrinths. This too is a kind of theology, and in one respect, it can be seen as an ordinary mysticism, an orthodox paradox. What is particular to *Paradise Lost* is that so much of its apophatic, its ineffable experience and its theo-vertigo, is associated with hell, not God. We are dizzy with (theologically speaking) the wrong thing and for all its Dionysian moments of excess, heaven proves insufficiently ineffable for many readers. But the most thoroughgoing and pervasive disorientation in the epic is

Milton's vertigo of resemblance, of things whose apparent similarity is all wrong.

The Hellish Ineffable and Doppelgänger Hermeneutics

If Milton is at best only fleetingly akin to Boehme or Eckhart, we might note also his not being like Nicholas of Cusa, whose *Of Learned Ignorance* and *The Idiot* also had some traction among the same radical circles and whose most fecund idea was the notion that opposites in ordinary reality can be reconciled in God, at infinity. Milton may or may not be indebted to or interested in Cusa, but *Paradise Lost* is rich in a kind of bastard "coincidence of opposites," in which we encounter distorted resemblance, the apparent cinching together of things that ought to be unalike.[59] Milton's insistent echoes produce a kind of doppelgänger hermeneutics, analogies that mislead even as they clarify. These ghostly echo-doubles are everywhere in *Paradise Lost*. They are its lifeblood, and work on both the small and large scale. A good deal of critical attention has been focused on the hermeneutic quandaries arising from them, driven in large part by a pervasive critical inclination for global explanatory devices—that what explains distortion in hell should also explain the warps in Milton's Eden.[60] The things of unthinkable eternity, and of the prelapsarian world, are paired relentlessly with things of the knowable world, whether words, saturated with fallen meaning, or will-o'-the-wisp classical resonances. A few such examples of this echo-logic are warranted, given how pervasive it proves in the epic, toward an argument that it constitutes a theological experience in the alogical abyss of unalike things twinned, their insoluble puzzles as apophatic moments.

One rich set of doppelgängers, though largely beyond the scope of this chapter, serves to *reduce* the distinction between prelapsarian and postlapsarian in Eden, so that Milton invests the primal state of Adam and Eve with qualities and associations, with emotions and actions, that seem positively fallen—bickering, labor, secret tears, a scattering of sexual allusion, or words used in prelapsarian etymological innocence that mislead when tainted with the associations we bring.[61] And yet all these tangled qualities of humanity must be reconciled with unfallenness; the associations need to be reengineered, such that it serves as one of the generative instabilities of the poem.[62] Another cluster of perplexing echoes emerges from Milton's manufacturing memories of a classical world that does not yet exist, and here too, whether it is epic heroism of the early books, or the Ovidian sexuality in Eden, the thing at issue is often the wrongness as much as the rightness of any such ghost in the poem, the need to disentangle layers of meaning and association.[63]

Those echoes that involve Satan are fraught in their own fashion, at times insisting that he is, after all, still an angel though fallen, at times recalling that he is still a devil, though pitiable. Sometimes these pairings can seem hell's parodic copy of heaven, its hierarchies, its grandeur, though at times, too, this almost works in reverse: the council chambers of both heaven and hell have their "whom shall we send?" moments, when the question is greeted by a cowed, if staged, silence, until Son and Satan, respectively, step in as champions. Solo martial prowess, chivalric or classical, with its concocted drama, is surely meant to be more jarring in heaven.[64] Or again, the paired instances of angelic mining create an equivalence as puzzle. The devils who ransack the soil in hell for gold, who "Rifled the bowels of their mother Earth," sluicing fire from a burning lake, have mining history behind them, having also pillaged the celestial soil, as part of Satan's chemico-military strategy.[65] It is a parallel designed to make heaven more rather than less baffling. Not only do we have the accommodated tale of war in heaven to transpose into thinkable human thought, but the geology of heaven. The monist explanation of the scene by Stephen Fallon—that the angels "mingle" their nitrous selves into the neutral matter of the earth, infusing their smutty selves into what they touch—is wholly convincing, but not less disorientating, turning as it does on the ambiguous character of each verb in turn ("mingled . . . concocted . . . adusted . . . reduced"), which can refer at once to the soil and to their own beings, reduced "to blackest grain."[66]

Hell's melancholy is all the more intense and twisted in that the autobiographical Milton in the poem has his own haunted presence there—another kind of doppelgänger. Blind Milton's misery, political and personal, is first expressed in his rolling eyes that meet only intractable dark, light seemingly withheld by God: "Thou / Revisitst not these eyes, that roll in vain / To find thy piercing ray, and find no dawn," he says in the proem to book 3. This entry into the useless light comes as the poet flies from hell, "Escaped the Stygian Pool, though long detained / In that obscure sojourn," the narrator co-sailing with Satan.[67] But the parallel extends back as well. The poet's rolling eyes recall Satan's attempt to grasp the immensity of the flamey emptiness around him, the darkness visible. He too throws his eyes around like a hammer hurled, to discover what vastness he has been cast into: "round he throws his baleful eyes / That witnessed huge affliction and dismay / Mixed with obdurate pride and steadfast hate."[68] As with the monist mingling in the soil of heaven, here too, we find, with a characteristic syntactical blur, Satan infusing himself into the already dismal surroundings and making them worse, a mixing that seems first to describe his environment, but which instantly becomes imbued with his own toxic pride and hate. He creates and becomes his hellish world. Milton's spectral place in this hall of mirrors that is fleetingly like and yet insistently dissimilar to his mundane world is encountered most fully in the irreconcilable political echoes of the opening books—monarchical here, Cromwellian there—its fleeting parallels that, though they cannot be maintained long under scrutiny, are nevertheless among the poem's most potent doppelgänger effects.[69]

Such prolepsis and recollection is the connective tissue that threads back and forth across *Paradise Lost,* a cat's cradle stringing together the devils and fallen humanity, in similarities and dissimilarity, although in the zigzag time of the epic the anticipatory and recollective are often inverted. Heaven and hell, or hell and Milton's grim present, are, in these echoes, in demented dance with each other.[70] Disorientation is not, by any means, only associated with Satan in *Paradise Lost,* but it is Milton's hell that sets the tone for all wrong-footedness in the poem. Hell is a realm that produces its disequilibrium most wholly in its capacity for eerie likeness: likeness to its Homeric and Virgilian epic predecessors, to parliamentary debate with its rhetorical grandeur and polemical manipulation, to Milton's own condition of dire defeat and defiance. But the character of this likeness remains intrinsically unsteady—whether or not (or how) hell belongs in the eternal or temporal presents the same problem as heaven, with sequentiality necessary for narration, even while, the poem insists that time and space in eternal punishment cannot be rendered in human terms.

———

Finding resemblance that is at best fleetingly similar is a characteristic of the apophatic, with its metaphors for the unthinkable God, its proliferation of divine names, each partial, each only temporary: the God who is like nothing can only be intuited by making him or her like something. *Paradise Lost,* in its polysimilitude, in its likenesses that so conspicuously undermine themselves, shares something with the relentless in-built failure of apophatic rhetoric. Similes accrue around Satan that are inexact and unstable, as do instabilities of scale and perspectival illusion. Hell is initially characterized by its uncertain measure and the insolidity of Leviathan, on whose diabolic rind seamen think to moor.[71] Satan's defiant and Titanic striding is wrought in a kaleidoscopic knot of similitudes, producing only an indecipherability of scale: his shield like the moon viewed though a telescope (is that big or small?), his spear outsizing "the tallest pine / Hewn on Norwegian hills, to be the mast / Of some great admiral." No sooner do we calibrate the scale of this than we find this pine "were but a wand" compared to the terrible spear, but this Satan, we discover, is something of a hobbling old man or ancient magician, needing his spear to walk with, "to support uneasy steps / Over the burning marl."[72] Milton's volatile similes, dense and wayward, construct a realm in which each and every clarification yields further bafflement, and the account of hell is particularly explosive with these terrible weapons of misdescription. The skewed experience of size and landscape is some kind of verbal and at times visual *anamorphosis,* the perspectival distortion beloved of early modern arts.[73] The scale of Pandaemonium, with its enstoned music that "rose like an exhalation," is conveyed in its vast digressive descriptions of mining and the tumbling of Mulciber-Hephaestus that attend its construction, before the digression itself is dismissed at it thuds to the bottom ("thus they relate, / Erring").[74] The finished magnificence of the Palace is subject immediately to perspectival recalibration in a series of similitudes that shift it from unthinkably vast to comically tiny—bees, dwarves, pygmies, and faeries that some peasant "sees / Or dreams he sees."[75] Erin Webster considers there to be a distinctly mathematical imagination at work in this, a manipulation of perspective that shares with seventeenth-century theories of the infinite an encounter with what will not yield to reason, not so much a borrowing of content between poetry and mathematics as a shared mimetic strategy in rendering what can only be encountered as paradox.[76] Is hell accommodated for the reader, in the way that heaven is? All of Raphael's cautions about the accommodated character of what he relates about heaven, that which "surmounts the reach / of human sense," is similarly true of hell.[77] Both have as one of their essential attributes that they are impenetrable to thought, and must, in the manner of the apophatic, render the sensation of the nondescribable thing, as much as the thing itself.

That the epic lures us into concocted resemblance, or that the stuff of hell is merely glitz, subject then to hard theological truths, or monist reality, is no doubt the case. The recognition of this—that we are meant to see through Satan (that well-worn pun) and recognize also our own proclivity to misdirected sympathy, setting our intellect to monitor our responses—is part of the interpretative theological work the poem demands. But it is not only Satan—brash, chiding and finagling—who embodies the dissonance of rebellion from God. The Miltonic uncanny extends also to the distended nature of hell's landscape, so earthy, malleable, and masterable by intrepid devils, when, left alone, disbanded, they discover boredom and Stygian ennui, each left "to entertain / The irksome hours."[78] Hell sprawls, seemingly alive with opportunity, offering the resourceful devils variously a sad philosophical idyll or the opportunity for adventure, and the angels are left apparently free to pursue their leisure and ambition unbounded, a *vita activa* or *vita contemplativa*, as they choose. The hellish uncanny of athletics, arts, and trailblazing is pursued with their endlessly detonating devilish energy. Some opt for sport and contend in their proto-Olympics and primitive quidditch, soaring in the "Air sublime" or raiding its underworld, ripping up hills, and exploding up through its depths to "ride the air / In whirlwind." Others set out to explore, in devilish imperial venture, "in Squadrons and gross Bands, / On bold adventure to discover wide / That dismal world." Its vastness may not produce what they hope to find (to "yield them easier habitation"), and the slog of those troops who go exploring may be far from appealing in a nation weary with war and turmoil, but the sheer unyielding immensity produces its own disorientating correlate of intrepid planters.[79] The world is all before them.

However, it is the lull between these two cacophonies, the frantic wargames and the pioneering in the barren outlands of hell, that most perplexes with its misresemblance. The "bottomless pit" wrought by "eternal wrath," as Raphael describes it, the "torture without end" that Satan awakes to, according to the narrator, proves to be not so bad after all, a pastoral respite with something like ordinary, slow time in it:[80]

> Others more mild,
> Retreated in a silent valley, sing
> With notes angelical to many a Harp
> Their own heroic deeds and hapless fall . . .
> Their Song was partial, but the harmony
> (What could it less when Spirits immortal sing?)
> Suspended Hell, and took with ravishment,
> The thronging audience.[81]

In this unfolding of artistic, civic, and philosophical longing, the character of hell is rendered newly strange. No longer a throng of Iliadic backbenchers, murmuring and manipulated in their parliamentary gaggle, this is hell in recess. No longer scorched on lavalike marl, the devils' off-duty eternity in humanist idyll is the epic's unfolding of what is lost to us postclassical poor banished children of Eve. It is not that our human damnation will resemble that of resourceful devils, but nevertheless, in this doppelgänger trace of the human future, with its brief likeness to the good life—its Athens, its Arcadian retreat—art, culture, everything, emerges as an always already lost interlude, as a thing that proves perished before it began. It may of course be that we should reason this distorted likeness through, exposing its frayed edges; the scene is riven with the immediate contradictions, paradoxes, and puns—its throng and solitude, its "partial" nature—that render it unmistakably fallen. But the tonal, emotional, and theological disorientation remains. By what unhellish logic can devils choose to suspend hell with soothing music?[82] What kind of ineffability and fleeting peace is this, in hell, where by rights all should be pain? Not only does the humanist pleasure-dome of this Xanadu offer its sublimity in a gothic sense, but there is also a hermeneutic sublime here, in its sheer uninterpretable character.

As the scene unfolds, the artistic bent of the devils gives way to the theological and the philosophical, and they muse

> Of Providence, Foreknowledge, Will and Fate
> Fixed Fate, free will, foreknowledge absolute
> And found no end, in wandering mazes lost.[83]

Of all hell's doppelgänger moments, this is its oddest, in that it pictures the devils' own engagement with Miltonesque theology, the whole of *Paradise Lost*—providence, foreknowledge, will, and fate—encompassed. Is Milton, is the poem's circuitous maze-walking in its theology of free will and foreknowledge, meant to be somehow less lost than the devils'? In the precipitous theological plunge of this, the doctrinal confidence of the poem is, surely, rendered doubtful. Some versions of Milton have him unshakeable in his Christian fundamentals, so that whatever else is whirling in *Paradise Lost*, a few bedrock certainties underlie it all: that the devils' logic is warped, and that they are incompetent and self-interested theologians.[84] The devils' deluded mess of thought, wrote Addison and Steele, "makes a Kind of Labyrinth in the very Words that describe it," and other responses have pointed to the chiasmic mirror of the lines, in the second part of which the devils have dropped that most crucial "providence."[85] The Richardsons, father and son, write in their commentary on this maze as "a very Proper Image here, a very Melancholly and Touching One," a melancholy that emerges from the poem's own lost wandering.[86] The seventeenth-century annotator, P.H., understood the devils not to be incompetent theologians ("They Discoursed and Reasoned subtily and refinedly of the wonderfull, various, and unaccountable Providence of that Eternal Being, who made this beauteous Universe"); rather, the problem was that they were intruding upon ineffable theology, probing "his inscrutable Will, not to be fathomed by the most discerning and enlightened Angels."[87] Just as Milton's rolling eyes recall Satan's, and just as there is a mirror in the political energies of hell and Milton's England, the doppelgänger here is the poem's entire theological gambit.

How would any theology of disorientation interact with the poem's knotty doctrinal cluster—of free will and grace, redemption and soteriology—that generates so many of the poem's puzzles and unshiftable certainties? These matters of dogmatic theology (though they themselves can seem abyssal) are, in the main, beyond the scope of the argument here. But if there is some dialectic between the two spheres, it no doubt corresponds to the uneasy relations between modalities of religious experience: doctrine in all its nearly legal qualities and mysticism or apophatic theology—realms sometimes at war, more often holding each other at arm's length, presuming each to have their own operative sphere. In *Paradise Lost*, they vie and perhaps jar. It is by no means certain that one trumps the other or is more evidently the center of things. The poem may turn on the crux that humans were sufficient to have stood, though free to fall, but it also whirls around other pivots, too—its cosmological and interpretative aporia—and it is the irreconcilable character of these theological modes that gives the poem its dark energy.

Chaos and Disequilibrium

> Silence, ye troubled waves, and thou deep, peace,
> Said then the Omnific Word, your discord end.[88]

The chaos of Raphael's hexameral creation in book 7 and the chaos that Satan hurls himself through in book 2 are not the same thing. Raphael's, though a "vast immeasurable abyss," though dark, wasteful, and wild, is the biddable chaos of Genesis—"without form, and void," a darkness "upon the face of the deep"—while Satan's demented experience recalls, rather, the chaos of Job, or at least in some respects: in its insolidity of scale, its terrible creative-destructive fecundity, its unfathomability rendered as atonality. The key difference between the two biblical creations (as explored in chapter 1) is perspectival: where in Genesis, God views the creation from afar, and with magisterial Word orchestrates things, in Job 38–41, God is ferociously busy, down and dirty as the birth waters of the cosmos gush, managing the tiny as well as the vast, the stupidity of the ostrich and the melancholy of the wild goats, as well as the immense live architecture of Leviathan. Job's creation, unlike that of Genesis, is all barbarous dissonance. But Satan's straining and swimming, lost in his anarchic neither-up-nor-down state, is not much akin to God's heaving strain in his Stakhanovite Jobean work, moving heaven and earth, producing emotional as well as ontological nuance across creation, tending at once to the weight of the seas, and the womb of the world, and to the character of the animals, in their haughty scorn of insignificant humans. The chaos of Job is what it is because of God's presence there, wrestling nonexistent things into being, into beginning. Satan, by contrast, is mere whirling atom in the vast abortive gulf, "a semi-place with semi-things," on the "border of being and non-being," everything always only transitory.[89] If we needed convincing that Satan's defiant comparisons of himself with God were all bluster, then his shrunken relation to an indifferent chaos amply demonstrates it. He is mere atom here. But chaos, unpredictable in its generic anarchy, does other work in the poem.

Milton's deranged chaos is at one moment a puzzle in theodicy, the next a philosophical maelstrom, with its proto-ontology probing the world's prime matter—his *ex-Deo* "dark materials." But the philosophical attention does not last long, before other allusive or allegorical energies take over. Speaking of the brief passage that describes Satan's tumbling, David Quint comments on the "amount of poetic memory that is crowded into this passage," Icarian or Odyssean, Lucretian and Virgilian, with Tasso and Dante glimmering in its texture.[90] As an ontology, the state of its warring atoms is one of volatility—none of its pre-elementary forces can hold sway for long, and the same is true of the generic character of Milton's chaos. Memory here may be long, but attention span is brief. The intelligibility of chaos, like its transitory atoms, is only ever fleeting.[91]

Satan's initial encounter with these secret and dark materials, as he stands on the outer ledge of hell, is, by some abyssal logic, depicted as a game, an elemental Olympics or martial exercise in a heaving half-reality of "embryon atoms" and the abortive qualities of being. Each is battered and batted around in what is simultaneously an "endless anarchy" and a well-arbitrated tournament, champions waiting by their standards, all overseen by its adjudicating umpire, seated over the fray, like the God of Genesis, perhaps.[92] At one and the same time, Satan witnesses the terrible enormity of unformed vastness—that very enormity that Job is confronted with—and a flea-circus battle, in which Hot, Cold, Moist, and Dry, none of which even ascend to nouns, send out their unborn atoms in chivalric farce, huddling "around the flag / Of each his faction, in their several clans."[93] Does Satan require microscopic vision to view the atomic tournament, or has he himself shrunk to the size of an atom, who has so failed in immensity that he, with the devils, shrinks in scale from Leviathan to "less than smallest dwarfs," in beelike huddle? Such a question is preposterous only in a certain sense. Satan, it has been noted, fleetingly resembles a Lucretian atom when he falls through chaos till, by chance and not by providence, he swerves upward again.[94] If precipitous shifts of scale and shape were qualities of hell, chaos, it seems, lacks scale at all, such is the volatility of things.

The idiot-games of chaos, though perhaps the doppelgänger of the devils' Olympics, or the "heroic games" of the angels on inattentive guard duty in Eden, are nevertheless more akin to the croquet game ruled over by the Queen of Hearts in *Alice in Wonderland*. They are at least a little ridiculous in their codified anarchy.[95] In his role as umpire, adjudicating momentary victory of the cosmological elements, Chaos is master-saboteur of his own realm, who "by decision more embroils the fray / By which he reigns."[96] He, along with Old Night, rules not to establish order, but toward entropy, and his or their own unstable continuance. Perhaps we have warrant to resort to that interpretative mainstay, that this is Satan's infusing whatever he encounters with his own poisoned nature: he experiences the realm of chaos, its war games on a dimensionless scale, as simultaneously anarchic and monarchical—hieranarchic, perhaps—because that describes something of his own entropic character, in its elaborate imbalance of order and confusion in the choreographed frenzy of its battles. But Satan does not overawe in chaos; he is a mere speck in the whirlwind. The games go on, indifferent to him. Lucretius, I noted in an earlier chapter, also includes swirling war-games, viewed from afar, as a simile to demonstrate the ungaugeable scale of things, that what is wild and chaotic close up can seem serene from sufficiently far away.[97] Such is the distortion and indeterminacy here.

This first encounter with what lies outside hell, when its unoiled gates open, is the near-apophatic sight of the invisible that swallows up dimension, the swell of its abyss without "time and place." This is the dark opposite of Dionysian hyperlight, in the register of negative theology, but shares something with it. This too demands, in response to its unspeakable character, hyperbole, negation, and paradox:

> Before their eyes in sudden view appear
> The secrets of the hoary deep, a dark
> Illimitable Ocean without bound,
> Without dimension, where length, breadth, and height,
> And time and place are lost;[98]

As Satan stands poised and hesitant on its cusp, it sounds, in some respects, like a place, although that is an error. In its enigmatic or merely mad (or nearly Behmenist) formulation, chaos is not formlessness, but dimensionlessness, not only indeterminate in length, breadth, and height, but wholly without coordinates of time and place.[99] The stripping back of the thinkable is neither the emptiness of the eternal, nor absolute non-entity, but its negation recalls such diabolic terrors, Satan's "void profound / Of unessential night" or Belial's reluctance to lose "this intellectual being, / Those thoughts that wander through Eternity."[100] It recalls too, in oblique fashion, Satan's defiant if disingenuous metaphysics, that he possesses "A mind not to be changed by place or time," mere attributes that cannot taint his essence.[101] Satan's uncertainty, about to plunge into nontime and nonspace, the illimitable in all its dead fullness, is the epic's closest brush with the Eternal and with the ineffable. Neither heaven nor God in heaven comes close, for all the synesthesic song we encounter there.

If we can entertain, in some fleeting fashion, the idea of timelessness and placelessness, it cannot last—we cannot remain in paradox. Time reasserts itself: Satan drops "Ten thousand fathom deep" through chaos and "to this hour / Down had been falling," but for a 'chance' countergust of wind.[102] Perhaps narrative trumps raw dimensionless ontology, and Milton needs must resort to sequence, but the illogic is more systemic than that implies. The poem has its timescape of chaos be insistently ancient, ruled by its near-senile god-monarchs, who while away the irksome millennia. Unlike the chaos of Job in its new-birthed raw world, the chaos Satan encounters is atrophied. Its ancient and near-abandoned kingdom is ruled over by a king, the "Imbecilic Anarch," as John Rumrich calls him.[103] Regina Schwarz notes of Anarch that, "visage incomposed," his very face will not stay still, and this instability "may well pose a greater threat in Milton's moral universe than the Satanic one."[104] This strobe monarch flickers, subject, it seems, to the same continual rearrangement as the "fray by which he reigns," the turmoil of elements and the only brief preeminence of one element over the other. This most ancient kingdom, with its "wasteful Deep" and its rulers who rule on a different timescale, may be the ultimate terror of the empty, the void profound, but it also appears a badly kept home for the elderly, Anarch-Chaos and Old Night enthroned in their bath-chairs, not really able to speak any longer, while around them, the ungoverned and underfed dogs—Rumor, Chance, Tumult, Confusion and Discord—yap ready to bite.[105] Anarch complains how his realm has been encroached upon, its view obscured: "first Hell / Your dungeon stretching far and wide beneath; / Now lately Heaven and Earth, another World / Hung o'er my Realm." With what may be listlessness, or a resurgence of destructive energy, he encourages Satan to wreak his revenge for "Havoc and spoil and ruin are my gain."[106] The forlorn condition of chaos may very well be abjection in the Kristevan sense, writes Eric Song, where listless despair is "silhouetted as non-being."[107]

This quasi-political alliance, albeit a passive and opportunistic alliance, has prompted debate on whether chaos, the realm, is in some fashion evil, despite its slurry being God's own dark materials: "Chaos and Night are the enemies of God. The fact is sufficiently obvious to all readers," went one such claim.[108] Against this, Rumrich has produced the most vigorous and convincing argument that chaos has more of God about it than might seem to be the case if we attend only to the "political terms" by which old Anarch waves Satan though. Chaos is excessive, and shares something with the "unpredictable plenitude of being" that he finds in unfallen Eve, a "procreative energy," in its seething creative juices.[109] Chaos is not not-evil, but it is ceaselessly something else again, in its turmoil and indeterminacy, ever more vertiginous as characterizations of it accrue, its logic ever more abyssal, and in demi-pantheist fashion, "God is the confused and dark matter of chaos," in one manifestation of divine fecundity, or elsewhere, that chaos is "the part of the deity . . . over which the eternal father does not exercise control."[110] Arguments that chaos gives rise to order, or that it is in some necessary cosmic dialectic with order, or that it is infused with a kind of passive divine presence, have been made and are not unconvincing.[111] However, it does little justice to the subtlety of the debates on this, to divide critics along the lines of whether they understand the pond of primal matter in its raw state as evil or good, not least because chaos would hardly allow for any such brute moral stability.[112]

In her brilliant account of chaos, Regina Schwartz, who is sometimes and a little crudely characterized as arguing that chaos is evil, traces a contrast between biblical hallowing, division, and dimension in the creation of Genesis—God's circumscribing the universe with golden compasses in Raphael's retelling of it—and what we are confronted with in the chaos of book 2, its endemic "lack of definition," a relentless "violation of categories," things immeasurable.[113] Again, perhaps, we are in the biblical territory of Job, where creation is all dissonance. The Book of Job, in its complex "exegetical gymnasium," as Emily Ransom terms it, has not featured heavily in accounts of Milton's chaos.[114] And perhaps it would not be right to suppose Job to be a "source," in the way that Lucretian, Hesiodic, or Ovidian sources lurk in the background, with their philosophical tidbits.[115] There is no ontology in the Book of Job, as such, no glimpse of the underphysics of things as they lurch into being, and certainly no gods on the edge of dementia. But the Book of Job's collapse of categories, its implosion of logic, and its vertiginous shifts of scale are a closer parallel to the antisense of chaos. Schwartz adds another analogy between the Book of Job and *Paradise Lost*, arguing that where Milton's skewed dialectic has a question about the origin of evil answered by an assertion of providence, so too the Book of Job has what looks like a question of theodicy, why Job suffers so, that is "'answered' in a very different key," asserting omnipotence and creation.[116] In both cases, theological misdirection intervenes in the (implicit) question, to insist that its terms of reference are the wrong ones. Divine discourse, it seems, need not descend to consistency.

Chaos has no physical structure, no stable ontology, that might not be obliterated by a new counter-gust, a generic wind, allegorical or epic, from elsewhere. If it is concocted of things that may become atoms or may coalesce into elements, if it has a Lucretian memory to it, it also lacks essence, like Satan's "unessential night." It is ruled by a volatile poetics as much as an intellectual history or a problem of classical scientific lineage, though fleetingly these may be the philosophical scenery. Satan, having tumbled till chance lofts him up, though perhaps "up" means nothing in particular, finds some boggy surface, but it is also one that refuses any steady state, "neither sea, nor good dry land" we hear, such that he traverses it "half on foot / Half flying," that might be "dense, or rare," and through which he tumbles, all erratic in the "universal hubbub wild" and "hollow dark."[117] We traverse chaos, all quagmire and stew, in just such ungainly fashion, but there is an important sense in which its capsized, alogical timelessness and placelessness is the very condition of the eternal in *Paradise Lost*.

Linda Gregerson comments—at least a little mischievously, I presume—that Stanley Fish "posits the poem as a *via negativa*," that each perception we have of the poem must, one by one, be rejected, each insufficient, in its fallen fashion. It is true that Fish requires us to negate and negate, to register and correct our waywardness by the yardstick of faith.[118] But Fish's is, nevertheless, the least mystic of readings. We need, when on reader-response guard duty, to *reason* a straight line through an epic whose every path is boggy and unstable, a Satanic chaos-landscape in which language and logic are tangled, and even angels can be tied in knots by duplicity and hypocrisy. Fish's reading, in which the reader comes to the epic with the answer—a firm and fixed faith and a good hermeneutic eye—already in the bag, remains important, while frustrating.[119] His most brilliant insight, I think, lies in his having the objects of the poem's theology be less its mazy questions of theodicy and divine justice than each micro-error of association and emotion, its disorderly allusions, and one's ungovernable sympathies in response. The theology is braided in with the poetry, and we cannot understand one without the other.

This chapter has argued that there is less a negative theology in *Paradise Lost* than a theology of disorientation: that in the poem's gluttonous scale, in its insistent reminders about its own irreality, set as it is in the Eternal or the Eviternal, the poem makes abundantly clear its stubbornly opaque character. In its haunted verbal texture, allusive, proleptic, and layered, the early modern reader was in a familiar terrain of theology—not formal creedal thought or doctrine, but the encounter with the unknowable. This experience of what is beyond words and all-consuming is a theological *mood* fundamental to the era. I take my cue in this from John Stachniewski's *The Persecutory Imagination,* which identified despair as a kind of characteristic religious mood of the seventeenth century, intractable and self-compounding.[120] Disorientation, like despair, overwhelms—one cannot reason oneself out of it; it swells and is abyssal. It is not always unpleasant. The "sublimity" of the poem, so long remarked upon in its reception, is in part a feature of its geocosmic immensity and in equal part its theological immensity, of the kind that the radical, John Saltmarsh, describes as "spiritual vertigo or turning in my Soule, a giddinesse, which makes mee unstable in all my wayes."[121] In its almost militant melancholy, Milton's is an epic in which the reader

CHAPTER 6

must attend not only to its small interpretable events—the thick foliage of wilfully misleading words, and prosodic traps—but also to the whirling universe, and the outer wheels of the eternal. The poem's dense interconnections of seemingly incommensurable matter shifts its perspective again and again, such that if one is not dizzy, one is not reading properly, and this interpretative spin is its own theological vortex. Vertigo is one of the ways of God that needs and resists justifying.

EPILOGUE

Ordinary and Exquisite Bafflement

RELIGION SIMPLY CANNOT DO without the mystical—mystery is at its heart—but neither does religion in its ecclesiastical form wholly embrace it. There is something wayward in a mode of heady illogic that needs to torture language and that demands a skewed poetics to represent a skewed reality. This book has made the case that in the seventeenth century, thinkers began to do new things with the *resources* of the apophatic, to deploy its paradoxes to new ends. At times, this took on religio-political form, such that radicals, Ranters, and latter-day prophets considered the apophatic and the enthusiastic to speak to a communal as much as a personal sphere. At times, too, it assumed a quasi-scientific bent, coinciding with, but not identical to, natural philosophy in its attention to the cosmological, the infinite and infinitesimal. Thinking about the unknowable—a contradiction in terms, strictly considered—can never quite proceed as an entirely intellectual endeavor; it also necessitated a poetic-prophetic-paradoxical embrace of our deficiencies and the limits of reason. To follow these different manifestations of the unknowable in seventeenth-century thought has involved at least one or two hairpin bends—accommodating Cavendish and Trapnel in close proximity, for example. The two of them would, I imagine, not get on, and their respective concerns—philosophy and prophecy—do not have much in common. Likewise, Milton would certainly want to hold the heady mysticism of Boehme at arm's length, even while his forays into the Eternal have some of the same generative energy that emerges from the perplexing, unthinkable character of the shadow world outside creation and before time, the unstable stuff of the Eternal that remained always, illogically, present. To consider the era's penchant for that which lies tantalizingly beyond thought produces strange alignments that made mystics out of temperamentally sober scientists. The creation in the Book of Job, taken here as the starting point, was, for early modern readers, descriptive of a brokenness of the world, seemingly there at its outset, a cacophony and disorder that had not gone away, a reality so complex that God, too, strained under the world's unfathomable variety. Across this whole terrain, and uniting these works, is the poetic prescription and desideratum for a constantly renewable rhetoric that outwits the dull self and outruns hobbled and fallen quotidian thought.

The idea that the seventeenth-century syncretic mind retooled the fecund notions it inherited produces important continuities that the era itself was not always keen to acknowledge. Regina Schwartz, looking at the Protestant ambivalence toward the "Holy" (or rather the "Holy" inherited in its Catholic forms, at least), notes one such act of reengineered sacred forms: "Of course no one claimed at the time to be bent on destroying sacramentality. They only applied an early modern logic to phenomena that were heretofore governed by premodern sacramental assumptions."[1] Perhaps the era's particular mystical gymnastics, its "excess of religious energy," as Michael Martin puts it, was ripe for this disciplinary muddle, on the strange cusp of religious experience and natural philosophy; he looks at John Dee, Kenelm Digby, and Henry Vaughan, among others. Its version of mysticism was far less institutionally contained than its pre-Reformation equivalent, and less resolutely inward in its focus on the annihilated self: "medieval mysticism had been effectively turned inside out," he writes.[2] Outside itself, this quasi-mystical mode of thinking—rich, playful, pained, or frustrating—discovered ways of encountering the world slantwise, not always amenable to logic.

Some early modern writers still pursued something akin to an apophatic discourse, and the experience of the absconding God, but it tends to sound very different in an early modern context. "O God, what shall I say thou art, when thou canst not be named?" begins Jacob Bauthumley's *The Light and Dark Sides of God* (1650), "what shall I speak of thee, when in speaking of thee, I speak nothing but contradiction?"[3] It might be considered an irony that the punishment for writing an apophatic text on exquisite speechlessness was to have a hole bored through the tongue with a hot iron. Such, however, was Bauthumley's painful fate. *The Light and Dark Sides of God* explores the inscription of and the surging of the divine in the creation, the illocal, inward, and supralogical manifestations of a God who enacts his divine drama of heaven and hell in the landscape of the fleshy self, allowing God to be obscurely present even in sin, "as sin is the dark appearance of God." Bauthumley is less intent on describing God's ever-receding character, however, than on his pulsing intimacy: "my seeking of thee is no other but thy seeking of thy selfe." Such counterintuitive inversion of God and God-seeker ("I have made God mutable as my self") is not wholly uncommon in the apophatic tradition's courting of paradox.[4] However, Bauthumley is also quite different from any medieval mystic lineage. He was a troublemaker, like Boehme a gentle though truculent shoemaker, later a quartermaster in the army, castigated as a Ranter, his writings condemned as "a very wide door to atheism and profaneness."[5] While apophatic writing is almost by its very nature about a state of the inarticulate, a failure of words, Bauthumley addresses in his book the actually illiterate—"I know the most unto whose hand it may come cannot read it," he begins—as well as those lacking the rhetorical aptitude to express their bursting, spiritual, inward knowledge, those "that travell with me in the same birth; yet are not able to bring forth their conceptions, for so much as many times, the Truth suffers by a weake delivery."[6]

The "mystical tradition," though often proud of its "holy fool" place outside dull ecclesiastical orthodoxy, has an uneasy relationship with the demotic, the unlearned, and the inarticulate. It can be haughty, at times venomously so, toward the down-at-heel apophatic of the politically radical, who will not be humble in worldly terms. This is one paradox that the apophatic tradition does not on the whole want to embrace: that, for all its stress on the fundamental inadequacy of language and the state of inarticulacy in encountering the divine, and for all its posture of learned ignorance as prerequisite to ineffable experience, it insistently distinguishes itself from those it sees as genuinely unlearned, the actually inarticulate, those whom Bauthumley speaks for and to, and who, he insists, have a fullness of religious experience. The apophatic tradition—and this is no less true in its newly evolved seventeenth-century variants—can be deeply antidemotic, if not a little misanthropic.

The twentieth-century theorist of the numinous, Rudolf Otto, is characteristically haughty and patrician about what and whom he will and will not allow into the orbit of the Holy. Speaking of the *mysterium tremendum*, the raw terror and vertiginous sublime at the heart of religion, utterly at odds with any domesticated theology, ethics, or ecclesiology, Otto describes "the *feeling* which remains when the *concept* fails," something qualitatively different from other kinds of not-knowing, such as "that which merely eludes our understanding for a time but is perfectly intelligible in principle."[7] Though this holy tremble constitutes the raw, almost savage, emotion at the center of religious being, it is one properly open only to the learned initiate, who has ascended an arduous and rigorously policed path: "no one ought to concern himself with the 'Numen ineffabile' who has not already devoted assiduous and serious study" to the lower tiers of religiosity. This is the imperious apophatic, violently jealous of its hard-won idiocy. It is several notches above ordinary bafflement, and wears its humility proudly; its priests do not to want their wordlessness to be confused with ordinary inarticulacy.[8] Others, in modernity, have theorized a far more generous and well-distributed idea of the holy. Rowan Williams explores how "ordinary" language is liable to rupture into eerie strangeness, and how it is in the character of being human to encounter the world, now and then, as disabling mystery. William Franke suggests that there is at least some relationship between ordinary inarticulacy and the apophatic. "Even very banal forms of silence," he writes, "may, after all, be akin to absolute silence and participate in the pregnant pauses characteristic of apophasis."[9]

In Sebastian Barry's beautiful novel, *Days without End* (2016), the violence of the uneducated fighting-Irish hero, hired to maim and savage at so doing, is immense. He is also (by the by) a man who lives as a woman, whose love is delicate, intense, and unmockable, not least because he will kill you if you do. There is a moment when, in the fighting pause of the winter, the soldiers come to a kind of calm because they have seen slaughter together. They pass the time playing cards, but it is a holy state, in which "stories tell another story just the whole while they are being told. Things you can't ever quite put your finger on." The experience, the temporary illumination, within their own excesses of violence, is one of brief luminosity, and of the apophatic, even while they may not have been able to articulate or understand the replete moment: "I ain't saying we knowed what we knowed . . . I ain't saying that."[10] Rendering violence as holy has an illustrious pedigree, of course—it's in the Bible, as the saying goes—but Barry's narrator makes no claim to religiosity. Nevertheless, the tremulous experience—how you might not know what you know, things ill understood speaking to something other than themselves, the discarnate moment—has about it a feel of the sacred, which will not remain within the confines of the strictly religious. The apophatic, by its wild nature, overspills and is liable to turn up in strange places.

Perhaps, if we are seeking some early modern version of the *numen ineffabile*, the absence of John Donne, George Herbert, or Thomas Traherne from this work might seem a strange omission—all of them produce, at points, an implosion and loss of the self, a mini-lyric version of semi-mystic self-annihilation—even if, as Gary Kuchar puts it, there is broadly speaking an "eclipse of mystery" in the era.[11] Donne's unholy Holy Sonnets construct the inimitable absence of a God who cannot be goaded into presence, while his grunting love-poems have at least something of the sacramental about them: "While John Milton takes the Eucharist to the cosmos, John Donne takes it to the bedroom," writes Schwartz.[12] Metaphysical poetry is what it is precisely because it produces its dazzling unpredictable flash at the edge of words. But the bastardization of and cynicism toward the mystical runs deep in Renaissance literature, which frequently borrows from and perhaps mocks the stock tropes of the apophatic: the clumsy "inexpressibility topos," in which the lover, courtier, or poet is unable to find words equal to their pitch of emotion, or unable to summon up the weasel words that duty requires of them, remains dimly tethered to the Petrarchan holy.[13] Much of the English sonnet tradition and some of its more political pastoral falls into such a category.[14] Most notably lost for words is King Lear. For Cordelia, who cannot heave her heart into her mouth, there is a precarious balance between the vomit of speaking and gut-twisting wordlessness by which she refuses the game of her soon-to-be-idiot father. Lear, in possession of the most dazzling curses and wordy violence toward his daughters, tumbles into an entropy where words are wholly insufficient to his fast-dissolving logic, in the wild periphery of reason and of England. There would be only slight reason, perhaps, to connect this bedlam to the apophatic, were it not for that inflection of the play in which Lear is a Job-like figure, the world rendered fathomless and wordless, as he sits collapsed upon his dunghill. Job too is wordy like Lear, and can curse and rail with the best of them, it being by no means clear that he avoids his wife's advice to "curse God and die."[15] The unknowable, as I trace it here, is something more thoroughgoing, than might be suggested in looking at any single play or body of poetry; it is a more pervasive kind of unthinkable, in its disciplinary sprawl, but its character is wholly bound up with the era's poetics. The prayerless, the inarticulate, the pain beyond words is a rich vein in the literature of the seventeenth century, insisting in its paradoxical heights of eloquence that it cannot go beyond mere groans and tears, when linguistic resources fail and are reduced to what Deleuze and Guattari see as the "snarls, squeals, stammers" we go through before coming anywhere near words.[16]

Notes

Introduction

1. Walter Charleton, *The darknes of atheism dispelled* (London: William Lee, 1652), 117, 348; Thomas Barton, Αντιτειχισμα or, *A counter-scarfe prepared anno 1642 for the eviction of those zealots* (London: Andrew Crooke, 1643), 19; Timothy Batt, *A treatise concerning the free grace* (London: Ed. Blackmore, 1643), 36.

2. Gilbert Burnet, *A modest and free conference betwixt a conformist and a non-conformist* (Edinburgh, 1669), 88; Henry More, *An explanation of the grand mystery of godliness* (London: Walter Kettilby, 1660), 493; Richard Linche, *The fountaine of ancient fiction* (London: Adam Islip, 1599), B1v, loosely translating Vincenzo Cartari, *Le Imagini de i Dei de gli Antichi* (Venetia, 1571); Thomas Morton, *A discharge of five imputations* (London: R. Milbourne, 1633), 174; Thomas Jackson, *A treatise of the consecration of the Sonne of God* (Oxford: Leonard Lichfield, 1638), 356 (mispaginated).

3. Joseph Glanvill, *The Vanity of Dogmatizing* (London: Henry Eversden, 1661), chap. 2, 15–16.

4. The term "apophasis," however, is not used with quite the same meaning in the early modern era, when it tends to be paired with *paralipsis*, or *occupatio*, pretending not to speak of a thing, while doing so; for example, John Smith, *The mysterie of rhetorique unveil'd* (London: George Eversden, 1665), 156–57: "a denying ... a kind of an Irony, whereby we deny that we say or doe that which we especially say or doe"; similarly, Richard Lloyd, *The Latine grammar* (London: Thomas Roycroft, 1653), 11.

5. William Franke speaks of the apophatic being "the basis of the mutual understanding and reciprocal appreciation among the three Abrahamic faiths during the Middle Ages. Islam, Judaism, and Christianity communicated cross-culturally on the basis of a common recognition of intrinsic limits to their ability to conceptualize God," though it would be difficult to find any such concord in the post-Reformation era. William Franke, *On the Universality of What Is Not: The Apophatic Turn in Critical Thinking* (Notre Dame, IN: University of Notre Dame Press, 2020), 9–10.

6. Richard Hooker, *Of the lawes of ecclesiasticall politie eight bookes* (London: John Windet, 1593), p. 49, Book 1.2, going on "yet our soundest knowledge is to know that wee know him not as in deed he is, neither can know him; and our safest eloquence concerning him is our silence" (buried reference to Job 36.36).

7. Robert Dallington, "A Briefe Inference upon Guicciardines Digression, In The

Fourth Part Of The First Quarterne of His Historie," 53, 56, appended (with separate pagination) to *Aphorismes civill and militarie* (London: Edward Blount, 1613).

8. There are exceptions, who invariably note the presumption that the field is thin: Sara Poor and Nigel Smith, eds., *Mysticism and Reform, 1400–1750* (Notre Dame, IN: University of Notre Dame Press, 2015), 10–11; Liam Peter Temple, *Mysticism in Early Modern England* (Woodbridge, UK: Boydell & Brewer, 2019), 1–2. Also see Bernard McGinn, "The Venture of Mysticism in the New Millennium," *New Theology Review* 21, no. 2 (2008): 70–79, at 71, taking issue with a characterization of early modernity, in which "mysticism as a creative aspect in the life of the church was moribund, if not quite dead" by the seventeenth century; and McGinn, *Mysticism in the Reformation (1500–1650)* (New York: Crossroad Publishing, 2017).

9. See, on the scholastic tradition, Thomas Bradwardine, *Insolubilia* (Insolubles), trans. Stephen Read (Leuven, 2010).

10. Rosalie L. Colie, *Paradoxia Epidemica: The Renaissance Tradition of Paradox* (Princeton: Princeton University Press, 1966), xi.

11. Claire Preston, *The Poetics of Scientific Imagination in Seventeenth-Century England* (New York: Oxford University Press, 2015), 88.

12. Frédérique Aït-Touati, *Fictions of the Cosmos: Science and Literature in the Seventeenth Century* (Chicago: University of Chicago Press, 2011), 1–2; Judith H. Anderson, *Light and Death: Figuration in Spenser, Kepler, Donne, Milton* (New York: Fordham University Press, 2017), 77–112, on analogy in literature and science; Elizabeth Spiller, *Science, Reading, and Renaissance Literature: The Art of Making Knowledge, 1580–1670* (Cambridge: Cambridge University Press, 2004), on the early modern fascination with perspective. See too Lorraine Daston and Katherine Park, *Wonders and the Order of Nature 1150–1750* (New York: Zone Books, 1998); Giuseppe Mazzotta, *Cosmopoiesis: The Renaissance Experiment* (Toronto: University of Toronto Press, 2001).

13. Marjorie Nicolson, *The Breaking of the Circle: Studies in the Effect of the 'New Science' upon Seventeenth-Century Poetry* (New York: W. W. Norton, 1960); Nicolson, *Mountain Gloom and Mountain Glory: The Development of the Aesthetics of the Infinite* (New York: W. W. Norton, 1963).

14. Katherine Eggert, *Disknowledge: Literature, Alchemy, and the End of Humanism in Renaissance England* (Philadelphia: University of Pennsylvania Press, 2015), 2.

15. Eggert, *Disknowledge*, 59–109.

16. Thomas Kuhn, *The Structure of Scientific Revolutions* (Chicago: University of Chicago Press, 1962).

17. Ernst Cassirer, *The Individual and the Cosmos in Renaissance Philosophy* (New York: Harper & Row, 1964), 42–43. C. A. Patrides, *The Cambridge Platonists* (Cambridge: Cambridge University Press, 1969), xxv, editing Henry More's *An Antidote Against Atheism* (London: J. Flesher, 1653) for the volume, says he will "flatter" him by omitting large portions of the work on bewitchment and magic. Ex-

amples of such sprawling subject matter within single works include Charleton, *The Darknes of Atheism*; Thomas Browne, *Religio Medici* (London: Andrew Crook, 1643); or Ralph Cudworth, *The true intellectual system of the universe* (London: Richard Royston, 1678).

18. Anne Cotterill, *Digressive Voices in Early Modern English Literature* (New York: Oxford University Press, 2004), 20. See too John Lennard, *But I Digress: The Exploitation of Parentheses in English Printed Verse* (Oxford: Clarendon Press, 1991).

19. Carla Mazzio, *The Inarticulate Renaissance: Language Trouble in an Age of Eloquence* (Philadelphia: University of Pennsylvania Press, 2009), 6–9, 28, citing the character, Titivillus, from the late medieval drama, *The Myrroure of Oure Lady* (1530), sig. F2v.

20. Amos Funkenstein, *Theology and the Scientific Imagination from the Middle Ages to the Seventeenth Century* (Princeton: Princeton University Press, 1986); Peter Harrison, *The Bible, Protestantism and the Rise of Natural Science* (Cambridge: Cambridge University Press, 1998).

21. A useful starting point is Katherine Park and Lorraine Daston, eds., *The Cambridge History of Science, Vol. 3: Early Modern Science* (Cambridge: Cambridge University Press, 2006). See too Kenneth J. Howell, *God's Two Books: Copernican Cosmology and Biblical Interpretation in Early-Modern Science* (Notre Dame, IN: University of Notre Dame Press, 2002).

22. John Sparrow, preface to Jacob Boehme, *Mysterium Magnum, or an exposition of the first book of Moses called Genesis*, trans. Sparrow (London: H. Blunden, 1654), sig A1v.

23. Joannes d'Espagnet, *Enchyridion physicae restitutae* (Paris, 1623), translated as *Enchyridion physicae restitutae: or, the summary of physicks recovered* (London: W. Bentley, 1651), 10.

24. Terry Eagleton, *Reason, Faith, and Revolution: Reflections on the God Debate* (New Haven: Yale University Press, 2010), 50.

25. Bo Andersson, Lucinda Martin, Leigh T. I. Penman, and Andrew Weeks, eds., *Jacob Böhme and His World* (Leiden: Brill, 2019), 17–18.

26. Boehme, *Mysterium Magnum*, 1.5, p. 2; 2.1, p. 3, "das Ausgehen des Geistes . . . der Wille des Ungrundes."

27. Gordon Teskey, *Delirious Milton: The Fate of the Poet in Modernity* (Cambridge, MA: Harvard University Press, 2006).

28. See Caroline van Eck, Stjn Bussels, Maarten Delbeke, and Jürgen Pieters, eds., *The Early Modern Reception and Dissemination of Longinus' Peri Hupsous in Rhetoric, the Visual Arts, Architecture and the Theatre* (Leiden: Brill, 2012); See too Thomas Matthew Vozar, *Abstracted Sublimities: Milton, Longinus and the Sublime in the Seventeenth Century* (Oxford: Oxford University Press, forthcoming).

29. Lorraine Daston, "The Empire of Observation, 1600–1800," in Daston and Elizabeth Lunbeck, eds., *Histories of Scientific Observation* (Chicago: University of Chicago Press, 2011); Daston, "On Scientific Observation," *Isis* 99, no. 1 (2008):

97–110. See too Ofer Gal and Raz Chen-Morris, *Baroque Science* (Chicago: University of Chicago Press, 2012).

30. Robert Boyle, *A Discourse of Things above Reason* (1681), in *Works of Robert Boyle*, ed. Michael Hunter and Edward B. Davis (London: Pickering & Chatto, 2000), 9:361–94 (at 366, 369). See Jan W. Wojcik, *Robert Boyle and the Limits of Reason* (Cambridge: Cambridge University Press, 2002). An earlier version appears in Michael Hunter's more broadly relevant collection of essays, *Robert Boyle Reconsidered* (Cambridge: Cambridge University Press, 1994), 139–55; Lotte Mulligan, "Robert Boyle, 'Right Reason' and the Meaning of Metaphor," *Journal of the History of Ideas* 55, no. 2 (1994): 235–57.

31. Alexander Wragge-Morley, *Aesthetic Science: Representing Nature in the Royal Society of London, 1650–1720* (Chicago: University of Chicago Press, 2020), 19, 47–72.

32. Thomas Browne, *Pseudodoxia Epidemica* (London: E. Dod, 1646), 2.2, p. 58.

33. On acatalepsy, see Francis Bacon, *Novum Organum*, in Graham Rees and Maria Wakely, eds., *The Instauratio Magna, Part II: Novum Organum and Associated Texts* (New York: Oxford University Press, 2004), with parallel texts, 1.37, p. 53; 1.75, p. 84. On latent process, 2.1. See the capacious account of the epistemological consequences of the Fall in Peter Harrison, *The Fall of Man and the Foundations of Science* (New York: Cambridge University Press, 2007), especially 73–88.

34. Paolo Rossi, *The Dark Abyss of Time* (Chicago: University of Chicago Press, 1987), xiii.

35. See, in particular, Kathryn Murphy, "The Anxiety of Variety: Knowledge and Experience in Montaigne, Burton and Bacon," in Yota Batsaki, Subha Mukherji, and Jan-Melissa Schramm, eds., *Fictions of Knowledge: Fact, Evidence, Doubt* (London: Palgrave Macmillan, 2012), 110–11.

36. Bacon, *Novum Organum*, 2.5.

37. Bacon, *Novum Organum*, 2.52.

38. Bacon, *Novum Organum*, on Heat, 2.11–20, elaborated into the prerogative instances, 2.21–52.

39. Boyle, *Things Above Reason*, 376. See Wojcik, *Robert Boyle and the Limits of Reason*. Sarah Mortimer and John Robertson, eds., *The Intellectual Consequences of Religious Heterodoxy 1600–1750* (Leiden: Brill, 2012), 1–46, on the coexistence of contradictory ideas.

40. This description from Sophie Weeks's forthcoming work on Bacon, and its roots in "Francis Bacon's Science of Magic," PhD diss., Leeds University, 2007, which includes some important attention to the role of ignorance and the *via negativa* in Bacon, 46–50, 136–48, 240–47.

41. Among the various studies of Bacon's sinuous poetics, see, in particular, Stephen Clucas, "'A Knowledge Broken': Francis Bacon's Aphoristic Style and the Crisis of Scholastic and Humanist Knowledge-Systems," in Neil Rhodes, ed., *English Renaissance Prose: History, Language, and Politics* (Tempe, AZ: MRTS Press,

1997); John C. Briggs, *Francis Bacon and the Rhetoric of Nature* (Cambridge, MA: Harvard University Press, 1989).

42. Maimonides, *The Guide of the Perplexed,* trans Shlomo Pines, 2 vols. (Chicago: University of Chicago Press, 1974), 7.

43. Frank Kermode, *The Sense of an Ending: Studies in the Theory of Fiction* (Oxford: Oxford University Press, 1966), 80. Maximilian De Gaynesford, *The Rift in the Lute: Attuning Poetry and Philosophy* (New York: Oxford University Press, 2017), 17, noting a different translation in René Descartes, *The Philosophical Writings of Descartes,* vol. 1, trans. John Cottingham, Robert Stoothoff, and Dugald Murdoch (Cambridge: Cambridge University Press, 1985), 4.

44. Michel de Certeau, *The Mystic Fable: The Sixteenth and Seventeenth Centuries,* trans. Michael B. Smith (Chicago: University of Chicago Press, 1992), 1–2.

45. de Certeau, *The Mystic Fable,* 7–8, 77.

46. Denys Turner, *The Darkness of God: Negativity in Christian Mysticism* (Cambridge: Cambridge University Press, 1995), 20. See too Oliver Davis and Denys Turner, *Silence and the Word: Negative Theology and Incarnation* (New York: Cambridge University Press, 2002); Eric Bugyis and David Newheiser, *Desire, Faith and Darkness of God: Essays in Honour of Denys Turner* (Notre Dame, IN: University of Notre Dame Press, 2015).

47. Turner, *The Darkness of God,* 260.

48. See William Franke, *On What Cannot Be Said: Apophatic Discourses in Philosophy, Religion, Literature, and the Arts,* 2 vols. (Notre Dame, IN: University of Notre Dame Press, 2007), an invaluable collection of texts from the apophatic traditions, learned and popular.

49. A starting point for the relevant scholarship is Bernard McGinn's multipart *Presence of God: A History of Western Christian Mysticism* (New York: Crossroad, 1991–).

50. See, for instance, Danielle Clarke, "Life Writing for the Counter-Reformation: The English Translation and Reception of Teresa de Ávila's Autobiography," *Journal of Medieval and Early Modern Studies* 50, no. 1 (2020–21): 75–94; Liam Temple, "'Have we any mother Juliana's among us?' The Multiple Identities of Julian of Norwich in Restoration England," *British Catholic History* 33, no. 3 (2017): 383–400.

51. For an overview of some of the key figures in northern mysticism, Ronald K. Rittgers and Vincent Evener, eds., *Protestants and Mysticism in Reformation Europe* (Leiden: Brill, 2019). Ranging geographically, see Dale Shuger, *God Made Word: An Archaeology of Mystic Discourse in Early Modern Spain* (Toronto: University of Toronto Press, 2022); Louis Cognet, *Crépuscule des mystiques: Bossuet, Fénelon* (Tournai, 1952).

52. Aquinas, *Summa Theologiae,* Ia, q. 13, arts. 1–10; and his treatise on Dionysius, *In librum Beati Dionysii De Diuinis Nominibus expositio,* ed. Ceslai Pera (Turin: Marietti, 1950). See David B. Burrell, *Knowing the Unknowable God: Ibn-Sina, Maimonides, Aquinas* (Notre Dame, IN: University of Notre Dame Press, 1987), attending in particular to the use of analogy as a conduit to knowledge of

what is, conceptually speaking, ungraspable. Deirdre Carabine, *The Unknown God: Negative Theology in the Platonic Tradition: Plato to Eriugena* (Eugene, OR: Wipf & Stock, 2015), 301–22; Andrew Louth, *The Origins of the Christian Mystical Tradition: From Plato to Denys* (Oxford: Oxford University Press, 1981); John Joseph O'Meara, *Eriugena* (Oxford: Oxford University Press, 1988); Paul Rorem, *The Dionysian Mystical Theology* (New York: Fortress Press, 2015), 79–100; Hugh of Saint Victor, *The Didascalicon*, ed. Jeromy Taylor (New York: Columbia University Press, 1991). On Hugh (albeit not particularly on his apophatic thought), see the idiosyncratic work of Ivan Illich, *In the Vineyard of the Text* (Chicago: University of Chicago Press, 1996); G. R. Evans, *Bernard of Clairvaux* (New York: Oxford University Press, 2000), 72–101.

53. Key modern points of reference include Marsilio Ficino, *Platonic Theology*, ed Michael J. B. Allen, 5 vols. (Cambridge, MA: Harvard University Press, 2001); Brian Copenhaver, *Hermetica: The Greek Corpus Hermeticum and the Latin Asclepius* (Cambridge: Cambridge University Press, 1995). As with much of the material in these synoptic paragraphs, the potential bibliography on this is vast. Starting points include Michael J. B. Allen, *Studies in the Platonism of Marsilio Ficino and Giovanni Pico* (New York: Routledge, 2017); Stephen Clucas, Peter Forshaw, and Valerie Rees, eds., *Laus Platonici Philosophi: Marsilio Ficino and His Influence* (Leiden: Brill, 2011). For an impressive synoptic account of the philosophical traditions in which this all sits, see Dmitri Levitin, *Ancient Wisdom in the Age of the New Science: Histories of Philosophy in England, c. 1640–1700* (Cambridge: Cambridge University Press, 2015).

54. See, for example, Elliot R. Wolfson, *Through a Speculum That Shines: Vision and Imagination in Medieval Jewish Mysticism* (Princeton: Princeton University Press, 1994); Sara Sviri, *Perspectives on Early Islamic Mysticism: The World of al-Ḥakīm al-Tirmidhī and His Contemporaries* (New York: Routledge, 2021).

55. See, on his influence, Simon J. G. Burton, Joshua Hollmann, and Eric M. Parker, eds., *Nicholas of Cusa and the Making of the Early Modern World* (Leiden: Brill, 2018); F. Edward Cranz and Thomas M. Izbicki, eds., *Nicholas of Cusa and the Renaissance* (New York: Routledge, 2000); Peter Casarella, ed., *Cusanus: The Legacy of Learned Ignorance* (Washington, DC: Catholic University of America Press, 2006); and Peter Casarella, *Word as Bread: Language and Theology in Nicholas of Cusa* (Münster: Aschendorff Verlag, 2017). Nicholas of Cusa, *Complete Philosophical and Theological Treatises*, ed. Jasper Hopkins, 2 vols. (Minneapolis: Arthur J. Banning Press, 2001).

56. Temple, *Mysticism in Early Modern England*; Sarah Apetrei, "Gender, Mysticism, and Enthusiasm in the British Post-Reformation," *Reformation & Renaissance Review* 17, no. 2 (2015): 116–28; Sarah Apetrei, "Prophecy and Mysticism in Seventeenth-Century England," in Louise Nelstrop and Simon Podmore, eds., *Exploring Lost Dimensions in Christian Mysticism* (Farnham, Surrey, UK: Ashgate, 2013); Poor and Smith, *Mysticism and Reform*.

57. Nigel Smith, *Perfection Proclaimed* (Oxford: Clarendon Press, 1999), 16.

58. Smith, *Perfection Proclaimed*, 107–43. Ariel Hessayon, *"Gold Tried in the Fire": The Prophet TheaurauJohn Tany and the English Revolution* (New York: Routledge, 2007); Hessayon, *Jane Lead and Her Transnational Legacy* (London: Palgrave Macmillan, 2016).

59. John Locke's phrase complaining about atomizing the Bible; John Locke, *A Paraphrase and Notes on the Epistles of St. Paul*, c. 1700 (1733), vi–vii. See the impressive rendering of a political apophatic in China Miéville, "Silence in Debris: Towards an Apophatic Marxism," in *Evidence of Things Not Seen, Salvage* 6 (New York: Verso, 2018), 115–54.

60. Abraham Caley, *A Glimpse of Eternity* (London: Thomas Parkhurse, 1679), 48.

61. Maximilianus Sandaeus, *Pro theologia mystica clavis* (Cologne, 1640), 6; Edward Stillingfleet, *An Answer to Mr. Cressy's Epistle apologetical* (London: Hen. Mortlock, 1675), 25.

62. Anthony Ossa-Richardson, *A History of Ambiguity* (Princeton: Princeton University Press, 2019), 2.

63. Stillingfleet, *Answer to Mr. Cressy's Epistle*, 25, regarding Carolus Hersentius, *Caroli Hersentii in D. Dionysii Areopagitae de Mystica Theologia* (Paris, 1626). This also exercises Meric Casaubon, *A treatise concerning enthusiasme, as it is an effect of nature, but is mistaken by many for either divine inspiration, or diabolical possession* (London, R. D., 1655), 112–13.

64. Louis Ellies Du Pin, *A New History of Ecclesiastical Writers* (London: Abel Swalle, 1693), 87, in the appended, *History of the Controversies . . . Transacted in the Fifteenth Century* (separate pagination).

65. Casaubon, *A treatise concerning enthusiasme*, 30. Bullshit is raised to its proper philosophical status in Harry G. Frankfurt, *On Bullshit* (Princeton: Princeton University Press, 2005).

66. Meric Casaubon, *A treatise concerning enthusiasme* (1656), A4v, pp. 149, 167, 173. Pseudo-Dionysius, a fifth- or sixth-century mystic, who presented himself as the figure converted by Paul in Acts 17.34. Casaubon is responding to *Life of Sister Katharine of Jesus* (1628). On the text's early modern fortunes, see Karlfried Froehlich, "Pseudo-Dionysius and the Reformation of the Sixteenth Century," in Colm Luibhéid, ed., *Pseudo-Dionysius: The Complete Works* (Mahwah, NJ: Paulist Press, 1987), 38–39. Lorenzo Valla, *Collatio Novi Testamenti*, ed. Alessandro Perosa (Florence, 1970), 167–68. On Acts 17.22–23, see Anne Reeve and M. A. Screech, eds., *Erasmus' Annotations of the New Testament*, 2 vols. (Leiden, 1990), 2:312–13. On the fluctuations of Pseudo-Dionysius's reputation, see Feisal G. Mohamed, "Renaissance Thought on the Celestial Hierarchy: The Decline of a Tradition?" *Journal of the History of Ideas* 65, no. 4 (2004): 559–82.

67. Isaac Casaubon, *De rebus sacris et ecclesiasticis exercitationes xvi* (Geneva, 1655). See Anthony Grafton, "Protestant versus Prophet: Isaac Casaubon on Hermes Trismegistus," *Journal of the Warburg and Courtauld Institutes* 46 (1983): 78–93.

68. See Steven E. Ozment, *Mysticism and Dissent: Religious Ideology and Social Protest in the Sixteenth Century* (New Haven: Yale University Press, 1973).

69. Clement Hawes, *Mania and Literary Style: The Rhetoric of Enthusiasm from the Ranters to Christopher Smart* (Cambridge: Cambridge University Press, 1996), 1–49; Michael Heyd, *Be Sober and Reasonable: The Critique of Enthusiasm in the Seventeenth and Early Eighteenth Centuries* (Leiden: Brill, 1995).

70. Jaroslav Pelikan, "The Odyssey of Dionysian Spirituality," in Luibheid, ed., *Pseudo-Dionysius: The Complete Works*, 11. Cited also in Richard H. Jones, *Philosophy of Mysticism: Raids on the Ineffable* (Albany: SUNY Press, 2016), 240.

71. Jacques Derrida, "How to Avoid Speaking: Denials," trans. Ken Frieden, in Harold Coward and Toby Foshay, *Derrida and Negative Theology* (Albany: SUNY Press, 1992), 73–142 (76). On the context of this essay, in debate with Jean-Luc Marion, see Arthur Bradley, *Negative Theology and Modern French Philosophy* (New York: Routledge, 2004), 81–111. See also Poor and Smith, *Mysticism and Reform*, 10, on works whose "broad approach seems to imply that nearly everything involves mysticism," with reference to Michael Kessler and Christian Sheppard, *Mystics: Presence and Aporia* (Chicago: University of Chicago Press, 2003).

72. John D. Caputo, *The Prayers and Tears of Jacques Derrida: Religion without Religion* (Bloomington: Indiana University Press, 1997), 11.

73. William Franke, *On the Universality of What Is Not: The Apophatic Turn in Critical Thinking* (Notre Dame, IN: University of Notre Dame Press, 2020). See too Rowan Williams, *The Edge of Words: God and the Habits of Language* (London: Bloomsbury, 2014).

Chapter 1

1. Hugh Broughton, *Job to the King. A Colon-Agrippina studie of one moneth, for the metricall translation: but of many yeres for Ebrew difficulties* (Amsterdam: Giles Thorp, 1610), 103–4. For a later elaboration of this use of Sadducees, see Joseph Glanvill, *Blow at Modern Sadducism in Some Philosophical Considerations about Witchcraft* (London: James Collins, 1668). "Epicure" is used with loose reference to Epicurus, as the source of Lucretian ideas.

2. Francis Bacon, *Of the advancement and proficience of learning . . . Nine books*, 1.6.2 (Oxford: Leon Lichfield, 1640), 44–45 (separate pagination); *De Dignitate & Augmentis scientiarum* (1623), in Spedding, ed., *The Works of Francis Bacon* (c. 1900), 2:148.

3. Bacon, *Advancement*, 44–45; Bacon, *Novum Organum*, in Graham Rees and Maria Wakely, eds., *The Oxford Francis Bacon, Vol. 11: The Instauratio magna Part II: Novum organum and Associated Texts* (New York: Oxford University Press, 2004), 1.65, 163.

4. John Spencer, *A discourse concerning prodigies wherein the vanity of presages by them is reprehended* (London: Will. Graves, 1663), 49. See too William Temple, *Miscellanea, in four essays* (London: Ri. Simpson, 1690), 308, "The Subject of *Job*, is Instruction concerning the Attributes of God and the Works of Nature."

5. Richard Franck, *A philosophical treatise of the original and production of*

things (London: John Gain, 1687), sig. B2r. See similarly Richard Ward, *Two very usefull and compendious theological treatises* (London: William Miller, 1673), 17.

6. Franck, *A philosophical treatise*, sig. B2r.

7. See Peter Harrison, *The Fall of Man and the Foundations of Science* (Cambridge: Cambridge University Press, 2007).

8. Franck, *A philosophical treatise*, 111.

9. William Clark, *The grand tryal, or, Poetical exercitations upon the book of Job* (Edinburgh: Andrew Anderson, 1685), sig. a1v.

10. See, for example, John Swan, *Speculum Mundi* (Cambridge: T. Buck and R. Daniel, 1635). Attention to the hexameral in Arnold Williams, *The Common Expositor: An Account of the Commentaries on Genesis, 1527–1633* (Chapel Hill: University of North Carolina Press, 1948).

11. See on this the account in William Franke, *A Theology of Literature* (Eugene, OR: Wipf & Stock/Cascade Books, 2017), 19.

12. Dionysius Longinus, *On the Sublime*, trans. W. Hamilton Fyfe (London: Heinemann, 1927), 9.9, "So, too, the lawgiver of the Jews no ordinary man having formed a worthy conception of divine power, and given expression to it, writes at the very beginning of his *Laws*: 'God said'—What? 'Let there be light' and there was light. 'Let there be earth', and there was earth."

13. Theophilus Gale, *The court of the Gentiles* (Oxford: Tho. Gilbert, 1660), 16. See similarly, John Beaumont, *Considerations on a book, entituled The theory of the earth* (London: Randal Taylor, 1693), 9–10.

14. J. V. C. (John Vincent Canes), *Fiat lux or, a general conduct to a right understanding in the great combustions and broils about religion here in England* (Douai, 1661), 82–84.

15. Clark, *The grand tryal, or, Poetical exercitations upon the book of Job*, 333.

16. Matthew Barker, *Natural theology* (London: Nathaniel Ranew, 1674), 80–81.

17. George Hutcheson, *An exposition of the book of Job being the sum of CCCXVI lectures* (London: Ralph Smith, 1669), sig. A3v.

18. Joseph Caryl, *Exposition . . . upon the thirty-eighth, thirty-ninth, fortieth, forty-first, and forty-second, being the five last, chapters of the Book of Job* (London: M. and S. Simmons, 1653), 98–99; Psalm 36.6; and Romans 11.33.

19. Joseph Caryl, *Exposition . . . of the Book of Job*, 149–51.

20. Joseph Caryl, *Exposition . . . of the Book of Job*, 146; Psalm 77.19.

21. Thomas Burnet, *The theory of the earth* (London: Walter Kettilby, 1697), 62. The work generally goes by the title *Sacred Theory of the Earth*, but was translated without the "sacred" (1684). I cite the 1697 version, which collates all its parts.

22. See chapter 5. Clement Hawes, *Mania and Literary Style: The Rhetoric of Enthusiasm from the Ranters to Christopher Smart* (Cambridge: Cambridge University Press, 2005), 9–10, on "mania as rhetoric" being in the tradition of "Longinian sublime." See, e.g. Henry More, *Enthusiasmus triumphatus, or a discourse of the Nature, Causes, Kinds, and Cure, of enthusiasme* (London: J. Flesher, 1656), in his spat with Thomas Vaughan.

23. Burnet, *The theory of the earth*, 1.7, 62–63.
24. Burnet, *The theory of the earth*, 1.7, 64.
25. William Hodson, *The divine cosmographer* (Cambridge: Roger Danie, 1640), 136; Edward Reyner, *A treatise of the necessity of humane learning* (London: John Field, 1663), 53.
26. Attributed to "a Member of the Athenian Society," collected in John Dunton's *The Young-students-library containing extracts and abridgments of the most valuable books* (London: Printed for John Dunton, 1692), 245.
27. On Moses as the author of Job, see, e.g., John Edwards, "Of the Excellency and perfection of the Holy Scriptures," appended to *A discourse concerning the authority, stile and perfection of the books of the Old and New Testament* (London: Jonathan Robinson, 1693), (separate pagination) 363; Matthew Hale, *The primitive origination of mankind* (London: William Shrowsbery, 1677), 138.
28. Recent writings on this include Kimberly Susan Hedlin, "The Book of Job in Early Modern England," PhD diss., UCLA, 2018, especially 301–50; Alison Knight, "Pen of Iron: Scriptural Text and the Book of Job in Early Modern English Literature," PhD diss., Cambridge University, 2012.
29. A sample of these: John Calvin, *Sermons sur le livre de Job* (1554), *Sermons of Master John Calvin, upon the booke of Job*, trans. Arthur Golding (London: George Byshop and Thomas Woodcocke, 1574); Johannes Oecolampadius, *Commentarii omnes in . . . Jobum* (Geneva, 1573); Théodore de Bèze, *Job expounded by Theodore Beza, partly in manner of a commentary* (London: Iohn Legatt, 1589); Johannes Coccejus, *Commentarius in librum Ijobi* (Franekerae [Franeker], 1644); Balthasar Cordier, *Iob Elucidatus* (Antwerp, 1646); Johannes Mercerus, *Commentarii, in Jobum* (Amsterdam, 1651); Nicolas Guillebert, *Le Livre de Job paraphrasé* (Paris, 1641); Jeremias Drexel, *Jobus divinae providentiae theatrum* (Antwerp, 1655). See also the dizzying decade-by-decade, pan-European list in David J. A. Clines, *Job 38–42: WBC Volume 18B* (London: Nelson, 2011), 1276–78.
30. George Hutcheson, *An exposition of the book of Job being the sum of CCCXVI lectures* (1669); Joseph Caryl, *An exposition with practical observations upon . . . the book of Job*, 12 vols. (1643–53). Other large-scale analysis in John Trapp, *A commentary or exposition upon . . . Job* (London: Thomas Newberry, 1657); Arthur Jackson, *Annotations upon . . . the Book of Job* (London: Roger Daniel, 1658); Simon Patrick, *The book of Job paraphras'd* (London: J. Macock, for R. Royston, 1679).
31. Du Bartas, *A Divine and True TragiComedy: Job Triumphant in His Triall* with *Divine Weeks* (London: Robert Young, 1633), 886–950; François Vavassor, *Jobus brevi commentario* (1679); Francis Quarles, *Job Militant* (London: Felix Kyngston for George Winder, 1624); George Abbott, *The Whole Book of job Paraphrased* (London: Edward Griffin for Henry Overton, 1640); George Sandys, *A paraphrase upon Job*, in *A paraphrase upon the divine poems* (London: John Legatt, 1638); Zacharie Boyd, *Book of Job*, in *The Second Volume of The garden of Zion* (Glasgow: George Anderson, 1644); Thomas Manley, *The Affliction and*

Deliverance of the Saints: or The Whole Booke of Iob (London: Iohn Tey, 1652); Arthur Brett, *Patientia victrix, or, The book of Job in lyrick verse* (London: Richard Gammon, 1661).

32. Hannibal Hamlin, *The Bible in Shakespeare* (New York: Oxford University Press, 2013), 305–33; Victoria Brownlee, *Biblical Readings and Literary Writings in Early Modern England, 1558–1625* (New York: Oxford University Press, 2018), 79–112; see too Steven Marx, *Shakespeare and the Bible* (New York: Oxford University Press, 2000), 59–78.

33. Alison Knight, "The Very, Very Words: Scriptural Misquotation in Lancelot Andrewes's and John Donne's Job Sermons," *Studies in Philology* 111, no. 3 (2014): 442–69.

34. This is beyond the scope of the chapter, but see, for instance, Robert Eisen, *The Book of Job in Medieval Jewish Philosophy* (New York: Oxford University Press, 2004).

35. John Gregory, *Notes and observations upon some passages of scripture* (London: R. Royston, 1646), 54.

36. Gregory, *Notes and observations* (1646), 55.

37. Thomas Browne, *Pseudodoxia Epidemica* (London: E. Dod, 1646), 2.2, p. 57; Vallesius, *Sacra Philosophia* (Francofurti [Frankfurt], 1600), 406.

38. John Arrowsmith, *Theanthropos; or, God-man: being an exposition upon the first eighteen verses of the first chapter of the Gospel according to St John* (London: Humphrey Moseley, 1660), 47, 52.

39. Diego de Zúñiga, *In Job Commentaria* (Toleti [Toledo], 1584), partially translated in "An Abstract of Some Passages in the Commentaries of Didacus a Stunica of Salamanca Upon Job," in *Mathematical Collections and Translations: In Two Tomes, Vol. 1, Part 1,* ed. Thomas Salusbury (London: William Leybourn, 1661), 468–70. Kimberly Hedlin, "The Book of Job in Early Modern England," PhD diss., UCLA, 2018, 259–300. See too Richard J. Blackwell, *Galileo, Bellarmine, and the Bible: Including a Translation of Foscarini's Letter on the Motion of the Earth* (Notre Dame, IN: University of Notre Dame Press, 1991).

40. Clark, *The grand tryal,* 331.

41. Clark, *The grand tryal,* 331.

42. Robert Boyle, *Of the High Veneration Man's Intellect owes to God* (1684–85), in *Works of Robert Boyle,* ed. Michael Hunter and Edward B. Davis (London: Pickering & Chatto, 2000), 9:157–204 (at 168), regarding Job 38.8–11.

43. John Wilkins, *A discourse concerning a new world & another planet* (1640), "That the Earth may be a planet," (sep. pag.) 10–11.

44. Alexander Ross, *The New Planet, No Planet: Or, The Earth No Wandering Star Except in the Wandering Heads of Galileans* (London: J. Young, 1646), 4–5.

45. See, for a collection of such comments, Kathryn Schifferdecker, *Out of the Whirlwind: Creation Theology in the Book of Job* (Cambridge, MA: Harvard University Press, 2008), 1–2.

46. Simone Weil, *Waiting for God* (Routledge, 2010), 46.

47. Not to do more than skim the surface of critical material on Job, notable are Carol Newsom, *The Book of Job: A Contest of Moral Imaginations* (New York: Oxford University Press, 2003), writing on the book's abstruse reality, its moral or amoral polyphony; Mark Larrimore, *The Book of Job: A Biography* (Princeton: Princeton University Press, 2013), 50, who talks of how the book's meaning plays hide-and-seek with the reader; Bruce Zuckerman, *Job the Silent: A Study in Historical Counterpoint* (Oxford: Oxford University Press, 1998). I exclude here the historical-critical tradition, which grapples with composition history.

48. Broughton, *Job to the King*, offering a dramatized version, "Job brought into dialogue: for our familiar speech," but excluding chaps. 28–42.

49. His impatience noted, for instance, by Thomas Byrdall, *A glimpse of God* (London: Thomas Parkhurst, 1665), 391. In Clark, *The grand tryal*, 351, God, once Job has been quietened, remarks, "I see thou hast some sense / Of *thy extravagant impatience*." Larrimore, *The Book of Job: A Biography*, 13, notes how the comment in James on his patience might refer to the apocryphal tale, the Legend of Job, or related oral traditions. The impatience is sometimes displaced onto Job's wife, which again is amplified in the Legend. See Jonathan Lamb, *The rhetoric of suffering: reading the book of Job in the eighteenth century* (Oxford: Oxford University Press, 1995).

50. Broughton, *Job To the King*, 103–4.

51. Robert Boyle, *Some Considerations touching the Style of the Holy Scriptures*, in *Works of Robert Boyle*, ed. Michael Hunter and Edward B. Davis (Pickering & Chatto, 2000), 2:414.

52. Lucy Hutchinson, *Order and Disorder*, ed. David Norbrook (Oxford: Blackwell, 2001) 1.53–60. Hutchinson's epic was only identified as hers, and published in its full form, with Norbrook's edition.

53. E.g., John Wollebius, *The Abridgement of Christian Divinity*, trans. Alexander Ross (London: John Saywell, 1650), 15.

54. Hutchinson, *Order and Disorder*, 1.300–305.

55. Hutchinson, *Order and Disorder*, 2.5–10.

56. See Georgia B. Christopher, *Milton and the Science of the Saints* (Princeton: Princeton University Press, 1982), 15. See, on the complexity of the "literal," Peter Harrison, *The Bible, Protestantism and the Rise of Natural Science* (Cambridge: Cambridge University Press, 1998).

57. Amos Funkenstein, *Theology and the Scientific Imagination from the Middle Ages to the Seventeenth Century* (Princeton: Princeton University Press, 1986), 3–4. See also the two volumes of Jitse M. van der Meer and Scott Mandelbrote, eds., *Nature and Scripture in the Abrahamic Religions: Up to 1700* (Leiden: Brill, 2008); Andrew D. Berns, *The Bible and Natural Philosophy in Renaissance Italy: Jewish and Christian Physicians in Search of Truth* (Cambridge: Cambridge University Press, 2015).

58. Lambert Daneau, *The wonderfull woorkmanship of the world* (London: Andrew Maunsell, 1578), fol. 7r. See Ann Blair, "Mosaic Physics and the Search for

a Pious Natural Philosophy in the Late Renaissance," *Isis* 91, no. 1 (March 2000): 23–58.

59. Harrison, *The Bible, Protestantism and the Rise of Natural Science*, 136–47.

60. Samuel Gott, *The divine history of the genesis of the world explicated & illustrated* (London: Henry Eversden, 1670), sig. A2r. Similarly, Beaumont, *Considerations on a book, entituled The theory of the earth*, 9–10, who suspects a Jobean origin of philosophy's "obscure and Aenigmatical manner."

61. Gott, *The divine history*, 5–6. Gott goes on to parse *"And the Earth was without form and void. And Darknes was upon the face of the Deep"* by reference to Job 38, with structured attention to natural philosophy.

62. George Hughes, *An analytical exposition of the whole first book of Moses, called Genesis* (n.p., 1672), sig. A5r. See similarly, Thomas Manningham, *Two discourses . . . the chief criterions of philosophical truth* (London: W. Brooke, 1578), 90–98.

63. Thomas White, *Institutionum Peripateticarum ad mentem . . . K. Digbæi pars theorica Item appendix theologica de Origine Mundi* (1646), translated as *Peripateticall institutions, In the way of that eminent person and excellent philosopher Sr. Kenelm Digby. The theoricall part. Also a theologicall appendix of the beginning of the world* (London: John Williams, 1656), 343. On the "Blackloist" philosopher, see Beverley Southgate, *Covetous of Truth: The Life and Work of Thomas White, 1593–1676* (New York: Kluwer, 1993), chap. 10, on cosmology; Stefania Tutino, *Thomas White and the Blackloists: Between Politics and Theology during the English Civil War: Catholic Christendom, 1300–1700* (Farnham, Surrey, UK: Ashgate, 2008), chap. 2, on natural philosophy.

64. White, *Beginning of the world*, 354.

65. White, *Beginning of the world*, 357–58.

66. White, *Beginning of the world*, 358–59.

67. Géraud de Cordemoy, *Copie d'une lettre écrite à un sçavant religieux de la Compagnie de Jésus, pour montrer: I, que le système de M. Descartes et son opinion touchant les bestes n'ont rien de dangereux; II, et que tout ce qu'il en a écrit semble estre tiré du premier chapitre de la Genèse* (Paris, 1668), 13, translated as *A discourse written to a learned frier by M. Des Fourneillis, shewing that this systeme of M. Des Cartes, and particularly his opinion concerning brutes, does contain nothing dangerous, and that all he hath written of both seems to have been taken out of the first chapter of Genesis* (London: Moses Pitt, 1670), 12–13.

68. De Cordemoy, *Copie d'une lettre*, 50.

69. Francis Oakley, *Omnipotence, Covenant and Order: An Excursion in the History of Ideas from Abelard to Leibniz* (Ithaca: Cornell University Press, 1984); and Oakley *Omnipotence and Promise: The Legacy of the Scholastic Distinction of Powers* (Toronto: Pontifical Institute of Mediaeval Studies, 2002); Anthony Kenny, *The God of the Philosophers* (Oxford: Oxford University Press, 1979), 100–115. An important debate around its significance in early modern science, which I can only hint at here, is found in Funkenstein, *Theology and the Scientific Imagination*, 117–

201; Margaret Osler, *Divine Will and the Mechanical Philosophy: Gassendi and Descartes on Contingency and Necessity in the Created World* (Cambridge: Cambridge University Press, 1994); Peter Harrison, "Voluntarism and Early Modern Science," *History of Science* 40 (2002): 63–89; John Henry, "Voluntarist Theology at the Origins of Modern Science: A Response to Peter Harrison," *History of Science* 47, no. 1 (2009): 79–113; Francis Oakley, "Voluntarist Theology and Early-Modern Science: The Matter of the Divine Power, Absolute and Ordained," *History of Science* 56 (2018): 72–96.

70. Edward Stillingfleet, *Origines Sacrae* (London: Henry Mortlock, 1662), 432.

71. Ralph Cudworth, *The true intellectual system of the universe* (London: Richard Royston, 1678), 738–67, for a detailed discussion of whether the axiom that nothing can come from nothing applies to the primal creation.

72. Moses Maimonides, *Doctor perplexorum*, ed. Johannes Buxtorf the Younger (Basel, 1629).

73. Stillingfleet, *Origines Sacrae*, 434.

74. Stillingfleet, *Origines Sacrae*, 434. See also Ibn Tufayl, *An account of the Oriental philosophy . . . particularly the profound wisdom of Hai Ebn Yokdan, both in natural and divine things*, trans. Edward Pocock the younger (from Arabic to Latin) and George Keith (into English) (London, 1674), 19–61, on the story of a boy brought up without parents and how he comes to understand the world. See Avner Ben-Zaken, *Reading Ḥayy Ibn-Yaqẓān: A Cross-Cultural History of Autodidacticism* (Baltimore: Johns Hopkins University Press, 2011).

75. Maimonides, *The Guide of the Perplexed*, trans. Shlomo Pines, 2 vols. (Chicago: University of Chicago Press, 1974), 21.7, 2:294–98. See Allan Nadler, "The 'Rambam Revival' in Early Modern Jewish Thought," in Jay Michael Harris, ed., *Maimonides after 800 Years: Essays on Maimonides and His Influence* (Cambridge, MA: Harvard University Press, 2007).

76. Stillingfleet, *Origines Sacrae*, bk. 2, on prophecy. Later editions of the work change the focus considerably. Beverley Southgate, "'The Fighting of Two Cocks on a Dung-Hill': Stillingfleet Versus Sergeant," in Allison P. Coudert, Sarah Hutton, Richard H. Popkin, and Gordon M. Weiner, *Judaeo-Christian Intellectual Culture in the Seventeenth Century* (New York: Springer, 1999). On the contexts of its philosophical engagements, see Dmitri Levitin, *Ancient Wisdom in the Age of the New Science: Histories of Philosophy in England, c. 1640–1700* (Cambridge: Cambridge University Press, 2015).

77. Samuel Taylor Coleridge, *Biographia Literaria*, 2: chap. 14 (London: Fenner, 1817), 10, how his work "furnish[es] undeniable proofs that poetry of the highest kind may exist without meter." See M. H. Abrams, *Natural Supernaturalism: Tradition and Revolution in Romantic Literature* (New York: Norton, 1973 [1971]), 99–106.

78. Isaac Newton, *The Correspondence of Isaac Newton*, 2:1667–87, ed. H. W. Turnbull (Cambridge, 1960), 319. On the correspondence, see Scott Mandelbrote, "Isaac Newton and Thomas Burnet: Biblical Criticism and the Crisis of Late

Seventeenth-Century England," in James E. Force and Richard H. Popkin, eds., *The Books of Nature and Scripture* (Dordrecht, 1994), 149–78; Stephen D. Snobelen, "'Not in the Language of Astronomers': Isaac Newton, the Scriptures and the Hermeneutics of Accommodation," in van der Meer and Mandelbrote, eds., *Nature and Scripture in the Abrahamic Religions*, 2:491–530, and in the same volume, Kerry Magruder, "Thomas Burnet, Biblical Idiom, and 17th-Century Theories of the Earth," 451–90.

79. Burnet, *The theory of the earth*, 9–10.
80. White, *Beginning of the World*, 407–18.
81. Burnet, *The theory of the earth*, 44–45.
82. Burnet, *The theory of the earth*, 60.
83. Paolo Rossi, *The Dark Abyss of Time: The History of the Earth and the History of Nations from Hooke to Vico*, trans. Lydia Cochrane (Chicago: University of Chicago Press, 1979), 33–41; Thomas Rossetter, "The Theorist: Thomas Burnet and His Sacred History of the Earth," PhD diss., Durham University, 2019. Harrison, *Bible*, pp. 138–46; Al Coppola, 'Imagination and Pleasure in the Cosmography of Thomas Burnet's *Sacred Theory of the Earth*', in Allison Kavey (ed.) *World-Building and the Early Modern Imagination* (Palgrave, 2010); William Poole, *The World Makers: Scientists of the Restoration and the Search for the Origins of the Earth* (Peter Lang, 2010), pp. 55–74; Looking at the strange character of the Burnetian 'literal', see Kevin Killeen, '"A Nice and Philosophical Account of the Origin of all Things": Accommodation in Burnet's *Sacred Theory* and Milton's *Paradise Lost*', *Milton Studies* 46 (2006): 106–22.
84. Thomas Burnet, *Telluris Theoria Sacra* (London: W. Kettilby, 1681), translated as *Theory of the Earth* (1684), 110. See too Marjorie Nicolson, *Mountain Gloom and Mountain Glory: The Development of the Aesthetics of the Infinite* (New York: Norton, 1959).
85. Thomas Burnet, *A review of the theory of the earth and of its proofs, especially in reference to Scripture* (London: Walter Kettilby, 1690), 35–37.
86. William Whiston, *New Theory of the Earth From its Original to the Consummation of all Things* (London: Benj. Tooke, 1696); John Woodward, *An Essay Towards a Natural History of the Earth* (London: Benj. Tooke, 1695); John Keill, *An Examination of Dr. Burnet's Theory of the Earth, Together with Some Remarks on Mr. Whiston's New Theory of the Earth* (Oxford: Theatre, 1698); Thomas Robinson, *New Observations on the Natural History of the World of Matter* (London: John Newton, 1696); John Edwards, *Brief Remarks upon Mr Whiston's New Theory of the Earth* (London: J. Robinson, 1697); John Arbuthnot, *An Examination of Dr Woodward's Account of the Deluge* (London: C. Bateman, 1697). See James E. Force, *William Whiston, Honest Newtonian* (Cambridge: Cambridge University Press, 1985), 32–63; Joseph M. Levine, *Dr Woodward's Shield: History, Science, and Satire in Augustan England* (Berkeley: University of California Press, 1977).
87. Thomas Burnet, *An answer to the late exceptions made by Mr. Erasmus Warren against The theory of the earth* (London: Walter Kettilby, 1690), 51–52;

Erasmus Warren, *Geologia, or, A discourse concerning the earth before the deluge* (London: R. Chiswell, 1690), 223–24.

88. Herbert Croft, *Some animadversions upon a book intituled The theory of the earth* (London: Charles Harper, 1685), 109–10, with reference to Francis Godwin, *The Man in the Moone; or, A Discourse of a Voyage Thither, by Domingo Gonsales* (London: Joshua Kirton, 1638).

Chapter 2

1. Jacob Boehme (Böhme), *Mysterium Magnum, or an exposition of the first book of Moses called Genesis*, trans. John Sparrow (London: M. Simmons for H. Blunden, 1654), 17.40, p. 77; *Mysterium magnum, oder Erklärung über das erste Buch Mosis* (1640), in *Theosophia Revelata. Das ist: Alle Göttliche Schriften Des Gottseligen und Hocherleuchteten Deutschen Theosophi Jacob Böhmens* (Amsterdam: Johann Georg Gichtel, 1730), 17.40, 8:115. The notes will give page numbers for both the English 1654 translation (cited as *Mysterium Magnum*) and the German in this 1730 standard edition (cited as *Theosophia*). *Theosophia* can be found online, in full scans, at https://www.digitale-sammlungen.de and at Google Books. A facsimile of *Theosophia*, with different volume numbering, is *Sämtliche Schriften*, ed. W.-E. Peuckert (Stuttgart: Frommann-Holzboog, 1955–61), vols. 7 and 8.

2. Boehme, *Mysterium Magnum*, 9.1, p. 31; *Theosophia*, 47.

3. Franz Rosenzweig, *The Star of Redemption*, trans. William W. Hallo (London: Routledge, 1971), 41. Hallo's translation is based on the second edition (1930). The triad of the unknowable is completed with an account of "negative psychology," of the evacuated self: "Mythic God, plastic world, tragic man," as he sums it up (83).

4. China Miéville, "Silence in Debris: Towards an Apophatic Marxism," in *Evidence of Things Not Seen*, *Salvage* 6 (2018): 115–54 (at 120).

5. Luther, in his use of *Deus absconditus*, was keen to distinguish his use of the term, meaning "hiddenness," from any tinge of the Dionysian. Bernard McGinn, "Vere tu es Deus absconditus: The Hidden God in Luther and Some Mystics," in Oliver Davies and Denys Turner, eds., *Silence and the Word: Negative Theology and Incarnation* (Cambridge: Cambridge University Press, 2002), 94–115 (at 99).

6. Boehme, *Mysterium Magnum*, 2.7, p. 4; *Theosophia*, 9.

7. Boehme, *Mysterium Magnum*, 2.9, p. 4, *Theosophia*, 9.

8. Boehme, *Mysterium Magnum*, 2.10, p. 5, *Theosophia*, 10.

9. I stint on biographical details here, but they will follow later. Among recent biographical work, see Ariel Hessayon, "Boehme's Life and Times," in Ariel Hessayon and Sarah Apetrei, eds., *An Introduction to Jacob Boehme: Four Centuries of Thought and Reception* (London: Routledge, 2018), 77–97; see too, several contextual essays in Bo Andersson, Lucinda Martin, Leigh T. I. Penman, and Andrew Weeks, eds., *Jacob Böhme and His World* (Leiden: Brill, 2019); Gerhard Wehr, "Jacob Böhme—Leben und Werk," and Carlos Gilly, "Zur Geschichte der Böhme-Biographien des Abraham von Franckenberg," both in Theodor Harmsen,

ed., *Jacob Böhmes Weg in die Welt. Zur Geschichte der Handschriftensammlung, Über-setzungen und Editionen von Abraham Willemsz van Bayerland* (Amsterdam: In de Pelikaan, 2007), 55–70, 329–63. John Joseph Stroud, *Sunrise to Eternity: A Study in Jacob Boehme's Life and Thought* (Philadelphia: University of Pennsylvania Press, 1957), 68–76, citing the account of Cornelius Weissner, *Wahrhaftige Relation* (1658).

10. On the publication history, Werner Buddecke, *Die Jacob Boehme Ausgaben: Teil 2. Die übersetzungen* (1957), 49–173. The first volume attends to the German publication history. See too Werner Buddecke, rev. Matthias Wenzel, *Jacob Boehme: Verzeichnis der Handschriften und frühen Abschriften* (2000).

11. Nigel Smith, *Perfection Proclaimed: Language and Literature in English Radical Religion, 1640–1660* (Oxford: Oxford University Press, 1989), 185–225. See too B. J. Gibbons, *Gender in Mystical and Occult Thought: Behmenism and Its Development in England* (Cambridge: Cambridge University Press, 1996); Wilhelm Struck, *Der Einfluss Jakob Boehmes auf die Englische Literatur des 17. Jahrhunderts* (Berlin: Junker & Dünnhaupt, 1936), 103–62; Nils Thune, *The Behmenists and the Philadelphians: A Contribution to the Study of Mysticism in the 17th and 18th Centuries* (Stockholm: Almqvist & Wiksell, 1948); Serge Hutin, *Les Disciples anglaises de Jacob Boehme* (Paris: Éditions Denoë, 1960). Paul Cefalu, *The Johannine Renaissance in Early Modern English Literature and Theology* (New York: Oxford University Press, 2017), especially 215–84, on the wider importance of the Word and antinominian thought; Nicolas McDowell, *The English Radical Imagination: Culture, Religion and Revolution, 1630–60* (New York: Oxford University Press, 2003). Ariel Hessayon's essays, toward a forthcoming book, include "Jacob Boehme's Writings during the English Revolution and Afterwards: Their Publication, Dissemination and Influence," in Hessayon and Apetrei, *Introduction to Jacob Boehme*, 77–97; Ariel Hessayon, "Jacob Böhme's Foremost Seventeenth-Century English Translator: John Sparrow (1615–1670) of Essex," in Andersson et al., *Böhme and His World*, 329–57; Hessayon, "Jacob Boehme and the Early Quakers," *Journal of the Friends Historical Society* 60 (2005): 191–223; Hessayon, "'The Teutonicks Writings': Translating Jacob Boehme into English and Welsh," *Esoterica* 9 (2007), online.

12. Used of Familist radicals, e.g., Henry More, *Enthusiasmus triumphatus* (1656), 37. See J. D. Moss, "'Godded with God': Hendrick Niclaes and His Family of Love," *Transactions of the American Philosophical Society* 71, no. 8 (1981); Smith, *Perfection*, 145–47.

13. Douglas Hedley, 'Censuring the Teutonic Philosopher? Henry More's Ambivalent Appraisal of Jacob Böhme', *Aries: Journal for the Study of Western Esotericism* 18, no. 1 (2018): 54–74, and the translation of More at http://www.cambridge-platonism.divinity.cam.ac.uk/view/texts/diplomatic/Hengstermann1679D.

14. Primary points of reference in Blake's Boehme are Kevin Fischer, *Converse in the Spirit: William Blake, Jacob Boehme, and the Creative Spirit* (Vancouver, BC: Fairleigh Dickinson University Press, 2004); Bryan Aubrey, *Watchmen of Eternity:*

Blake's Debt to Jacob Boehme (Lanham, MD: University Press of America, 1986); Elisabeth Engell Jessen, "Boehme and the Early English Romanics," in Hessayon and Apetrei, *Introduction to Jacob Boehme*, 180–95.

15. See, in particular, the excellent account by Cecilia Muratori, *The First German Philosopher: The Mysticism of Jakob Böhme as Interpreted by Hegel* (New York: Springer, 2018); Kristine Hannak, "Boehme and German Romanticism," in Hessayon and Apetrei, *Introduction to Jacob Boehme*, 162–79.

16. Attention to the seventeenth-century philosophical reception in Lucinda Martin, ed., *Jacob Böhme and Early Modern Philosophy*, special issue of *Aries: Journal for the Study of Western Esotericism* (2018); see too the broad Europe-wide cultural reception in the impressive volume of Wilhelm Kühlmann and Friedrich Vollhardt, eds., *Offenbarung und Episteme. Zur europäischen Wirkung Jakob Böhmes im 17. und 18. Jahrhundert* (Berlin: De Gruyter, 2012); see also Struck, *Der Einfluss Jakob Boehmes*, 189–230.

17. Boehme, *Mysterium Magnum*, 2.6, p. 4, *Theosophia*, 8–9.

18. Boehme, *Mysterium Magnum*, 2.11, p. 5: "In the inward *Spirituall world*, the Word conceiveth it selfe into a *Spirituall Essence* as one onely *Element,* wherein the foure lie hid: but when God, *viz.* the Word moved this one *Element*: then the hidden Properties did manifest themselves." *Theosophia*, 10. Compare 8.24, "where his love is hid in any thing, then his anger is manifest"; 24.2, on cursing the earth understood as the holy element in things hiding itself; similarly, 13.9.

19. Boehme, *Mysterium Magnum*, 2.6, 12.35, 12.39, 21.8, with "pullulate" and "pullulation" translating various German terms for growth and budding through: *grünete, das Ausdringen, Ausgrünen*.

20. Boehme does deploy this more naïvely straightforward microcosm elsewhere, in *Aurora, That is, the Day-Spring* (1656), 2.31–58. On the logic of correspondence, see the first part of Michel Foucault, *The Order of Things: An Archaeology of the Human Sciences* (London: Routledge, 1989), 19–50.

21. *Mysterium Magnum*, 2.10, p. 5; *Theosophia*, 10.

22. See Arnold Williams, *The Common Expositor: an account of the commentaries on Genesis, 1527–1633* (Chapel Hill: University of North Carolina Press, 1948); Philip Almond, *Adam and Eve in Seventeenth-Century Thought* (Cambridge: Cambridge University Press, 1999); Kathleen Crowther, *Adam and Eve in the Protestant Reformation* (Cambridge: Cambridge University Press, 2010).

23. John Sparrow, in Boehme, *Aurora*, sig. B1v.

24. The *nunc stans*, the scholastic "everlasting now," a condition of existence outside time.

25. Cyril O'Regan, *Gnostic Apocalypse: Jacob Boehme's Haunted Narrative* (Albany: SUNY, 2002), 17–18. See too David Walsh, *The Mysticism of Innerworldly Fulfillment: A Study of Jacob Boehme* (Tallahassee: University of Florida Press, 1983).

26. Muratori, *The First German Philosopher*, 26–27, describing Schlegel's idea of Boehme's *poesie*, language that burns with the "real" through imagination.

27. Catherine Keller, *Cloud of the Impossible: Negative Theology and Planetary Entanglements* (New York: Columbia University Press, 2015), 26.

28. John D. Caputo, *The Insistence of God: A Theology of Perhaps* (Bloomington: Indiana University Press, 2013), 9–11.

29. A lineage from Boehme back to Luther has been noted, but it tends to involve isolating single doctrines as its "unit ideas." The classic point of reference is Heinrich Bornkamm's *Luther and Böhme* (Berlin: De Gruyter, 2015 [1925]). See too Arlene A. Miller, "The Theologies of Luther and Boehme in the Light of Their Genesis Commentaries," *Harvard Theological Review* 63, no. 2 (1970): 261–303.

30. See also Roland Faber and Jeremy Fackenthal, eds., *Theopoetic Folds: Philosophizing Multifariousness* (New York: Fordham University Press, 2013), 179–94.

31. John Sparrow, preface to Boehme, *Aurora*, sig. B1v.

32. *Mysterium Magnum*, 12.9, p. 50; *Theosophia*, 76.

33. See Andrew Weeks, *Boehme, An Intellectual Biography of the Seventeenth-Century Philosopher and Mystic* (Albany: SUNY Press, 1991), 100. See too Bo Andersson, "The Rhetoric of Presence: Reflections on Jacob Böhme's Writing," in Andersson et al., *Böhme and His World*, 20–69 (at 43); Hans Grunsky, *Jacob Böhme* (Stuttgart: Frommanns-Holzboog, 1956), "Die Lehre als geschlossenes System."

34. The *clavis* is appended, in the English translation to *XL. questions concerning the soule* (1647), with separate page numeration. *Mysterium Magnum* (1654) includes as appendices *A Brief Abstract of the Sublime Considerations*, *The life of the author* (by Durand Holland, based on Abraham van Frankenberg's biography), and *Foure tables of divine revelation*. See Buddecke, *Die Jakob Boehme Ausgaben*, 2:39–41, 167.

35. John Sparrow, in Jacob Boehme, *Aurora*, sig. B1v.

36. *Mysterium Magnum*, 9.9, 11.1, 17.16. See Stroud, *Sunrise to Eternity*, 229, 270–71.

37. An exhibition on Boehme, originally at the Staatliche Kunstsammlungen Dresden, was accompanied by a useful catalogue and introduction, edited by Claudia Brink and Lucinda Martin: *Grund und Ungrund: Der Kosmos des Mystischen Philosophen Jacob Bohme* (Dresden: Sandstein, 2018). See too C. Brink and L. Martin, eds., *Alles in Allem: Die Gedankenwelt Des Mystischen Philosophen Jacob Bohme—Denken—Kontext—Wirkung* (Dresden: Sandstein, 2017); Claudia Brink, Lucinda Martin, and Cecilia Muratori, eds., *Light in Darkness: The Mystical Philosophy of Jacob Böhme* (Dresden: Sandstein 2019).

38. Alexander Koyré, *La Philosophie de Jacob Boehme* (Paris: J. Vrin, 1929), 281, makes the case that they need to be kept distinct; discussed by Weeks, *Boehme*, 148–49.

39. On the latter, *Aurora*, 23.17, p. 542: "God Himself knoweth not what He is: For He knoweth no Beginning of himself, also he knoweth not anything that is like Himself, as also he knoweth no End of himself." Stroud, *Sunrise*, 197–212.

40. Gibbons, *Gender in Mystical and Occult Thought*, 89.

41. O'Regan's account in *Gnostic Apocalypse*, 32–42 (at 39).

42. *Mysterium Magnum*, chap. 4, p. 10; *Theosophia*, 17, 29. See Koyré, *La Philosophie de Jacob Boehme*, on the Three Principles (169–236).

43. Gibbons, *Gender in Mystical and Occult Thought*, 91–92, noting D. P. Walker, *The Decline of Hell: Seventeenth-Century Discussions of Eternal Torment* (Chicago: University of Chicago Press, 1964), 120; O'Regan, *Gnostic Apocalypse*, 39.

44. See Lucinda Martin, "Jakob Böhmes 'göttliche Sophia' und Emazipationesansätze bei pietistischen Autorinnen," in Wilhelm Kühlmann and Friendrich Vollhardt, eds., *Offenbarung und Episteme. Zur europäischen Wirkung Jakob Böhmes im 17. und 18. Jahrhundert* (Berlin: De Gruyter, 2012). On the schemes of seven, see, for instance, Hans Lassen Martensen, *Jacob Boehme: Studies in His Life and Teaching* (1882; English trans., London: Hodder & Stoughton, 1885), 67–98; Basarab Nicolsecu, *Science, Meaning and Evolution: The Cosmology of Jacob Boehme*, trans. Rob Baker (n.p., Parabola, 1991), 21–35.

45. *Aurora*, 18.5.

46. *Mysterium Magnum*, p. 22; *Theosophia*, 34. See Cecilia Muratori, "'We Shall Remove the Sun': Henry More's Neoplatonic Adaptation of Jacob Böhme," in Christian Hengstermann, Douglas Hedley, and Benedikt Göcke, eds., *The Abyss and the One: Henry More's Critique of Jacob Boehme* (Peeters, forthcoming), to whom, my thanks for letting me see this essay in advance of publication. A rich iconography developed around Boehme's writings, on which see Christoph Geissmar-Brandi, *Das Auge Gottes: Bilder zu Jakob Böhme* (Wiesbaden: Harrassowitz, 1993); Frank van Lamoen, "Der Unbekannte Illustrator: Michael Andreae," in Harmsen, ed., *Jakob Böhmes Weg in die Welt*, 255–308.

47. See Weeks, *Boehme*, 101.

48. See Elliot R. Wolfson, "The Holy Cabala of Changes: Jacob Böhme and Jewish Esotericism," in Lucinda Martin, ed., *Jacob Böhme and Early Modern Philosophy*, special issue of *Aries: Journal for the Study of Western Esotericism* 18, no. 1 (2018): 21–53, tracing the critical literature on Boehme and Kabbalah.

49. Lawrence Principe and Andrew Weeks, "Jacob Boehme's Divine Substance Salitter: Its Nature, Origin and Relationship to Seventeenth-Century Scientific Theories," *British Journal of the History of Science* 22 (1989): 52–61. In *Aurora*, he writes, "Do not take me for an alchymist . . . [having] only knowledge in the spirit, not experience" (22.104).

50. Robert D. Denham, *Northrop Frye and Others: The Order of Words* (University of Toronto Press, 2017), 2: chap. 4, "Frye and Jacob Boehme," notes how a term such as "turba," by no means the most problematic of ideas, has attracted some thirteen different critical definitions, and that while there may be a "family resemblance" between such definitions, there can also be considerable distance (70).

51. Gibbons, *Gender in Mystical and Occult Thought*, 89–102 (at 90), elaborating most fully on this.

52. *Mysterium Magnum*, 1.2, p. 1; *Theosophia*, 5. See Martensen, *Jacob Boehme: Studies in His Life and Teaching*, 56–66.

53. Nicolas Berdyaev, "Unground [sic] and Freedom," translated as the introduction to Boehme, *Six Theosophic Points* (Ann Arbor: University of Michigan Press, 1971 [1958]), xviii.

54. *Mysterium Magnum*, 3.5, p. 6; *Theosophia*, 12.

55. Alexandre Koyré, *La Philosophie de Jacob Boehme*, 325. See too George Pattison, *Eternal God/Saving Time* (New York: Oxford University Press, 2015), 60–61.

56. *Mysterium Magnum*, 6.10, p. 20; *Theosophia*, 32.

57. *Mysterium Magnum*, 3.9, p. 7; *Theosophia*, 13.

58. *Mysterium Magnum*, 8.24, p. 29; *Theosophia*, 44.

59. See, for example, Michael Stoeber's chapter "The Origin of Evil in Human Nature: Jacob Boehme's *Ungrund*," in his *Evil and the Mystics' God: Towards a Mystical Theodicy* (London: Palgrave Macmillan, 1992), 143–64. One of the few instances of this in early modern England is that of the ranter, Jacob Bauthumley, *The Light and Dark Sides of God* (London: William Learner, 1650).

60. *Mysterium Magnum*, 12.10, pp. 50–51; *Theosophia*, 76.

61. *Mysterium Magnum*, 8.28, p. 30; *Theosophia*, 45.

62. *Mysterium Magnum*, 8.19, pp. 28–29; *Theosophia*, 43.

63. *Paradise Lost* 4.677. Stephen M. Fallon, *Milton among the Philosophers: Poetry and Materialism in Seventeenth-Century England* (Ithaca: Cornell University Press, 1991); Margaret Bailey, *Milton and Jakob Boehme: A Study of German Mysticism in Seventeenth-Century England* (Oxford: Oxford University Press, 1914), has a fair account of the English reception of Boehme, but its account of Milton shows its age.

64. *Mysterium Magnum*, 3.20, p. 9; *Theosophia*, 15.

65. *Mysterium Magnum*, 8.10, p. 27; *Theosophia*, 41.

66. *Mysterium Magnum*, 31.32, p. 191; *Theosophia*, 284.

67. Boehme, *Aurora*, 3.64, p. 64; *Theosophia Revelata*, vol. 1, p. 45, §3.25 (the section numbering differs in the English); compare *Aurora*, 1.38: "a stirring Boyling flowing joy in every thing" for *"eine quellende Freude"* (*Theosophia*, 1.23, p. 28).

68. *Mysterium Magnum*, Preface, §6, sig. A1v; *Theosophia*, 2.

69. *Mysterium Magnum*, 8.32, pp. 30–31; *Theosophia*, 46.

70. *Aurora*, in *Theosophia Revelata*, vol. 1, 3.29, p. 46.

71. *Mysterium Magnum*, 8.24, p. 29; *Theosophia*, 44.

72. *Mysterium Magnum*, 24.2, p. 119; *Theosophia*, 179–80.

73. *Mysterium Magnum*, 12.18, p. 52; *Theosophia*, 77; compare 14.1, 15.2.

74. *Mysterium Magnum*, 8.15, p. 28; *Theosophia*, 42.

75. *Mysterium Magnum*, 16.16, p. 69; *Theosophia*, 103; compare 12.18.

76. *Mysterium Magnum*, 17.40, p. 77; *Theosophia*, 115. On the proliferation of Adam's sins, see for example David Pareus, *In Genesin Mosis Commentarius* (1614), col. 494, in which Arnold Williams counts seventeen antecedent sins (*The Common Expositor*, 121–22).

77. *Mysterium Magnum*, 17.39, p. 77, though in this instance citing from *Mys-*

terium Magnum, ed. C. J. B. (London: J. M. Watkins, 1965). *Theosophia*, 115. The "Law Edition," with its wonderful illustrations of Boehme's ideas is William Law, ed., *The works of Jacob Behmen, the Teutonic theosopher* (London: M. Richardson, 1764–81), *Mysterium Magnum* in vol. 3. This can be viewed at https://archive.org. On Behmenist imagination (and image), see Joshua Levi Ian Gentzke, "Imagining the Image of God: Corporeal Envisioning in the Theosophy of Jacob Böhme," in Peter Forshaw, ed., *Lux in Tenebris: The Visual and the Symbolic in Western Esotericism* (Leiden: Brill, 2017), 103–29 (at 114–16).

78. Genesis 1.11. Readers of Milton might again recall the devils' not dissimilar trick when they "discover" gunpowder in the soil of heaven and gold in the soil of hell (5.11–14).

79. *Mysterium Magnum*, 17.16, p. 73; *Theosophia*, 110.

80. *Mysterium Magnum*, 17.13, p. 73; *Theosophia*, 110.

81. *Mysterium Magnum*, 18.6, 18.2, p. 78; *Theosophia*, 117.

82. *Mysterium Magnum*, 18.11, p. 79; *Theosophia*, 119–20. See Gibbons, *Gender in Mystical and Occult*, 95–97, on Adam's two falls from androgyny into gender, and a fall into matter, and his noting that for Boehme, "Christ is as much a second Eve as a second Adam."

83. Koyré, *La Philosophie de Jacob Boehme*, 207–8, "une erreur d'optique."

84. *Mysterium Magnum*, 25.4, p. 125; *Theosophia*, 188–89.

85. *Mysterium Magnum*, 21.3, p. 94; *Theosophia*, 142.

86. *Mysterium Magnum*, 18.10, p. 79; *Theosophia*, 119.

87. *Mysterium Magnum*, 18.14, p. 80; *Theosophia*, 120. See too an inflection of this, by which the "play" relates to his "knowledge of all tinctures" (16.11).

88. *Mysterium Magnum*, Preface, §6, sig. A1r; *Theosophia*, 2. See Milton, *Paradise Lost* 2.243, on forced *Halleluiahs*.

89. *Mysterium Magnum*, 54.17, p. 389; *Theosophia*, 571.

90. *Mysterium Magnum*, 41.49, p. 289; *Theosophia*, 421.

91. *Mysterium Magnum*, 44.24, p. 312; *Theosophia*, 456–75. See too the discussion of the rainbow: *Mysterium Magnum*, 33.27, 33.32.

92. *Mysterium Magnum*, 43.57, p. 307; *Theosophia*, 448.

93. A counterargument to this might be that Bohme expresses his deep antipathy to predestination in a number of places, but this does not feature extensively in *Mysterium Magnum*.

94. *Aurora*, 10.45, 12.92–96, 13.18, 20.12.

95. *Mysterium Magnum*, 9.1, p. 31; *Theosophia*, 47.

96. The "magical" in this ("*auf magische Art*") might be more closely associated with imagination than magic in the trickster sense, or at least it was so interpreted in the Romantic reception.

97. *Mysterium Magnum*, 9.2, p. 31; *Theosophia*, 48.

98. *Mysterium Magnum*, 9.10; other intrusions in the voice of Reason in §7, 9, 14, 15.

99. *Mysterium Magnum*, 12.22, p. 53; *Theosophia*, 79.

100. *Mysterium Magnum*, 12.9, p. 50; *Theosophia*, 68–9.
101. *Aurora*, 10.45, p. 184; *Theosophia*, vol. 1, §10.27, p. 119.
102. *Mysterium Magnum*, 18.1, pp. 77–78; *Theosophia*, 117.
103. Nigel Smith, "Did Anyone Understand Boehme?" in Hessayon and Apetrei, *Introduction to Jacob Boehme*, 98–119.
104. John Elliston, in Jacob Boehme, *The epistles of Jacob Behmen* (London: Gyles Calvert, 1649), a2v.
105. "Beemist" in Thomas Gumble, *The Life of General Monck* (London: Thomas Basset, 1671), 60, cited by Ariel Hessayon, "John Sparrow (1615–1670) of Essex," in Andersson et al., *Böhme and His World*, 329–57 (at 342).
106. John Webster, *Academiarum Examen* (Oxford: Leonard Litchfield, 1654); Morgan Llwyd, *Llyfr y tri Aderyn* (The Book of the Three Birds; 1653). Charles Hotham, *An Introduction to the Teutonick Philosophie*, trans. D. F. (Daniel Foote?) (London: Nath. Brooks, 1650), discussing Boehme, *Forty questions of the soul* (London: Matt. Simmons, 1665), has been identified as perhaps the earliest sustained attention, noted by Smith, "Did Anyone Understand Boehme?" 107–8. On Tany, see Ariel Hessayon, *"Gold Tried in the Fire": The Prophet TheaurauJohn Tany and the English Revolution* (Farnham, Surrey, UK: Ashgate, 2007), 290–97.
107. Details of the key texts—Nils Thune, Serge Hutin, Wilhelm Struck, and others—noted in the introduction. Ariel Hessayon, *Jane Lead and Her Transnational Legacy* (London: Palgrave Macmillan, 2016). See too Burkhard Dohm, "Böhme-Rezeption in England und deren Rückwirkung auf den frühen deutschen Pietismus," in Kühlmann and Vollhardt, eds., *Offenbarung und Episteme. Zur europäischen Wirkung Jakob Böhmes*, 219–40.
108. Gibbons, *Gender in Mystical and Occult Thought*, 103–42.
109. E.g., Richard Baxter, *A key for Catholicks, to open the jugling of the Jesuits* (London: New Simmons, 1659), a4r; *Reliquiae Baxterianae* (London: T. Parkhurst, 1696), 77–78, using the term and complaining of Boehme that "his bombasted words do signifie nothing more than before was easily known by common familiar terms." John Anderdon, *One blow at Babel in those of the people called Behmenites whose foundation is not upon that of the prophets . . . but upon their own carnal conceptions begotten in their imaginations upon Jacob Behmen's writings* (London, 1662), 2, on the "imaginary conceptions of *Iacob Behmen's* writings, the tendencie of whose spirit ye can never fathom."
110. Gerardus Croese, *The general history of the Quakers* (London: John Dunton, 1696), 257–61.
111. Anon., *The Eternal gospel once more testified unto and vindicated against the ignorance, or malice of the bishops and teachers of the now Church of England* (London: Allen Banks, 1681), 62–63.
112. Henry More, *Conway Letters*, ed. Marjorie Hope Nicolson, rev. Sarah Hutton (Oxford, 1930/1992), Ep. 200 (September 15, 1670), 306.
113. Henry More, *Censura Philosophiae Teutonica* (c. 1670), in *Henrici Mori Cantabrigiensis Opera omnia* (London: J Macock, 1679), 1:536–61. See too com-

ments in *Dialogi Divini*, in *Opera omnia* (1679), 2:718–20. On More's understanding of Boehme, see Sarah Hutton, "Henry More and Jacob Boehme," in Hutton, ed., *Henry More (1614–1687) Tercentenary Studies* (Alphen aan den Rijn: Kluwer, 1990), 157–71; Douglas Hedley, "The Reception of More's *Censura Philosophiae Teutonica*," in Martin, ed., *Jacob Böhme and Early Modern Philosophy*, 54–74; Cecilia Muratori, "'A Philosopher at Randome': Translating Jacob Böhme in Seventeenth-Century Cambridge," in Douglas Hedley and David Leech, eds., *Revisioning Cambridge Platonism: Sources and Legacies* (New York: Springer, 2017); Eric Achermann, "Fromme Irrlehren. Zur Böhme-Rezeption bei More, Newton and Leibniz," in Kühlmann and Vollhardt, eds., *Offenbarung und Episteme. Zur europäischen Wirkung Jakob Böhmes*, 313–62.

114. On the radical Dutch interest, see Freya Sierhuis, "Transnational Networks and Radical Religion: Johannes Rothe and the Construction of Prophetic Charisma," in Jan Bloemendal, Nigel Smith, and James Parente Jr., eds., *Transnational Exchange in the Early Modern Low Countries*, special issue of *Renaissance Studies* 36, no. 1 (2022).

115. Smith, *Perfection Proclaimed*, 192.

116. John Ellistone, preface to Jacob Boehme, *The epistles of Jacob Behmen aliter, Teutonicus philosophus* (London: Gyles Calvert, 1649), A2v.

117. J. P. (John Perrot), *Battering rams against Rome* (London: Robert Wilson, 1661), 11–12; the bracketed interpolations are mine. Nigel Smith, *Perfection Proclaimed*, 109.

Chapter 3

1. Denys Turner, *The Darkness of God: Negativity in Christian Mysticism* (Cambridge: Cambridge University Press, 1995), 1, 24–25; Pseudo-Dionysius, *Mystical Theology*, in *Pseudo-Dionysius: The Complete Works*, trans. Colm Luibheid (Mahwah, NJ: Paulist Press, 1987), 1033B, p. 139.

2. Thomas Browne, *Religio Medici*, 1.13. I cite from *21st Century Oxford Authors: Thomas Browne*, ed. Kevin Killeen (New York: Oxford University Press, 2014), 15.

3. Exodus 33.20–23, concluding "I will put thee in a clift of the rock and will cover thee with my hand while I pass by, and I will take away mine hand, and thou shalt see my back parts: but my face shall not be seen." See Gregory of Nyssa, *The Life of Moses*, trans. Everett Ferguson and Abraham Malherbe (Mahwah, NJ: Paulist Press, 1978), §152–68. A thorough early modern digest of patristic and scholastic views on these verses in the 55 Questions raised by Andrew Willet, *Hexapla in Genesin & Exodum* (London: John Haviland, 1633), 639–65; Ovid, *Metamorphoses* 3.273–315.

4. Claire Preston, *Thomas Browne and the Writing of Early Modern Science* (Cambridge: Cambridge University Press, 2009), 175–210. On the careful Platonic disorder, see, in particular, Kathryn Murphy, "'A Likely Story': Plato's *Timaeus* in *The Garden of Cyrus*," in Reid Barbour and Claire Preston, eds., *Sir Thomas*

Browne: The World Proposed (New York: Oxford University Press, 2008), 242–57; Mary E. Zimmer, "Seeking to Become All Things: The Neoplatonic Soul and the Next World in Sir Thomas Browne's *The Garden of Cyrus*," *Modern Language Review* 112, no. 1 (2017): 35–53. Also, Thomas C. Singer, "Sir Thomas Browne's 'Emphaticall Decussation, or Fundamentall Figure': Geometrical Hieroglyphs and *The Garden of Cyrus*," *English Literary Renaissance* 17 (1987): 85–102; and Janet E. Halley, "Sir Thomas Browne's 'The Garden of Cyrus' and the Real Character," *English Literary Renaissance* 15 (1985): 100–121.

5. Browne, *The Garden of Cyrus*, in *21st Century Oxford Authors: Thomas Browne*, 591; throughout this chapter I cite from this edition, with page numbers given parenthetically in the text.

6. Preston, *Thomas Browne and the Writing of Early Modern Science*, 203–4, 208, notes the litotical rhythm of *The Garden of Cyrus*, its characteristically negative professions of what it is not, in endlessly paraliptical profusion ("we shall decline," "to omit," and "we shall not insist"). See also Verena Olejniczak Lobsien, *Transparency and Dissimulation: Configurations of Neoplatonism in Early Modern English Literature* (Berlin: De Gruyter, 2010), 124–39, on paralipsis deployed to Platonic ends.

7. Browne, *Pseudodoxia Epidemica*, "To the Reader," in *Thomas Browne*, ed. Killeen, 88. On *Pseudodoxia*, see Kevin Killeen, *Biblical Scholarship, Science and Politics in Early Modern Culture: Thomas Browne and The Thorny Place of Knowledge* (Farnham, Surrey, UK: Ashgate, 2009).

8. "Remotion" noted by, for example, Ralph Cudworth, *The true intellectual system of the universe* (London, 1678), 656; and Edward Polhill, *Christus in corde* (1680), 24.

9. Noam Reisner, *Milton and the Ineffable* (New York: Oxford University Press, 2009), 54–104 (at 99, 124), on post-Reformation negotiations of the ineffable; the fullest attention to post-Reformation ideas of the divine is Richard Muller, *Post-Reformation Reformed Dogmatics: The Rise and Development of Reformed Orthodoxy*, 4 vols. (Ada, MI: Baker Academic, 2003), vol. 3, *The Divine Essence and Attributes*. See also Bernard McGinn, "*Vere tu es Deus absonditus*: The Hidden God in Luther and Some Mystics," in Oliver Davies and Denys Turner, eds., *Silence and the Word: Negative Theology and Incarnation* (Cambridge: Cambridge University Press, 2008).

10. Thomas Jackson, *Treatise of the divine essence and attributes* (London: John Clarke, 1628); William Twisse, *A Discovery of D. Jacksons Vanitie* (Amsterdam: Giles Thorp, 1631).

11. Jackson, *Treatise of the divine essence and attributes*, chap. 1, pp. 3–4. The treatise is itself part of a more extensive commentary project on the Apostles' Creed, the final parts of which appeared posthumously (c. 1613–57). This is Thomas Jackson of Newcastle, later dean of Peterborough, not to be confused with Thomas Jackson of Canterbury.

12. Jackson, *Treatise*, 4.

13. Jackson, *Treatise*, 4.

14. Jackson, *Treatise*, 27. As he goes on, he suggests that "things sensible, or by imagination numerable, are but so many severall representations of his incomprehensible being, who is one."

15. Barbour, *Sir Thomas Browne: A Life* (New York: Oxford University Press, 2013), 83–88.

16. "*Deus est sphaera, cujus Centrum est ubique, cujus peripheria nusquam*" (55), occasioning a lengthy discussion of its paradox and metaphorical probity. See William Twisse, *A Discovery of D. Jacksons Vanitie* (1631), 124–25; in *Religio Medici* (1643), 1.10; and in *Pseudodoxia Epidemica* (1646), 1.2. See also *Mercurii Trismegisti Pimander, de potestate et sapientia Dei* (Basil, 1532), 12.14, p. 97; *Liber XXIV philosophorum*, in Georg Graf von Hertling, ed., *Abhandlungen aus dem Gebiete der Philosophie und ihrer Geschichte* (Freiberg, 1913), 31, aph. 2. My thanks to Reid Barbour for suggestions about connections between Browne and Jackson and to Katie Murphy, who pointed to the republication of Jackson's and other broadly Arminian works by Barnabas Oley in the 1650s, in which context we might see the *Garden of Cyrus*. The political implications of the work are explored in Anne Cotterill, *Digressive Voices in Early Modern English Literature* (New York: Oxford University Press, 2004), 126–64.

17. *Corpus Hermeticum ('Poimandres')*, trans. Brian Copenhaver, *Hermetica: The Greek Corpus Hermeticum and the Latin Asclepius* (Cambridge: Cambridge University Press, 1992), I.31, p. 7; see also, within Copenhaver's edition, *Poimandres* V.9–11, p. 20, and *Asclepius*, 20, pp. 78–79. See William Franke, *On What Cannot Be Said: Apophatic Discourses in Philosophy, Religion, Literature and the Arts*, 2 vols. (Notre Dame, IN: University of Notre Dame Press, 2007). Key points of reference are Clement, *Stromata*, trans. William Wilson (London, 1869), 2:267–70, bk. 5.7, pp. 78–82; Gregory of Nyssa's *The Abyss of Knowledge*, on Ecclesiastes, in Jean Daniélou, ed., *From Glory to Glory; Texts from Gregory of Nyssa's Mystical Writings* (New York: Scribner, 1961), 122–29; and Moses Maimonides, *Guide of the Perplexed*, ed. Shlomo Pines, 2 vols. (Chicago: University of Chicago Press, 1963), 1: chaps. 52–53, 56–58, on the impossibility of predicating attributes to God.

18. Pseudo-Dionysius, *The Divine Names*, in *Pseudo-Dionysius: The Complete Works*, trans. Luibheid, 51–56 (589D, 592D, 597A). See also Marsilio Ficino, *On Dionysius the Areopagite*, trans. Michael J. B. Allen, 2 vols. (Cambridge, MA: Harvard University Press, 2015), XII, XX, and XXX.

19. Translation from Luibheid, *Pseudo-Dionysius: The Complete Works*, 636B–C; in Ficino, ed. Allen, XXXII, "Que in Trinitate communia sint, que propria . . . omnes semper denominationes Deo dignas non divisim per partes, sed in tota, perfecta, integra, plena deitate a sanctis eloquiis celebrari, ipsasque omnes individue, absolute, preter omnem discriminis observantiam, integra videlicet ratione, universe integritati perfecte totiusque deitatis attribui."

20. Luibheid, *Pseudo-Dionysius*, 641B, 644A, Allen XL.4, "quemadmodum lumina lampadum, ut sensibilibus propriisque utamur exemplis, in domo una cum

sint et tota in totis mutuo sunt et sincera interim enactaque a se invicem discretione propria secernuntur, discretione quidem coniuncta et vicissim unione inter se discreta." Dionysius was known in early modernity via Ficino's translation and commentary, but also appeared in several other editions, including, in Browne's sales catalogue, *S. Dionysii Areopag. Opera omnia*, 2 vol. (1644), with notes by Balthasar Cordier.

21. Hugh of St. Victor, *Commentariorum in Hierarchiam coelestem Sancti Dionysii Areopagitae*, ed. J.-P. Migne, Patrologia Latina 175 (Paris, 1854); Robert Grosseteste, *Mystical Theology: The Glosses by Thomas Gallus and the Commentary of Robert Grosseteste on "De Mystica Theologia,"* ed. J. McEvoy (Leuven: Peeters, 2003); Albert the Great, *Super Dionysium de divinis nominibus*, ed. P. Simon, in *Opera omnia*, vol. 37, part 1 (Münster: Aschendorff, 1972); Thomas Aquinas, *In librum beati Dionysii De divinis nominibus,* ed. C. Pera (Turin: Marietti, 1950). John Colet, *On the Ecclesiastical Hierarchy of Dionysius: A New Edition and Translation with Introduction and Notes*, ed. Daniel J. Nodes and Daniel Lochman (Leiden: Brill, 2014); and see Feisal G. Mohamed, *In the Anteroom of Divinity: The Reformation of the Angels from Colet to Milton* (Toronto: University of Toronto Press, 2008), 15–32.

22. Johannes Scotus Eriugena, *Periphyseon* (The Division of Nature), trans. I. P. Sheldon-Williams, rev. John J. O'Maera (Montreal: Bellarmin, 1968, rev. 1987), pp. 45–51, 456d–462d, on predicating qualities of God; Scotus, a ninth-century Irish mystic, was the translator of and conduit for Dionysius. He deploys in his version the idea of God's containing a union of all opposites, a paradox-absorbing black hole of the unthinkable. See Dierdre Carabine, *The Unknown God: Negative Theology in the Platonic Tradition: Plato to Eriugena* (Leuven: Peeters, 1995), 301–23; Thomas Carlson, *Indiscretion: Finitude and the Naming of God* (Chicago: University of Chicago Press, 1999), 154–89. Similarly on existence as something that we cannot attribute to God in the way we might to humans, see Maimonides, *Guide of the Perplexed,* ed. Shlomo Pines, 2 vols. (Chicago: University of Chicago Press, 1963) vol. 1, chap. 56, pp. 130–31.

23. Meister Eckhart, *Essential Sermons, Commentaries, Treatises and Defense,* trans. Edmund Colledge and Bernard McGinn (Mahwah, NJ: Paulist Press, 1981), 188, 203. Eckhart, though he seems not to have courted confrontation, was condemned as a heretic, but died before the issue could go further.

24. Angelus Silesius, *The Cherubinic Wanderer*, ed. Maria Shrady (Mahwah, NJ: Paulist Press, 1986), 1.202, 1.197, 1.256, 1.278. The aphoristic poems were first published in 1657 as *Heilige Seelenlust* and a collection *Geistreiche Sinn- und-Schlussreime zur göttlichen Beschaulichkeit*, collected then, in the second edition of 1674, which gave it the name it has become known by, *Cherubinischer Wandersmann.*

25. Silesius's other life, as a grappling and somewhat crabby, convert Catholic polemicist, has tended to disappoint his admirers, but the crabby and the mystical are hardly exclusive of each other.

26. Nicholas of Cusa, *De Deo Abscondito* (1444), *Dialogue on the Hidden God*, in Jasper Hopkins, *Complete Philosophical and Theological Treaties of Nicholas of Cusa*, 2 vols. (Minneapolis: Arthur J. Banning Press, 2001).

27. Franke, *On What Cannot Be Said*, 1:340; Nicholas of Cusa, *On Learned Ignorance: A Translation and an Appraisal of De Docta Ignorantia*, ed. Jasper Hopkins (Minneapolis: Arthur J. Banning Press, 1985), 1.13–14, pp. 35–39; see also F. Edward Cranz, Thomas M. Izbicki, and Gerald Christianson, eds., *Nicholas of Cusa and the Renaissance* (Farnham, Surrey, UK: Ashgate, 2000).

28. Sanches, *That Nothing is Known (Quod Nihil Scitur)*, ed. Elaine Limbrick, trans. Douglas Thomson (Cambridge: Cambridge University Press, 1988). Seventeenth-century deployments of Sanches as shorthand for skepticism include, for example, Richard Baxter, *Fair-warning, or, XXV reasons against toleration* (London: S.U.N.T.F.S, 1663), 22: "And then we must not only subscribe to Fransc. Sanchez, Quod nihil scitur, but also say that Nihil certo creditur."

29. William Franke, *A Philosophy of the Unsayable* (Notre Dame, IN: University of Notre Dame Press, 2014), 14. A good deal of modern philosophical-theological attention has been devoted to the lineage of Dionysius, Gregory of Nyssa, and Cusa in the apophatic; see Catherine Keller, *Cloud of the Impossible: Negative Theology and Planetary Entanglement* (New York: Columbia University Press, 2015), 50–126.

30. See Turner, *Darkness*, 4.

31. Jackson, *Treatise*, 4.

32. As noted in the introduction, the terms "apophatic" and "apophasis" in the seventeenth century seem not to have taken on quite the theological connotations they later do but are rather treated as a rhetorical trope, related to or synonymous with *paralipsis*, the trope in which one professes not to mention a topic, but in doing so emphasizes it. See Hanserd Knollys, *Rhetoricae adumbratio opera & studio* (London, 1663), 5; Richard Lloyd, *The Latine grammar* (London: Thomas Roycroft, 1653), 11; John Newton, *The English academy, or, A brief introduction to the seven liberal arts* (London: W. Godbid, 1677), 163; and Robert Day, *Free thoughts in defence of a future state . . . a refutation of the reviv'd Hylozoicism of Democritus and Leucippus* (London: Dan Brown, 1700), 91, who summarizes "Apophasis, which promises not to mention those things which are most industriously mention'd and offer'd to the Hearers consideration."

33. Edward Evans, *Verba dierum, or, The dayes report of Gods glory* (London: Robert Bulmer, 1615), 87–89. Jackson's *A treatise containing the originall of unbeliefe* (London: John Clarke, 1625), 94–95, writes of the "vertuall similitude which our soules have with all things" by virtue of being "wooven by the finger of God in its essentiall constitution" as a multivalent residual image of God. See similarly, on the idea of God's similitude to everything, Thomas Morton of Berwick, *A treatise of the nature of God* (London: Ralph Jackson, 1599), 205, in an extensive discussion on the attributes of God; and Robert Fludd, *Philosophia Moysaica* (Goudae: Petrus Rammazenius, 1638), fols. 67–71; trans. *Mosaicall philosophy grounded upon the essentiall truth, or eternal sapience* (London: Humphrey Moseley, 1659), 129–38.

34. Nathanael Culverwel, *Spiritual Opticks*, in *An elegant and learned discourse of the light of nature, with several other treatises* (London: John Rothwell, 1652), preface, p. 181.

35. Nathanael Fairfax, *A treatise of the bulk and selvedge of the world* (London: Robert Boulter, 1674), 12, 19. On Browne's relationship to the younger Fairfax, both Norfolk physicians in East Anglia, see Barbour, *Browne*, 389–90.

36. Fairfax, *Bulk and selvedge*, 1, 12, 14–16.

37. Emily Thomas, *Absolute Time: Rifts in Early Modern British Metaphysics* (New York: Oxford University Press, 2018), 99–100 on Fairfax. See too Claire Preston, "Utopian Intelligences: Scientific Correspondence and Christian Virtuosos," in Anne Dunon-Page and Clotilde Prunier, eds., *Debating the Faith: Religion and Letter Writing in Great Britain, 1550–1800* (New York: Springer, 2013), 139–57; Steven Connor, "Bodily Wayfare: Nathaniel Fairfax on Matter and Limit," http://stevenconnor.com/bodilywayfare.html.

38. *Advancement of Learning*, ed. Michael Kiernan (Oxford: Clarendon Press, 2000), 31, 56, 124; *Novum Organum*, ed. Graham Rees and Maria Wakely (Oxford: Clarendon Press, 2004), p. 139, Aph. 1.86. See Stephen Clucas, "'A Knowledge Broken': Francis Bacon's Aphoristic Style and the Crisis of Scholastic and Humanist Knowledge Systems," in Neil Rhodes, ed., *English Renaissance Prose: History, Language, and Politics* (Albany: SUNY Press, 1997), 152–53.

39. *Garden of Cyrus*, 569–70.

40. See Scott Mandelbrote, "Early Modern Natural Theologies," in Russell Re Manning, ed., *The Oxford Handbook of Natural Theology* (New York: Oxford University Press, 2013), 75–99.

41. Early modern attention to "wonder," as a prompt to Renaissance scientific thought, is explored impressively in Katharine Park and Lorraine Daston, *Wonders and the Order of Nature: 1150–1750* (New York: Zone Books, 1998); Mary Baine Campbell, *Wonder and Science: Imagining Worlds in Early Modern Europe* (Ithaca: Cornell University Press, 2004).

42. The profusion of invented words in *Cyrus*, perched between "Joycean verbal fancy" and technical, scientific precision is explored in Claire Preston, "'Meer Nomenclature' and the Description of Order in the *Garden of Cyrus*," *Renaissance Studies* 28 (2014): 299.

43. The text references fleetingly Xenophon's *Oeconomicus*, Plutarch's *Artaxerxes*, and Varro's *De Re Rustica*, along with more recent sources in Benedict Curtius's *Hortorum libri triginta* (Lyon, 1560) and Giambiattista della Porta's *Villae* (Frankfurt, 1592).

44. Johnson, "Life of Browne," published with Browne, *Christian Morals*, 2nd ed. (1756), xxv.

45. Preston, *Browne and the Writing of Early Modern Science*, 207; Browne, *Cyrus*, 567–83. See too Benjamin P. Lomas, "'That Universall and Publik Manuscript': The Book of Nature and *The Garden of Cyrus*," *Journal of Literature and Science* 11, no. 1 (2018): 20–32. On Browne's extensive interest in seminal principles

in natural philosophy, see my *Thomas Browne and the Thorny Place of Knowledge*, 120–36.

46. Christopher D'Addario, "Raining Mice and Russian Leather: The Production of Knowledge in the Early Royal Society and Thomas Browne's *The Garden of Cyrus*," *English Literary History* 84, no. 1 (2017): 1–32 (at 24).

47. Jacques Gaffarel, *Unheard-of Curiosities* (London: Humphrey Moseley, 1650), 352–53, 257; Browne and Gaffarel are noted together by John Edwards, *A demonstration of the existence and providence of God, from the contemplation of the visible structure of the greater and the lesser world* (London: Jonathan Robinson, 1696), 68, which takes *The Garden of Cyrus* as the quintessential work of physico-theology, with Browne as "Great Man, of a very inquisitive Brain."

48. Milton, *Paradise Lost*, 5.479–82.

49. "[T]he first parity and imparity, the active and passive digits, the material and formall principles in generative societies" (595).

50. Plutarch, *The Ei at Delphi*, in *The Philosophie, Commonlie called the Morals*, trans. Philemon Holland (London: Arnold Hatfield, 1603), 1357.

51. Plutarch, *The Ei at Delphi*, 1357.

52. Marsilio Ficino, *On Dionysius the Areopagite*, trans. Michael Allen, 2 vols. (Cambridge, MA: Harvard University Press, 2015), xxv, a notion that is ascribed to Plotinus, *Enneads* 3.5.9, 6.7.35: "Better to be drunk in a drunkenness like this than to be more respectably sober," describing the "orphic manner" of Dionysius's reeling. On the role of the Delphic in early modern thought, see Anthony Ossa-Richardson, *The Devil's Tabernacle: The Pagan Oracles in Early Modern Thought* (Princeton: Princeton University Press, 2013).

53. Plutarch, *The Ei at Delphi*, 1358. This in turn produces a Heraclitan task for the mind in similar flux: "all humane nature being ever in the midst betweene generation and corruption, giveth but an obscure apparence, a darke shadow." (1361)

54. Plutarch, *The Ei at Delphi*, 1361.

55. Philemon Holland is a phenomenon with his brilliant if idiosyncratic translations into English of a vast classical corpus, both Greek and Latin, including Plutarch, *The philosophie, commonlie called, the morals* (1603); Pliny, *The naturall historie* (1601); Livy, *Romane historie* (1600); Suetonius, *The historie of twelve Caesars emperors of Rome* (1606); Xenophon, *Cyrupaedia* (1632); Ammianus Marcellinus, *The Roman historie* (1609), as well as William Camden, *Britain, or A chorographicall description* (1610).

56. Plutarch, *The Ei at Delphi*, 1352.

57. *Hydriotaphia*, in Killeen, ed., *Thomas Browne*, 544.

58. *Hydriotaphia*, 547, the phrase repeated in the posthumously published *Christian Morals*, 785.

Chapter 4
1. On this phrase, from Claude Lévi-Strauss's discussion of animals in *Totemism* (London: Merlin Press, 1964), see Marjorie Garber, *Loaded Words* (New York: Fordham University Press, 2012), 94–103.

2. Robert Boyle, *A Discourse of Things above Reason* (1681), in *Works of Robert Boyle*, ed. Michael Hunter and Edward B. Davis (London: Pickering & Chatto, 2000), 9:361–94 (at 366, 369). See the impressive work of Alexander Wragge-Morley, *Aesthetic Science: Representing Nature in the Royal Society of London, 1650–1720* (Chicago: University of Chicago Press, 2020); Jan W. Wojcik, *Robert Boyle and the Limits of Reason* (Cambridge: Cambridge University Press, 1997), 151–88. An earlier version of Wojcik's chapter appears in Michael Hunter's collection, *Robert Boyle Reconsidered* (Cambridge: Cambridge University Press, 1994), 139–55. Lotte Mulligan, "Robert Boyle, 'Right Reason' and the Meaning of Metaphor," *Journal of the History of Ideas* 55, no. 2 (1994): 235–57.

3. A good deal has been written around this, but a skimpy list would include Gerard Reedy, SJ, *The Bible and Reason: Anglicans and Scripture in Late Seventeenth-Century England* (Philadelphia: University of Pennsylvania Press, 1985); Justin Champion, *The Pillars of Priestcraft Shaken* (Cambridge: Cambridge University Press, 1991); Sarah Mortimer, *Reason and Religion in the English Revolution: The Challenge of Socinianism* (Cambridge: Cambridge University Press, 2010).

4. Boyle, *Discourse of Things above Reason*, 369. On voluntarism, see Francis Oakley, *Omnipotence, Covenant and Order: An Excursion in the History of Ideas from Abelard to Leibniz* (Ithaca: Cornell University Press, 1984); and in the early modern context, Amos Funkenstein, *Theology and the Scientific Imagination* (Princeton: Princeton University Press, 1986), 117–201; Margaret Osler, *Divine Will and the Mechanical Philosophy: Gassendi and Descartes on Contingency and Necessity in the Created World* (Cambridge: Cambridge University Press, 1994); Peter Harrison, "Voluntarism and Early Modern Science," *History of Science* 40 (2002): 63–89; John Henry, "Voluntarist Theology at the Origins of Modern Science: A Response to Peter Harrison," *History of Science* 47, no. 1 (2009): 79–113; Francis Oakley, "Voluntarist Theology and Early-Modern Science: The Matter of the Divine Power, Absolute and Ordained," *History of Science* 56 (2018): 72–96.

5. Boyle, *Things above Reason*, 368–69. The latter quotation from the appended "Advices in Judging of Things said to transcend Reason," in *Works*, 9:395–424 (at 398–99).

6. Boyle, *Things above Reason*, 385, 379; compare "Advices in Judging of Things said to transcend Reason," 396–97, elaborating on the criteria for judging this.

7. Boyle, *Of the High Veneration Man's Intellect owes to God* (1684–85), in *Works*, 9:157–200 (at 177), going on to discuss (185) "if the other Worlds or Vortexes . . . be peopled with intelligent, though not visible, inhabitants?"

8. Claire Preston, *The Poetics of Scientific Investigation* (Oxford: Oxford University Press, 2015), 88.

9. Catherine Wilson, *The Invisible World: Early Modern Philosophy and the Invention of the Microscope* (Princeton: Princeton University Press, 1995), 7.

10. Christoph Meinel, "Early Seventeenth-Century Atomism: Theory, Epistemology, and the Insufficiency of Experiment," *Isis* 79, no. 1 (1988): 68–103 (at 81–84); also Catherine Wilson, "Corpuscular Effluvia: Between Imagination and Experiment," in Wolfgang Detel and Claus Zittel, eds., *Wissensideale und Wissenskulturen in der frühen Neuziet / Ideas and Cultures of Knowledge in Early Modern Europe* (Berlin: Akademie Verlag, 2002), 168–69.

11. Robert Boyle, *Experiments and considerations about the porosity of bodies* (London: Sam. Smith, 1684), 9.

12. Boyle, *Porosity of bodies*, 2.

13. Vera Keller, *Knowledge and the Public Interest, 1575–1725* (Cambridge: Cambridge University Press, 2015), 167–98; Michael Hunter, *Boyle Studies: Aspects of the Life and Thought of Robert Boyle (1627–91)* (London: Routledge, 2015), 26–32.

14. Boyle, *Porosity of bodies*, 11.

15. Meinel, *Atomism*, 70–71.

16. Robert Boyle, *History of Fluidity and Firmness*, in *Certain physiological essays and other tracts written at distant times* (London: Henry Herringman, 1669), 189–90.

17. Useful background material here includes: Antonio Clericuzio, *Elements, Principles and Corpuscles: A Study of Atomism and Chemistry in the Seventeenth Century* (New York: Springer, 2001), 103–48; Lawrence Principe, *The Aspiring Adept: Robert Boyle and His Alchemical Quest* (Princeton: Princeton University Press, 2000), 63–90; Wojcik, *Robert Boyle and the Limits of Reason*, 151–88; Peter Anstey, *The Philosophy of Robert Boyle* (London: Routledge, 2011).

18. Boyle, *Fluidity and Firmness*, 164.

19. Boyle, *Fluidity and Firmness*, 184–89.

20. Boyle, *Fluidity and Firmness*, 165, 189, 210.

21. Max Weber, *Wissenschaft als Beruf* (Tübingen: Mohr Siebeck, 1917; 1994), 9; Michel Foucault, *The Order of Things* (London: Routledge, 1970).

22. Liz Oakley-Brown, Introduction: "Scrutinizing Surfaces in Early Modern Thought," in special issue of *Journal of the Northern Renaissance* (2017), online; Bruno Latour, "An Attempt at a 'Compositionist Manifesto,'" *New Literary History* 41 (2010): 471–90; Michel de Certeau, *The Mystic Fable: The Sixteenth and Seventeenth Centuries*, trans. Michael B. Smith (Chicago: University of Chicago Press, 1992).

23. Joseph Amato, *Surfaces: A History* (Berkeley: University of California Press, 2013), 119, 127.

24. Amato, *Surfaces: A History*, 135.

25. Keith Hutchison, "What Happened to Occult Qualities in the Scientific Revolution?" *Isis*, 73, no. 2 (1982): 233–53; John Henry, "Occult Qualities and the Experimental Philosophy: Active Principles in pre-Newtonian Matter Theory," *History of Science* 24 (1986): 335–81.

26. Christiane Frey, "The Art of Observing the Small: On the Borders of the Subvisibilia (from Hooke to Brockes)," *Monatshefte* 105, no. 3 (2013): 376–88 (at 380).

27. Peter Harrison, *The Fall of Man and the Foundations of Science* (Cambridge: Cambridge University Press, 2009).

28. Paul K. Feyerabend, *Realism, Rationalism, and Scientific Method* (Cambridge: Cambridge University Press, 1985), 1:17–36; Thomas Kuhn, *The Structure of Scientific Revolutions* (Chicago: University of Chicago Press, 1962; 1996), 111–15. See too Lorraine Daston and Elizabeth Lunbeck, Introduction, in Daston and Lunbeck, eds., *Histories of Scientific Observation* (Chicago: University of Chicago Press, 2011), 1–3.

29. Ofer Gal and Raz Chen-Morris, *Baroque Science* (Chicago: University of Chicago Press, 2013), 4.

30. Walter Charleton, *Physiologia Epicuro-Gassendo-Charltoniana, or, A fabrick of science natural, upon the hypothesis of atoms founded by Epicurus* (London: Thomas Heath, 1654); Jean Fernel, *De abditis rerum causis* (1642), "Atomos veteres jam ridimus"; translated as *On the Hidden Causes of Things,* ed. and trans. John M. Forrester (Leiden: Brill, 2005), 398–99.

31. Henry Power, *Experimental philosophy* (London: John Martin and James Allestry, 1664), 51, 53.

32. Robert Hooke, *Micrographia* (London: Jo. Martin and Ja. Allestry, 1665), 4–5. Hooke's natural philosophy has received a good deal of attention, See, e.g. Francesco G. Sacco, *Real, Mechanical, Experimental: Robert Hooke's Natural Philosophy* (New York: Springer, 2020); Robert D. Purrington, *The First Professional Scientist: Robert Hooke and the Royal Society of London* (New York: Springer, 2009); Michael Cooper and Michael Hunter, eds., *Robert Hooke: Tercentennial Studies* (Farnham, Surrey, UK: Ashgate, 2006).

33. Matthew C. Hunter, *Wicked Intelligence: Visual Art and the Science of Experiment in Restoration London* (Chicago: University of Chicago Press, 2013); Michael Hunter, *Boyle: Between God and Science* (New Haven: Yale University Press, 2010); Lisa Jardine, *Ingenious Pursuits: Building the Scientific Revolution* (New York: Little, Brown, 1999).

34. John Hughes, *Henry Power of Halifax: A Seventeenth-Century Physician and Scientist* (Oxford: Rimes House, 2010).

35. Power, *Experimental philosophy*, sig. C2r.

36. Power, *Experimental philosophy*, sigs. B4v–C1r.

37. Alessandro Palazzo, "Eckhart's Islamic and Jewish Sources," in Jeremiah Hackett, ed., *A Companion to Meister Eckhart* (Leiden: Brill, 2013), 267–71; Michael Fagge and Gwendolen Jackson, "The Godhead beyond God and Proclus's Henads: A Reading of Eckhart's Trinity," *Medieval Mystical Theology* 25, no. 1 (2016): 57–68.

38. Power, *Experimental philosophy*, sig. C3v.

39. Power, *Experimental philosophy*, sig. A4r; Joseph Glanvill, *The vanity of dogmatizing* (1661), 5.

40. Power, *Experimental philosophy*, sigs. C2v–c3r.
41. Power, *Experimental philosophy*, 58; regarding Browne, *Pseudodoxia Epidemica*, 2.2, in *21st Century Oxford Authors: Sir Thomas Browne*, ed. Kevin Killeen (Oxford: Oxford University Press, 2014), 168.
42. Christoph Lüthy, "Atomism, Lynceus, and the Fate of Seventeenth-Century Microscopy," *Early Science and Medicine* 1, no. 1 (1996): 1–27, on the optical limits and lack of trust in the technology. See too Marian Fournier, *The Fabric of Life: Microscopy in the Seventeenth Century* (Baltimore: Johns Hopkins University Press, 1996); Edward Ruestow, *The Microscope in the Dutch Republic* (Cambridge: Cambridge University Press, 1996).
43. Boyle, *Fluidity and Firmness*, 191; Thomas Browne, *Pseudodoxia Epidemica*, in *Browne*, ed. Killeen, 194. See Clare Neanon, "The Matter of Dust in Renaissance Literature," PhD diss., Oxford University, 2020, on the poetic, as well as the scientific understandings of motes and flecks.
44. Boyle, *Fluidity and Firmness*, 203. See Catherine Wilson, *Epicureanism at the Origins of Modernity* (Cambridge: Cambridge University Press, 2008); Meinel, *Atomism*, 1988.
45. Wilson, *Invisible World*, 62.
46. Ralph Cudworth, *The true intellectual system of the universe* (London: Richard Royston: 1678), 98.
47. Steven Connor, *The Book of Skin* (Ithaca: Cornell University Press, 2004), 39.
48. Charleton, *Physiologia Epicuro-Gassendo-Charltoniana*, 100; also Boyle, *Fluidity and Firmness*, 165. See Reid Barbour, *English Epicures and Stoics: Ancient Legacies in Early Stuart Culture* (Amherst: University of Massachusetts Press, 1998); Adam Rzepka, "Discourse *Ex Nihilo*: Epicurus and Lucretius in Sixteenth-Century England," in Brooke Holmes and W. H. Shearin, eds., *Dynamic Reading: Studies in the Reception of Epicureanism* (New York: Oxford University Press, 2012), 113–32. Stephen Clucas, "Poetic Atomism in Seventeenth-Century England: Henry More, Thomas Traherne and 'Scientific Imagination,'" *Renaissance Studies* 5, no. 3 (1991): 327–40.
49. Christoph Lüthy, John E. Murdoch, and William R. Newman, eds., *Late Medieval and Early Modern Corpuscular Matter Theories* (Leiden: Brill, 2001); Andrew Pyle, *Atomism and Its Critics* (Bristol: Thoemmes, 1995); Robert Hugh Kargon, *Atomism in England from Hariot to Newton* (Oxford: Clarendon Press, 1966).
50. Martin Fotherby, *Atheomastix* (London: Nicholas Okes, 1622), 122–23.
51. Thomas Heywood, *Gynaikeion* (London: Adam Islip, 1624), 217; Michel de Montaigne, *Essays*, trans. Florio (London: Edward Blount and William Barret, 1613), 191; Anon., *Another collection of philosophical conferences of the French virtuosi* (London: Thomas Dring and John Starkey, 1665), 451.
52. Ada Palmer, *Reading Lucretius in the Renaissance* (Cambridge, MA: Harvard University Press, 2014); Stuart Gillespie, "Lucretius in the English Renais-

sance," in Stuart Gillespie and Philip Hardie, eds., *The Cambridge Companion to Lucretius* (Cambridge: Cambridge University Press, 2007), 242–53; Alison Brown, *Return of Lucretius to Renaissance Florence* (Cambridge, MA: Harvard University Press, 2010).

53. John Edwards, *A demonstration of the existence and providence of God* (London: Jonathan Robinson, 1696), 119; James Wright, *Country conversation* (London: Henry Bonwicke, 1694), 4–5.

54. The two scenes in Lucretius, from 2.309–33., citing from Lucretius, *De Rerum Natura*, in *The Works of Lucy Hutchinson, vol. 1: Translation of Lucretius*, ed. Reid Barbour and David Norbrook (New York: Oxford University Press, 2012). The standard Latin, from the Loeb edition of W. H. Rouse, rev. Martin Smith, *On the Nature of Things* (Cambridge, MA: Harvard University Press, 1992), is ". . . Omnia cum rerum primordia sint in motu, summa tamen summa videatur stare quiete . . ." (2.309–10); "nam saepe in colli tondentes pabula laeta / lanigerae reptant pecudes quo quamque vocantes / invitant herbae gemmantes rore recenti, /et satiati agni ludunt blandeque coruscant" (2.317–20); "praeterea magnae legiones cum loca cursu / camporus complent, belli simulacra cientes . . . et tamen est quidam locus altis montibus unde / stare videntur et in campis consistere fulgor" (2.323–32). R. E. Latham's translation, *On the Nature of the Universe* (Harmondsworth, UK: Penguin, 1951), remains an engaging version.

55. Lucretius, trans. Hutchinson, Bk. 2, 115–22, 553–57, 263–68, 345–47.

56. Lucy Hutchinson, *Order and Disorder*, ed. David Norbrook (Oxford: Blackwell, 2001), preface, p. 1. On the links between the two works, see Cassandra Gorman, "Lucy Hutchinson, Lucretius and Soteriological Materialism," *Seventeenth Century* 28, no. 3 (2013): 293–309; Reid Barbour, "Between Atoms and the Spirit : Lucy Hutchinson's Translation of *Lucretius*," in Mihoko Suzuki, ed., *Anne Clifford and Lucy Hutchinson, Ashgate Critical Essays on Women Writers in England, 1550–1700* (Farnham, Surrey, UK: Ashgate, 2009), 333–48; Hugh de Quehen, "Ease and Flow in Lucy Hutchinson's Lucretius," *Studies in Philology* 93, no. 3 (1996): 288–303.

57. John Evelyn, *An essay on the first book of T. Lucretius Carus De rerum natura. Interpreted and made English verse* (London: Gabriel Bedle and Thomas Collins 1656), 127.

58. Gerard Passannante, *The Lucretian Renaissance* (Chicago: University of Chicago Press, 2011), 76–82; W. H. Shearin, *The Language of Atoms: Performativity and Politics in Lucretius' De Rerum Natura* (Oxford: Oxford University Press, 2015).

59. Lucretius, trans. Thomas Creech, *T. Lucretius Carus the Epicurean philospher his six books De natura rerum done into English verse, with notes* (Oxford: L. Lichfield 1682), separate pagination, 39, 22, 17–18.

60. Boyle, *Fluidity and Firmness*, 161–62. The "he" here, means the author himself.

61. Boyle, *Fluidity and Firmness*, 165, 235.

62. Lucretius, *De Rerum Natura* 2.434.

63. Boyle, *Fluidity and Firmness*, 235, quoting Lucretius, *De Rerum Natura* 2.444–49.

64. Michel Serres, *The Birth of Physics*, trans. Jack Hawkes (Manchester, UK: Clinamen Press, 2000), 107, 104–5.

65. Charleton, *Physiologia Epicuro-Gassendo-Charltoniana*, 248.

66. Charleton, *Physiologia Epicuro-Gassendo-Charltoniana*, 249. See Emily Booth, *A Subtle and Mysterious Machine: The Medical World of Walter Charleton (1619–1707)* (Dordrecht: Springer, 2006).

67. Walter Charleton, *The darknes of atheism dispelled by the light of nature: a physico-theologicall treatise* (London: William Lee, 1652), 41–42.

68. Charleton, *The darknes of atheism*, 46.

69. Charleton, *The darknes of atheism*, 198–99.

70. Henry More, *Divine Dialogues* (London: Henry Playford, 1668), 182, 185. Similarly commenting on his poetic brilliance, but moral degradation, see, e.g., Meric Casaubon, *A discourse concerning Christ his incarnation* (London: R. Mynne, 1646), 9–10; Nathanael Culverwel, *An elegant and learned discourse of the light of nature* (London: Tho. Roycroft for John Rothwell, 1652), 196.

71. William Ramesey, *Helminthologia, or, Some physical considerations of the matter, origination, and several species of wormes macerating and direfully cruciating every part of the bodies of mankind* (London: George Sawbridge, 1668).

72. Gideon Harvey, *The conclave of physicians in two parts, detecting their intrigues, frauds, and plots, against their patients, and their destroying the faculty of physick* (London, 1686), 25.

73. See, in particular, Cassandra Gorman, *The Atom in Seventeenth Century Poetry* (Rochester, NY: D. S. Brewer, 2021), 117–174; and Jesse Hock, *The Erotics of Materialism: Lucretius and Early Modern Poetics* (Philadelphia: University of Pennsylvania Press, 2021), 145–70. Useful, too, is the introduction by Brandie R. Siegfried to her edition of Margaret Cavendish, *Poems and Fancies with The Animal Parliament* (Tempe: Arizona Center for Medieval & Renaissance Studies, 2018).

74. Margaret Cavendish, *Observations upon Experimental Philosophy* (London: A. Maxwell, 1666), 7.

75. Cavendish, *Observations*, 10–11.

76. Deborah Boyle, *The Well-Ordered Universe: The Philosophy of Margaret Cavendish* (Oxford: Oxford University Press, 2018); David Cunning, *Cavendish* (London: Routledge, 2016); Emily Thomas, ed., *Early Modern Women on Metaphysics* (Cambridge: Cambridge University Press, 2018). See too Stephen Clucas, "Variation, Irregularity and Probabilism: Margaret Cavendish and Natural Philosophy as Rhetoric," in Clucas, ed., *A Princely Brave Woman: Essays on Margaret Cavendish, Duchess of Newcastle* (Farnham, Surrey, UK: Ashgate, 2003); and Stephen Clucas, "The Atomism of the Cavendish Circle: A Reappraisal," *Seventeenth Century* 9 (1994): 247–73; Jacqueline Broad, *Women Philosophers of the Seventeenth Century* (Cambridge: Cambridge University Press, 2002); Lisa T. Sarasohn,

The Natural Philosophy of Margaret Cavendish: Reason and Fancy during the Scientific Revolutions (Baltimore: Johns Hopkins University Press, 2010), 149–72; Sara H. Mendelson, ed., *Ashgate Critical Essays on Women Writers in England, 1550–1700*, vol. 7, *Margaret Cavendish* (Farnham, Surrey, UK: Ashgate, 2009); Line Cottegnies and Nancy Weitz, eds., *Authorial Conquests: Essays on Genre in the Writings of Margaret Cavendish*. (Vancouver, BC: Fairleigh Dickinson University Press, 2003). Anna Battigelli, *Margaret Cavendish and the Exiles of the Mind*, (Lexington: University of Kentucky Press, 1998); Aït-Touati, *Fictions of the Cosmos*, 174–90, on Cavendish.

77. Cavendish, *The Description of a New World, Called The Blazing World*, 28–33, appended to *Observations upon experimental philosophy* (1666), separate pagination. See Ian Lawson, "Bears in Eden, or, This Is Not the Garden You're Looking For: Margaret Cavendish, Robert Hooke and the Limits of Natural Philosophy," *British Journal for the History of Science* 48, no. 4 (December 2015): 583–605.

78. Cavendish, *Observations*, 135–36; compare 69: "that Nature is a perpetually self-moving body, dividing, composing, changing, forming and transforming her parts by self-corporeal figurative motions."

79. Cavendish, *Observations*, 191. Karen Detlefsen, "Reason and Freedom: Margaret Cavendish on the Order and Disorder of Nature," *Archiv für Geschichte der Philosophie* 89 (2007): 157–91 (at 163–64).

80. See, on this remarkable idea, Susan James, "The Philosophical Innovations of Margaret Cavendish," *British Journal for the History of Philosophy* 7, no. 2 (1999): 219–44 (at 222–25); Eileen O'Neill, "Introduction," in Margaret Cavendish, *Observations upon Experimental Philosophy*, ed. O'Neill (Cambridge: Cambridge University Press, 2001) xxix–xxxiii.

81. Cavendish, *Observations*, 196.

82. See Stephen Clucas, "'A double perception in all creatures': Margaret Cavendish's Philosophical Letters and Seventeenth-Century Natural Philosophy,' in Brandie R. Siegfried and Lisa T. Sarasohn, eds., *God and Nature in the Thought of Margaret Cavendish* (Farnham, Surrey, UK: Ashgate, 2014).

83. Boyle, *Well-Ordered Universe*, 90.

84. Cavendish, *Observations*, 197–98.

85. Cavendish, *Observations*, 198. See too, Margaret Cavendish, *Grounds of Natural Philosophy* (London: A. Maxwell, 1668), 48; compare Avrum Stroll, *Surfaces* (Minneapolis: University of Minnesota Press, 1988), 10.

86. Plutarch, *The Ei at Delphi*, in *The Philosophie, Commonlie called the Morals*, trans. Philemon Holland (London: Arnold Hatfield, 1603), 1361.

87. On the ascription of will to matter, see Cunning, *Cavendish*, 210–42; Karen Detlefsen, "Atomism, Monism, and Causation in the Natural Philosophy of Margaret Cavendish," *Oxford Studies in Early Modern Philosophy* 3 (2006): 199–240.

88. Cavendish, *Observations*, 159–60.

89. Kourken Michaelian, "Margaret Cavendish's Epistemology," *British Jour-*

nal for the History of Philosophy 17, no. 1 (2009): 31–53 (at 45–46); Detlefsen, "Reason and Freedom," 166.

90. Cavendish, *Observations*, 159–60.

91. Margaret Cavendish, *Philosophical Letters* (London, 1664), 444–45; see O'Neill, "Introduction," xxix–xxxiii.

92. Cavendish, *Observations*, 160–61.

93. Cavendish, *Observations*, 198.

94. Cavendish, *Observations*, 1, 3, 164.

Chapter 5

1. Anna Trapnel, *The Cry of a Stone* (London, 1654), 67–68 [71–72] Here and throughout, the 1654 text is cited, followed in square brackets by the corresponding page(s) in Hilary Hinds's edition (Tempe, AZ: ACMRS Press, 2000).

2. Ezekiel 4.12, Isaiah 20.3, Hosea 1.2, Isaiah 6.6. The instruction to cook with human dung is commuted to cooking with cow dung.

3. William Greenhill, *An exposition continued upon the XX . . . XXIX, chapters of the prophet Ezekiel* (London: Hanna Allen, 1658), 291, 314. See too Giovanni Diodati, *Pious annotations, upon the Holy Bible* (1643), on Ezekiel 23 (separaate pagination), explaining how this is "[a] figurative description . . . taken from a Whores preparation, when she entertaineth her expected Ruffian" (on 23.40); John Mayer, *A commentary upon the whole Old Testament* (London: Robert and William Laybourn, 1653), 428 (on Ez. 23.25, "*They shall take away thy nose and thine eares,* because they used to do thus to adulteresses, to cut off their noses"). The names are sometimes rendered Oholah and Oholibah.

4. Yvonne Sherwood, *Biblical Blaspheming: Trials of the Sacred for a Secular Age* (Cambridge: Cambridge University Press, 2012), 129–76, "Prophetic Scatology"; Hugh Pyper, *An Unsuitable Book: The Bible as Scandalous Text* (Sheffield, UK: Sheffield Phoenix Press, 2005), 22–23; William Ian Miller, *The Anatomy of Disgust* (Cambridge, MA: Harvard University Press, 1997). See too Yvonne Sherwood, *The Prostitute and the Prophet: Hosea's Marriage in Literary-Theoretical Perspective* (Sheffield, UK: Sheffield Academic Press, 1996).

5. Rowan Williams, *The Edge of Words: God and the Habits of Language* (London: Bloomsbury, 2014), 149.

6. Ezekiel 4.9, where the prophet is commanded to bake "barley cakes, and thou shalt bake it with dung that cometh out of man, in their sight."

7. Henry More, *A modest enquiry into the mystery of iniquity* (London: W. Morden, 1664), 212–13.

8. William Day, *An exposition of the Book of the Prophet Isaiah* (London: Joshua Kirton, 1654), A3r.

9. Thomas Barlow, *The genuine remains of that learned prelate* (London: John Dunton, 1693), 250.

10. Lambert Daneau, *A fruitfull commentarie upon the twelve small prophets* (Cambridge: John Legate, 1594), 23–24.

NOTES TO CHAPTER 5

11. On the fast sermons of the era, Achsah Guibbory, "England's 'Biblical' Prophets, 1642–60," in Roger D. Sell and A. W. Johnson, eds., *Writing and Religion in England, 1558–1689: Studies in Community-Making and Cultural Memory* (Farnham, Surrey, UK: Ashgate, 2009), 305–26; Kevin Killeen, *The Political Bible in Early-Modern England* (Cambridge: Cambridge University Press, 2017), 105–34.

12. See Nicholas Woltersorff, *Divine Discourse: Philosophical Reflections of the Claim That God Speaks* (Cambridge: Cambridge University Press, 1995).

13. Edward Stillingfleet, *Origines Sacrae* (London: Henry Mortlock, 1662), 170. The mock-Merlinic prophecy is something else again, on which see Tim Thornton, *Prophecy, Politics and the People in Early Modern England* (Woodbridge, UK: Boydell & Brewer, 2006); Jonathan Green, *Printing and Prophecy: Prognostication and Media Change 1450–1550* (Ann Arbor: University of Michigan Press, 2011). Sometimes the term covers preaching. On the Delphic oracle, see Anthony Ossa-Richardson, *The Devil's Tabernacle: The Pagan Oracles in Early Modern Thought* (Princeton: Princeton University Press, 2013). See too Emily Jennings, "Prophetic Rhetoric in the Early Stuart Period," PhD diss., Oxford University, 2015, on the suspicion about and strategic uses of prophetic rhetoric.

14. As noted in Harold Bloom, *Ruin the Sacred Truths* (Cambridge, MA: Harvard University Press, 1989), 13–14 on Jeremiah 4.19.

15. John Milton, *Paradise Lost* 4.127–9.

16. Leonard Cohen, "Going Home," on *Old Ideas* (2012).

17. John Oldham, "A Dithyrambick. The Drunkards Speech in a Mask," in *Poems, and translations* (London: Jos. Hindmarsh, 1683), 213; George Fox, *A distinction between the phanatick spirit and the spirit of God and the fruits of each spirit* (London: Robert Wilson, 1660), broadsheet. For a good survey of the parameters of prophecy, see Ariel Hessayon and Lionel Laborie, eds., *Early Modern Prophecies in Transnational, National and Regional Contexts*, 3 vols. (Leiden: Brill, 2020), vol. 3: *The British Isles*.

18. Needham to Protector, 7 February 1654, *Calendar of State Papers, 1600–1700*, vol. 66, http://www.british-history.ac.uk/cal-state-papers/domestic/interregnum/1653-4/pp381-426.

19. A much debated trope of radical rhetoric, deployed quite frequently by those who evidently did have university learning, as noted in Nicolas McDowell, *The English Radical Imagination: Culture, Religion and Revolution, 1630–1660* (Oxford: Clarendon Press, 2003), 89–136, on the Ranter, Abiezer Coppe, and against the idea of an "efflorescence of an autochthonous folk irreligion, welling up from the depths of popular culture" (11), ascribed to Christopher Hill, *The World Turned Upside Down: Radical Ideas during the English Revolution* (Harmondsworth, UK: Penguin, 1972/1991).

20. Hilary Hinds, *God's Englishwomen: Seventeenth Century Radical Sectarian Writing and Feminist Criticism* (Manchester, UK: Manchester University Press, 1996), 1.

21. Teresa Feroli, *Political Speaking Justified: Women Prophets and the English*

Revolution (Newark: University of Delaware Press, 2006), 29. On Eleanor Davies, see Diane Watt, *Secretaries of God: Women Prophets in Late Medieval and Early Modern England* (Woodbridge, Suffolk, UK: Boydell and Brewer, 2001), 118–54; Esther S. Cope, *Handmaid of the Holy Spirit: Dame Eleanor Davies, Never Soe Mad a Ladie* (Ann Arbor: University of Michigan Press, 1993).

22. Phyllis Mack, *Visionary Women: Ecstatic Prophecy in Seventeenth-Century England* (Berkeley: University of California Press, 1994), 119.

23. See, for example, Kate Chedgzoy, "Female Prophecy in the Seventeenth Century: The Case of Anna Trapnel," in William Zunder and Suzanne Trill, eds., *Writing and the English Renaissance* (London: Longman, 1996), 238–54; Naomi Baker, "'Break Down the Walls of Flesh': Anna Trapnel, John James and Fifth Monarchist Self-Representation," in Sylvia Brown, ed., *Women, Gender, and Radical Religion in Early Modern Europe* (Leiden: Brill, 2007), 117–37, along with other essays in the volume.

24. Susan Wiseman, "Unsilent Instruments and the Devil's Cushions: Authority in Seventeenth-Century Women's Prophetic Discourse," in Isobel Armstrong, ed., *New Feminist Discourses* (London: Routledge, 1992), 176–96; Diane Purkiss, "Producing the Voice, Consuming the Body: Women Prophets of the Seventeenth Century," in Isobel Grundy and Susan Wiseman, eds., *Women, Writing, History 1640–1740* (Athens: University of Georgia Press, 1992), 141.

25. James Holstun, *Ehud's Dagger: Class Struggle in the English Revolution* (London: Verso, 2000), 257–304 (at 267, 282); see too the political readings of Catie Gill, "'All the Monarchies of This World Are Going Down the Hill': The Antimonarchism of Anna Trapnel's *The Cry of a Stone* (1654)," *Prose Studies* 29, no. 1 (2007): 19–35; Maria Magro, "Spiritual Autobiography and Radical Sectarian Women's Discourse: Anna Trapnel and the Bad Girls of the English Revolution," *Journal of Medieval and Early Modern Studies* 34, no. 2 (2004): 405–37.

26. Katharine Gillespie, *Domesticity and Dissent in the Seventeenth Century: English Women Writers and the Public Sphere* (Cambridge: Cambridge University Press, 2004), 62–114; David Loewenstein, *Representing Revolution in Milton and His Contemporaries: Religion, Politics, and Polemics in Radical Puritanism* (Cambridge: Cambridge University Press, 2001), 92–124; Erica Longfellow, *Women and Religious Writing in Early Modern England* (Cambridge: Cambridge University Press, 2009), 149–79; Marcus Nevitt, 'Blessed, Self-Denying, Lambe-like'? The Fifth Monarchist Women," *Critical Survey* 11, no. 1 (1999): 83–97.

27. Rachel Adcock, *Baptist Women's Writings in Revolutionary Culture, 1640–1680* (Farnham, Surrey, UK: Ashgate, 2015); Carme Font, *Women's Prophetic Writings in Seventeenth-Century Britain* (London: Routledge, 2017), 114–38; W. Scott Howard, "Prophecy, Power and Religious Dissent," in Patricia Phillippy, *A History of Early Modern Women's Writing* (Cambridge: Cambridge University Press, 2018); Alexis Butzner, "'Taken Weak in My Outward Man': The Paradox of the Pathologized Female Prophet," *Early Modern Women* 13, no. 1 (2018): 30–57.

28. Ramona Wray, "'What Say You to [This] Book? [. . .] Is It Yours?': Oral and Collaborative Narrative Trajectories in the Mediated Writings of Anna Trapnel,"

Women's Writing 16, no. 3 (2009): 408–24. On Trapnel's life-writing, see Rebecca Bullard, "Textual Disruption in Anna Trapnel's *Report and Plea* (1654)," *Seventeenth Century* 23, no. 1 (2008): 34–53; Susannah B. Mintz, "The Specular Self of Anna Trapnel's *Report and Plea*," *Pacific Coast Philology* 25 (2000): 1–16; Laura Williamson Ambrose, "Moved by God: Mobility and Agency in Anna Trapnel's *Report and Plea*," *Renaissance Studies* 33, no. 4 (2019): 609–23.

29. See Claire McGann, "'To Print Her Discourses & Hymmes': The Typographic Features of Anna Trapnel's Prophecies," *Seventeenth Century* 36, no. 2 (2021): 233–52.

30. Jane Baston, "History, Prophecy, and Interpretation: Mary Cary and Fifth Monarchism," *Prose studies* 21, no. 3 (1998): 1–18; David Loewenstein, "Scriptural Exegesis, Female Prophecy, and Radical Politics in Mary Cary," *SEL Studies in English Literature 1500–1900* 46, no. 1 (2006): 133–53. On Poole, see, e.g., Susan Wiseman, *Conspiracy and Virtue: Women, Writing, and Politics in Seventeenth Century England* (New York: Oxford University Press, 2006), 143–78; Marcus Nevitt, "Elizabeth Poole Writes the Regicide," *Women's Writing* 9, no. 2 (2002): 233–48; Font, *Women's Prophetic Writings*, 56–82; Gillespie, *Domesticity and Dissent*, 115–65, 215–61.

31. M. H. Abrams, "Apocalypse: Themes and Variations," in C. A. Patrides and Joseph Wittreich, eds., *The Apocalypse in English Renaissance Thought and Literature* (Ithaca: Cornell University Press, 1984), 353–56, and in Abrams, *Natural Supernaturalism; Tradition and Revolutions in Romantic Literature* (New York: Norton, 1971), 47.

32. Wiseman, *Conspiracy and Virtue*, 176.

33. This link has been suggested by Christine Berg and Philippa Berry, "'Spiritual Whoredom': An Essay on Female Prophets in the Seventeenth Century," in Francis Barker et al., eds., *1642: Literature and Power in the Seventeenth Century* (Colchester, UK: University of Essex, 1981), 37–54; Paul Salzman, *Reading Early Modern Women's Writing* (New York: Oxford University Press, 2008), 109–34.

34. David Como, *Blown by the Spirit: Puritanism and the Emergence of an Antinomian Underground in Pre-Civil-War England* (Stanford: Stanford University Press, 2004); Ariel Hessayon, "Abiezer Coppe and the Ranters," in Laura Lunger Knoppers, ed., *The Oxford Handbook of Literature and the English Revolution* (New York: Oxford University Press, 2012); McDowell, *The English Radical Imagination*, 89–136. On the nonreality of a "group" known as the Ranters, see J. C. Davis, *Fear, Myth and History, The Ranters and the Historians* (Cambridge: Cambridge University Press, 1986).

35. Smith, *Perfection Proclaimed*, 16–18.

36. Clement Hawes, *Mania and Literary Style: The Rhetoric of Enthusiasm from the Ranters to Christopher Smart* (Cambridge: Cambridge University Press, 1996), 2, 10.

37. Thanks to Jenny Richards for this metaphor, in a passing discussion of Thomas Nashe and Thomas Browne, on a traffic-swarming Euston Road.

38. Natasha Simonova, "New Evidence for the Reading of Sectarian Women's Prophecies," *Notes and Queries* 60, no. 1 (2013): 66–70. Luke 19.40 itself contains a reference to wailing objects in Habakkuk 2.11, "For the stone shall crie out of the wall, and the beame out of the timber shall answere it." Or perhaps even Job 5.23, "For thou shalt be in league with the stones of the field." My thanks to the Stanford reader for pointing these out.

39. Hinds, ed., *Cry of a Stone*, 81; Wiseman, "Unsilent Instruments," 186.

40. Hinds, *God's Englishwomen*, 89–91.

41. *Cry of a Stone*, on the city's inhabitants, 25–27, 56 [24–28, 61–62].

42. On universities, 42, 50, 57, 62 [45–46, 54, 62, 67]. On Cromwell's betrayals, 40, 43, 47, 50, 62 [43, 47, 50, 54, 67].

43. *The Cry of a Stone* appears in two editions in 1654, designated in Hinds's edition via the Cambridge University Library copy (CUL) and the British Library version (BL). See the textual note, and collation of editions, xlix–l. The EEBO copy is the BL version. The differences are in typesetting and layout, most notably the introduction of stanzaic form in the BL (presumably the later) copy, which Hinds suggests serves to "emphasise the 'poetic' nature of Trapnel's spontaneous prophesying."

44. There is an impressive critical literature on psalm culture and its musical aesthetics. See, for instance, the useful survey by Rachel Willie, "'All Scripture Is Given by Inspiration of God': Dissonance and Psalmody," in Kevin Killeen, Helen Smith, and Rachel Willie, eds., *The Oxford Handbook of the Early Modern Bible, 1530–1700* (New York: Oxford University Press, 2015); Linda Phyllis Austern, Kari Boyd McBride, and David L. Orvis, eds., *Psalms in the Early Modern World* (Farnham, Surrey, UK: Ashgate, 2011).

45. 1 Samuel 1; Judges 4–5. Cited by, for example, Katherine Chidley, *Justification of the Independent Churches of Christ* (1641), Judges 4.21, cited on title page.

46. 1 Corinthians 11.4–5 and 14.34–35; 1 Timothy 2.11–12.

47. Gerrard Winstanley, *Fire in the Bush*, in Thomas Corns, Ann Hughes, and David Loewenstein, eds., *The Complete Works of Gerrard Winstanley*, 2 vols. (Oxford University Press, 2009), 2:200.

48. Thomas Hall, *An exposition . . . of the prophecy of Amos* (London: Henry Mortlock, 1661), 6.

49. Nicholas of Cusa, *The idiot in four books* (London: William Leake, 1650).

50. Durant Hotham, *The life of one Jacob Boehmen* (London: Richard Whitaker, 1644), A2v, absorbing the charge of idiocy by Gregor Richter.

Chapter 6

1. *Paradise Lost* [PL] 4.127–29; 3.68, 71–74. All quotations from John Milton, *Paradise Lost*, ed. Alastair Fowler, 2nd ed. (London: Longman, 1998).

2. PL 3.80.

3. PL 4.37, 75.

4. P.H., *Annotations on Milton's Paradise Lost* (1695), long understood to be Patrick Hume. On the misattribution and revealing the nonconformist, Peter Hume,

as the annotator, see David Harper, "The First Annotator of *Paradise Lost* and the Makings of English Literary Criticism," *SEL Studies in English Literature 1500–1900* 59, no. 3 (2019): 507–30. On Milton and Job, see Emily A. Ransom, "Digesting Job in *Paradise Lost*," *Studies in Philology* 111, no. 1 (2014): 110–31; Harold Fisch, "Creation in Reverse: The Book of Job and *Paradise Lost*," in James H. Sims, ed., *Milton and Scriptural Tradition: The Bible into Poetry* (Columbia: University of Missouri Press, 1984). James H. Sims collates numerous references to Job in *The Bible in Milton's Epics* (Tallahassee: University of Florida Press, 1962).

5. *PL* 4.196.

6. *PL* 3.555–56. See Joad Raymond, *Milton's Angels: The Early Modern Imagination* (New York: Oxford University Press, 2010), 301–8, citing the phrase "strange velocitie" taken from Thomas Heywood, *Hierarchie of the Blessed Angells* (1635), 438–39. On the pliability of angelic shape, *PL* 1.423–31, 6.344–53.

7. *PL* 8.66–84 (at 83).

8. See, for a view of the poem as less vehemently focused on right reason, David Carroll Simon, *Light without Heat: The Observational Mood from Bacon to Milton* (Ithaca: Cornell University Press, 2018), 169–212.

9. Victoria Silver, *Imperfect Sense: The Predicament of Milton's Irony* (Princeton: Princeton University Press, 2001), 9, 223, 98; Theodor Adorno, *Negative Dialectics*, trans. E. B. Ashton (New York: Continuum, 1973), 31–33.

10. Michael Lieb, *Poetics of the Holy* (Chapel Hill: University of North Carolina Press, 1981) makes the case for a "cultic" and priestly element to *Paradise Lost*; William Kerrigan, *The Prophetic Milton* (Charlottesville: University Press of Virginia, 1974); Gordon Teskey, *Delirious Milton: The Fate of the Poet in Modernity* (Cambridge, MA: Harvard University Press, 2006), 15, 95.

11. *PL* 3.99, 5.488–89. Thanks to Namratha Rao for this comment on the line's balance and more broadly for astute comments on a draft of the chapter. See the useful collection edited by Richard J. DuRocher and Margaret Olofson Thickstun, *Milton's Rival Hermeneutics: "Reason is but Choosing"* (Pittsburgh, PA: Duquesne University Press, 2012).

12. Karen Edwards, *Milton and the Natural World* (Cambridge: Cambridge University Press, 1999), 15–39.

13. Teskey, *Delirious Milton*, 4.

14. *PL* 1.63, 4.110.

15. *PL* 3.56–62, 380.

16. Noam Reisner, *Milton and the Ineffable* (New York: Oxford University Press, 2021), 202, 215. See too Michael E. Bryson, "The Mysterious Darkness of Unknowing: *Paradise Lost* and the God Beyond Names," in Michael Lieb and John Shawcross, eds., *"Paradise Lost: A Poem Written in Ten Books": Essays on the 1667 First Edition* (Pittsburgh, PA: Duquesne University Press, 2007), 183–212. Both works focus on Milton's alertness to idolatry and "the distinction between the image and that which is imagined" (198). Michael E. Bryson, *The Atheist Milton* (Farnham, Surrey, UK: Ashgate, 2012), 75–107, on "The apophatic Milton," use-

fully tracing the "mystical" context. On the inheritance of Pseudo-Dionysius, and his angelic hierarchies for Milton, see Feisal G. Mohamed, *In the Anteroom of Divinity: The Reformation of the Angels from Colet to Milton* (Toronto: University of Toronto Press, 2008).

17. N. G. Sugimura, *Matter of Glorious Trial: Spiritual and Material Substance in Paradise Lost* (New Haven: Yale University Press, 2009), 215; Michael Lieb, "Reading God: Milton and the Anthropopathetic Tradition," *Milton Studies* 25 (1985): 213–43 (at 232). See too Paul Cefalu, "Incarnational Apophatic: Rethinking Divine Accommodation in John Milton's *Paradise Lost*," *Studies in Philology* 113, no. 1 (2016): 198–228; Neil D. Graves, "Milton and the Theory of Accommodation," *Studies in Philology* 98, no. 2 (2001): 251–72.

18. *PL* 3.3. Peter Herman, *Destabilizing Milton: Paradise Lost and the Poetics of Incertitude* (Basingstoke, UK: Palgrave Macmillan, 2005), 44–45. Similarly, William Kerrigan, *Sacred Complex: On the Psychogenesis of Paradise Lost* (Cambridge, MA: Harvard University Press, 1983), 159–60.

19. Christopher Ricks, *Milton's Grand Style* (Oxford: Clarendon Press, 1963), 96. In keeping with Milton's truculence, Miltonic criticism is more brutal than most other fields of literary studies. However, the blade-inflicted wounds are never mortal, due to the critics' liquid texture.

20. Irene Montori, *Milton, The Sublime and the Dramas of Choice: Figures of Heroic and Literary Virtue* (Rome: Studium, 2020), 32–46; Philip Shaw, *The Sublime* (London: Routledge, 2017), 4, as a "signifier for that which exceeds the grasp of reason"; Patrick Cheney, *English Authorship and the Early Modern Sublime* (Cambridge: Cambridge University Press, 2018), 21, on the sublime as a quality of style. David L. Sedley, *Sublimity and Skepticism in Montaigne and Milton* (Ann Arbor: University of Michigan Press, 2006), 1–2. See too Thomas Matthew Vozar, *Abstracted Sublimities: Milton, Longinus and the Sublime in the Seventeenth Century* (Oxford: Oxford University Press, forthcoming).

21. David Norbrook, *Writing the English Republic: Poetry, Rhetoric and Politics, 1627–1660* (Cambridge: Cambridge University Press, 1999), 212–21, 433–95; David Norbrook, "Milton, Lucy Hutchinson, and the Lucretian Sublime," *Tate Papers* 13 (2010); on Lucretius, *De rerum natura*, 3.1–4, 13–30, citing Hutchinson's translation.

22. Mary Wollstonecraft, *Thoughts on the Education of Daughters* (1787), 52, "Reading." Gordon Teskey, *The Poetry of John Milton* (Cambridge, MA: Harvard University Press, 2015), 409–35.

23. Kerrigan, *Sacred Complex*, 231–35.

24. *PL* 2.1053–4.

25. *PL* 3.418.

26. See John Leonard, *Faithful Labourers: A Reception History of Paradise Lost, 1667–1970*, 2 vols. (New York: Oxford University Press, 2013), 2:705–819 (at 721), "The Universe," for a discussion of the interpretative history of this.

27. Neil Forsyth, *The Satanic Epic* (Princeton: Princeton University Press, 2003), 121, on *PL* 1.200–208.

28. Regina M. Schwartz, *Remembering and Repeating: Biblical Creation in Paradise Lost* (Cambridge: Cambridge University Press, 1988), 40.

29. Thomas Blount, *Glossographia or a Dictionary* (1656), "a dizziness, giddiness or swimming in the head; a disease in the head, caused by wind, wherein the Patient thinks all things turn round; a whirling or turning about."

30. PL 3.418, 490–92.

31. PL 3.418–30, 3.440–97. See Catherine Gimelli Martin, "'What if the Sun be the Center of the World': Milton's Epistemology, Cosmology, and Paradise of Fools Reconsidered," *Modern Philology* 99 (2001): 231–65 (at 262), against the notion that the convex globe Satan lands upon can be associated with the *primum mobile*, with attention to the "sources" in Du Bartas and Dante (Paradiso 28). Leonard's account, *Faithful Labourers*, 2:711–30, traces the collateral assumptions that accrued, century upon century, from reading it without its satirical bite. John King, "Milton's Paradise of Fools: Ecclesiastical Satire in *Paradise Lost*," in Arthur Marotti, ed., *Catholicism and Anti-Catholicism in Early Modern English Texts* (London: Palgrave Macmillan, 1999), 198–217.

32. PL 3.494, 542–43.

33. Dennis Danielson, *Paradise Lost and the Cosmological Revolution* (Cambridge: Cambridge University Press, 2014), xvii–xx, taking to task some of the earlier accounts of a scientifically conservative, Ptolemaic-inclined Milton; Harinder Singh Marjara, *Contemplation of Created Things: Science in "Paradise Lost"* (Toronto: University of Toronto Press, 1992); Kester Svendsen, *Milton and Science* (Cambridge, MA: Harvard University Press, 1969); William Poole, "Milton and Science: A Caveat," *Milton Quarterly* 38, no. 1 (2004): 18–34. See too Leonard, *Faithful Labourers*, 2:711–30, making a similarly damning case. Michael Slater, "Surprised by Science: The 'Original Errors' of *Paradise Lost*," *Early Modern Culture* 14 (2019): 1–20; Catherine Gimelli Martin, *The Ruins of Allegory: Paradise Lost and the Metamorphosis of Epic Convention* (Durham, NC: Duke University Press, 1998), 101–2.

34. David Masson, *The Poetical Works of John Milton*, 3 vols. (1874), 1:85. The misleading effects of this and others, by for example Thomas Orchard, *Milton's Astronomy* (1913), 64, are reviewed in Leonard, *Faithful Labourers*, 2.735–46.

35. Johann Georg Locher and Christoph Scheiner, *Disquisitiones Mathematicae de Controversiis et Novitatibus Astronomicis* (1614).

36. Danielson, *Cosmological Revolution*, 49–50.

37. The Richardsons, father and son, *Explanatory Notes and Remarks on Milton* (1734), 128, on line 3.574–75, write in their commentary on Satan's spatial confusion at the sight of the universe ("up or down . . . hard to tell"), "Milton says so because he Determines not whether the Sun or Earth is the Centre of the Creation."

38. PL 3.527, 588–90; compare 1.282–91, 5.261.

39. Amy Boesky, "Milton, Galileo and Sunspots: Optics and Certainty in *Paradise Lost*," *Milton Studies* 34 (1997): 23–42; Malabika Sarkar, *Cosmos and Character in Paradise Lost* (London: Palgrave Macmillan, 2012), 145–60; Danielson, *Cosmological Revolution*, 78–128, and at 140–45 noting an anti-Copernican ac-

count of sunspots; Christoph Scheiner, *Tres Epistolae de maculis Solaribus* (1612), p. 61, sig. A2r. There is a large critical literature on Milton and Galileo, e.g., Maura Brady, "Galileo in Action: The 'Telescope' in *Paradise Lost*," *Milton Studies* 44 (2005): 129–52; Mario A. DiCesare, ed., *Milton in Italy: Contexts, Images, Contradictions* (Binghamton, NY, 1991); Denise Albanese, *New Science, New World* (Durham, NC: Duke University Press, 1996), 121–47.

40. *PL* 5.261–66, 8.110.

41. Revelation 19.17, on the "angel standing in the sun," the association with Uriel in 2 Esdras 4.1–5.

42. Amy Boesky, "*Paradise Lost* and the Multiplicity of Time," in Thomas Corns, ed., *A Companion to Milton* (Oxford: Blackwell, 2001), 380–92 (at 382).

43. Ayelet Langer, "Milton's *Aevum*: The Time Structure of Grace in *Paradise Lost*," *Early Modern Literary Studies* 17, no. 1 (2014): 1–21 (at 2), explored also in Rory Fox, *Time and Eternity in Mid-Thirteenth-Century Thought* (New York: Oxford University Press, 2006), 244–81. Raymond, *Milton's Angels*, 30–31, showing how Aquinas in his *Summa Theologiae* figured angels as mediate beings, "angels were intellectually necessary as a way of grasping the divine." See too, on the timefulness of God, Stephen J. Schuler, "Eternal Duration: Milton on God's Justice in Everlasting Time," *Milton Studies* 61, no. 2 (2019): 163–85.

44. Judith Scherer Herz, "Meanwhile: (un)making Time in *Paradise Lost*," in Peter C. Herman and Elizabeth Sauer, eds., *The New Milton Criticism* (Cambridge: Cambridge University Press, 2012), 85–101 (at 94).

45. *PL* 8.15–21, 26–27; Eve's question at 4.657–58.

46. For example, *PL* 5.453–56, 508–9, 7.118–20, 8.66–68, 277–81, 12.558–59. Marjara, *Contemplation of Created Things*, 289–99, taking his title from Adam's licit voracious appetite for knowledge.

47. *PL* 8.123, 128; Karen Edwards, *Natural World*, 66.

48. On the telescopic producing its particular aesthetic and sense of perspective, see Marjorie Nicholson, *Science and Imagination* (Archon Books, 1976), 80–109.

49. See Nigel Smith, *Perfection Proclaimed: Language and Literature in English Radical Religion, 1640–60* (Oxford: Clarendon Press, 1989), 185–225; and see chapter 2 for more details.

50. Joad Raymond devotes a chapter of his *Milton's Angels*, 125–61, to the Pordages, father and son, among the most Behmenist figures in Milton's England.

51. Denis Saurat, *Blake and Milton* (Bordeaux: Y. Cadoret, 1920), 3, writes that "Blake is a wild brother of Milton," distorted and transfigured; he is "Milton gone mad"; and further, that Milton is a little afraid of his havoc, while Blake "careers recklessly through shattered solar systems."

52. Margaret Lewis Bailey, *Milton and Jakob Boehme: A Study of German Mysticism in Seventeenth-Century England* (Oxford: Oxford University Press, 1914).

53. Meister Eckhart, *The Essential Sermons, Commentaries, Treatises and Defense* (Mahwah, NJ: Paulist Press, 1981), German sermons: Sermon 83, p. 207; Sermon 48, p. 197.

54. Eckhart, Sermon 52, p. 203; Sermon 6, p. 188. If Eckhart's aphorisms were, as I say here, beyond heresy, his accusers evidently did not agree, and he died indicted and mid-trial, albeit having made an initial retraction.

55. Beryl Smalley, *Study of the Bible in the Middle Ages* (Notre Dame, IN: University of Notre Dame Press, 1952, 1964), 288–89, banding Eckhart with Joachim of Fiore, cited by Donald Declow, "Meister Eckhart's Latin Biblical Exegesis," in Jeremiah Hackett, *A Companion to Meister Eckhart* (Leiden: Brill, 2013), 321. Smalley retracts her metaphor, partially, in a later edition (1964), xiii, saying that this "spiritual exposition in its old age produced a thriving child, though not one that I should care to adopt."

56. *PL* 5.860.

57. Angelus Silesius, born Johann Scheffler (1627–77), Lutheran turned Catholic, produced his large collection of mystical aphorisms, in the epigrammatic, hyperbolic, and paradoxical style of Eckhart, claiming divinity indebted to him (1.259), that God was unfathomable to himself (1.265), or "I am God's other self" (1.278). See Silesius, *The Cherubinic Wanderer* (Mahwah, NJ: Paulist Press, 1986).

58. Rosalie L. Colie, "Time and Eternity: Paradox and Structure in *Paradise Lost*," *Journal of the Warburg and Courtauld Institutes* 23, no. 1 (1960): 127–38 (at 127), noting his distaste for these paradoxes in *De Doctrina Christiana*; Ralph Venning, *Orthodox paradoxes, theological and experimental, or, A believer clearing truth by seeming contradictions* (1654).

59. A good starting point on his early modern reputation is Simon J. G. Burton, Joshua Hollmann, and Eric M. Parker, eds., *Nicholas of Cusa and the Making of the Early Modern World* (Leiden: Brill, 2018). On the "coincidence of opposites," see Nicholas of Cusa, *On Learned Ignorance: A Translation and an Appraisal of De Docta Ignorantia*, ed. Jasper Hopkins (Minneapolis: Arthur J. Banning Press, 1985), 1.24–26.

60. Two of the most influential works of Miltonic criticism owe much of their power to this, that they can be brought to bear, in so capacious a manner, across the epic in all its variety: Stanley Fish, *Surprised by Sin: The Reader in Paradise Lost*, 2nd ed. (Cambridge, MA: Harvard University Press, 1997); and Stephen Fallon, *Milton among the Philosophers* (Ithaca: Cornell University Press, 1991).

61. John Leonard, *Naming in Paradise: Milton and the Language of Adam and Eve* (Oxford: Clarendon Press, 1990), 239, how Milton "courts the savage associations of his vocabulary," luring the reader into connotative excess. Dayton Haskin, *Milton's Burden of Interpretation* (Philadelphia: University of Pennsylvania Press, 1994), 186–87, notes that the "tangles and thick obscurity" ascribed to the landscape and life of Eden "generally show[] up in contexts where harm seems to be lurking, for Satan is present."

62. A phrase used in a different context by Linda Gregerson, *The Reformation of the Subject: Spenser, Milton and the English Protestant Epic* (Cambridge: Cambridge University Press, 1995), 4.

63. Critical writing on the classical heritage of *Paradise Lost* is large. Starting

points might include Maggie Kilgour, *Milton and the Metamorphosis of Ovid* (New York: Oxford University Press, 2012); Charles Martindale, *John Milton and the Transformation of Ancient Epic* (London: Bristol Classical Press, 2002).

64. PL 2:466–70, 3.217–18. We might note a biblical moment when a "champion" is called for, in the David and Goliath story, 1 Samuel 17, but this is not, I think, evoked in either instance in *Paradise Lost*.

65. PL 6.511–15, 1.685–704.

66. Fallon, *Milton among the Philosophers*, 196–97.

67. PL 3.23–24, 3.14–15.

68. PL 1.55–57.

69. This, too, is a large field with impressive works of scholarship, e.g., Eric B. Song, *Dominion Undeserved: Milton and the Perils of Creation* (Ithaca: Cornell University Press, 2015); David Williams, *Milton's Leveller God* (Montreal: McGill-Queen's University Press, 2017); Walter S. H. Lim, *John Milton, Radical Politics, and Biblical Republicanism* (Newark: University of Delaware Press, 2006); David Loewenstein, *Representing Revolution in Milton and His Contemporaries: Religion, Politics, and Polemics in Radical Puritanism* (Cambridge: Cambridge University Press, 2001); Sharon Achinstein, *Milton and the Revolutionary Reader* (Princeton: Princeton University Press, 1994), 177–223.

70. PL 1.685–704.

71. PL 1.192–208. On the intricate critical history of Milton's similes, Leonard, *Faithful Labourers*, 1:310–90. Amlan Das Gupta, "The Miltonic Dissimile: Language and Style in *Paradise Lost*, Book 4," in Sukanta Chaudhuri, ed., *Renaissance Themes: Essays Presented to Arun Kumar Das Gupta* (New York: Anthem Press, 2009), 113–26; Earl Miner, "The Reign of Narrative in *Paradise Lost*," *Milton Studies* 17 (1983): 3–25.

72. PL 1.283–96.

73. Jen E. Boyle, *Anamorphosis in Early Modern Literature: Mediation and Affect* (London: Routledge, 2010), 91–110.

74. PL 1.701–7, 1.747–48.

75. PL 1.775–84; Nicholson, *Science and Imagination*, 93–96.

76. Erin Webster, "Milton's Pandæmonium and the Infinitesimal Calculus," *English Literary Renaissance* 45, no. 3 (2015): 425–58; Joanna Picciotto, *Labors of Innocence in Early Modern England* (Cambridge, MA: Harvard University Press, 2010), 13. See too Webster's *The Curious Eye: Optics and Imaginative Literature in Seventeenth-Century England* (New York: Oxford University Press, 2020).

77. PL 5.571–72.

78. PL 2.506, 513, 525–26.

79. PL 2.540, 2.570–72; John Martin Evans, *Milton's Imperial Epic: Paradise Lost and the Discourse of Colonialism* (Ithaca: Cornell University Press, 1996), 41–42.

80. PL 1.65, 6.865–66.

81. PL 2.546–55.

82. On the puns, Fowler notes that "suspended" did not have the musical valence in the seventeenth century.

83. *PL* 2.559–61.

84. The touchstone for this idea of a basic "mere Christianity" underlying all variations remains C. S. Lewis, *A Preface to Paradise Lost* (Oxford: Oxford University Press, 1942). Benjamin Myers, *Milton's Theology of Freedom* (Berlin: de Gruyter, 2006).

85. Joseph Addison and Richard Steele, *Tatler* 114, 31 December 1709, in John T. Shawcross, ed., *Milton: The Critical Heritage* (London: Routledge, 1970), 142. See Paul Hammond, *Milton's Complex Words* (New York: Oxford University Press, 2018), "Chance, Fate and Providence" (17), elaborating on the critical history and theology of these lines.

86. Richardsons, *Explanatory Notes and Remarks on Milton* (1734), 62–63.

87. P.H., *Annotations on Milton's Paradise Lost* (1695), 72.

88. *PL* 7.210–17.

89. Teskey, *Delirious Milton*, 69; Fallon, *Milton among the Philosophers*, 191–92.

90. David Quint, "Fear of Falling: Icarus, Phaethon, and Lucretius in *Paradise Lost*," *Renaissance Quarterly* 57, no. 3 (2004): 847–81 (at 857), on *PL* 2.927–38.

91. Catherine Gimelli Martin, *The Ruins of Allegory: Paradise Lost and the Metamorphosis of Epic Convention* (Durham, NC: Duke University Press, 1998), 162–200, argues against the idea of such poetic inconsistency, incorporating earlier essays "'Pregnant Causes Mixt': The Wages of Sin and the Laws of Entropy in Milton's Chaos," in Kristin McCoglan and Charles Durham, eds., *Arenas of Conflict: Milton and the Unfettered Mind* (Selinsgrove, PA: Susquehanna University Press, 1997), 161–82; and "Fire, Ice, and Epic Entropy: The Physics and Metaphysics of Milton's Reformed Chaos," *Milton Studies* 35 (1997): 73–113. On Milton's materialism, Juliet Lucy Cummins, "Milton's Gods and the Matter of Creation," *Milton Studies* 40 (2001): 81–105; Kerrigan, *Sacred Complex*, 193–262; John Rogers, *The Matter of Revolution: Science, Poetry and Politics in the Age of Milton* (Ithaca: Cornell University Press, 1996), 103–76.

92. The tumble of battling elements has a long hexameral history. Basil, *Homilia in Hexaemeron*, Patrologia Graeca, 29:20; Gregory, *In Hexameron*, Patrologia Graeca, 44:72, noted in A. B. Chambers, "Chaos in *Paradise Lost*," *Journal of the History of Ideas* 24, no. 1 (1963): 55–84, on early modern understandings—More, Cudworth, and Gassendi—of the classical and para-biblical history of chaos.

93. *PL* 7.210–17, 2.898–906.

94. Quint, *Fear of Falling*, 859, building on Leonard, "Void Profound," (note 115).

95. *PL* 4.551–54.

96. *PL* 2.908–9.

97. Noted in chapter 4 in regard to disorientation of the microscopic. Lucretius, *De Rerum Natura*, in *The Works of Lucy Hutchinson, vol. 1: Translation of Lucretius*, ed. Reid Barbour and David Norbrook (New York: Oxford University Press, 2012), 2.319–33.

98. *PL* 2.890–93.
99. *PL* 2.890–93.
100. *PL* 2.438–39, 2.146–48.
101. *PL* 1.253.
102. *PL* 2.933–34.

103. John P. Rumrich, *Milton Unbound: Controversy and Reinterpretation* (Cambridge: Cambridge University Press, 1996), 132; Robert M. Adams, "A Little Look into Chaos," in Earl Miner, ed., *Illustrious Evidence: Approaches to English Literature of the Early Seventeenth Century* (Berkeley: University of California Press, 1975), 71–89.

104. Schwartz, *Remembering and Repeating*, 18; Yaakov Mascetti, "Satan and the "Incompos'd" Visage of Chaos: Milton's Hermeneutic Indeterminacy," *Milton Studies* 50 (2009): 35–63.

105. On the "sources," Hesiodic and otherwise, of Chaos and Night, see Walter Clyde Curry, *Milton's Ontology, Cosmogony, and Physics* (Lexington: University of Kentucky Press; 1957), 48–73; A. B. Chambers, "Chaos in *Paradise Lost*," *Journal of the History of Ideas* 24, no. 1 (1963): 55–84, on early modern understandings of the classical and religious history of chaos. William B. Hunter, "Milton's Power of Matter," *Journal of the History of Ideas* 13, no. 4 (1952): 551–62.

106. *PL* 2.1002–9.

107. Song, *Dominion Undeserved*, 6–7, citing Julia Kristeva, *Powers of Horror: An Essay on Abjection*, trans. Leon S. Roudiez (New York: Columbia University Press, 1982), 4.

108. Chambers, "Chaos," 65.

109. Rumrich, *Milton Unbound*, 130. On the procreative chaos, see Louis Schwartz, *Milton and Maternal Mortality* (Cambridge: Cambridge University Press, 2009), 245–60; Michael Lieb, *The Dialectics of Creation: Patterns of Birth and Regeneration in Paradise Lost* (Amherst: University of Massachusetts Press, 1970).

110. Rumrich, *Milton Unbound*, 141–42. The ontological dimensions of this are explored further in Rumrich, "Milton's God and the Matter of Chaos," *PMLA* 110 (1995): 1035–46 (at 1043). See too Rumrich, *Matter of Glory* (Pittsburgh: University of Pittsburgh Press, 1987).

111. Dennis Danielson, *Milton's Good God: A Study in Literary Theodicy* (Cambridge: Cambridge University Press, 1982); Mary F. Norton, "The Rising World of Waters Dark and Deep: Chaos Theory and *Paradise Lost*," *Milton Studies* 32 (1995): 91–110. At the root of any such account of matter is Milton's statement on the *prima materia* in *De Doctrina Christiana*, that "original matter was not an evil thing, nor to be thought of as worthless: it was good, and it contained the seeds of all subsequent good," and Milton's materialist denying *ex nihilo* creation. See *Complete Prose Works of John Milton*, ed. Don M. Wolfe (New Haven: Yale University Press, 1953), 6:307.

112. See the survey of these debates, Sarah Smith, "The Ecology of Chaos in *Paradise Lost*," *Milton Studies* 59 (2017): 31–55.

113. Schwartz, *Remembering and Repeating*, 12, 18.

114. See Emily Ransom, "Digesting Job in *Paradise Lost*," for a good overview of Miltonic uses of Job in Milton's works elsewhere, and in relation to the moral and theodical framework of *Paradise Lost*. For links to Job's creation narrative, Leviathan, and more, see Fisch, "Creation in Reverse: The Book of Job and *Paradise Lost*"; Barbara Lewalski, *Milton's Brief Epic: The Genre, Meaning, and Art of Paradise Regained* (Providence: Brown University Press, 1966).

115. Phillip Hardie, "The Presence of Lucretius in *Paradise Lost*," *Milton Quarterly* 29, no. 1 (1995): 23–24; John Leonard, "Milton, Lucretius, and 'the Void Profound of Unessential Night," in K. A. Pruitt and C. W. Durham, eds., *Living Texts: Interpreting Milton* (Selinsgrove, PA: Susquehanna University Press, 2000); Katherine Calloway, "Milton's Lucretian Anxiety Revisited," *Renaissance and Reformation / Renaissance et Réforme* 32, no. 3 (2009): 79–97.

116. Schwarz, *Remembering and Repeating*, 36.

117. *PL* 2.939–52.

118. Linda Gregerson, "The Limbs of Truth: Milton's Use of Simile in *Paradise Lost*," *Milton Studies* 14 (1980): 135–52 (at 135).

119. See the special issue of *Milton Quarterly* 52:4 (2018) on the fiftieth anniversary of Stanley Fish, *Surprised by Sin* (London: Macmillan, 1967).

120. John Stachniewski, *The Persecutory Imagination: English Puritanism and the Literature of Religious Despair* (Oxford: Clarendon Press, 1991).

121. John Saltmarsh, *Holy discoveries and flames* (1640), 25; compare John Brinsley, *The spirituall* vertigo, or, *Turning sickensse of soul-unsettlednesse in matters of* religious *concernment* (1655).

Epilogue

1. Regina Schwartz, *Sacramental Poetics at the Dawn of Secularism: When God Left the World* (Stanford: Stanford University Press, 2008), 15.

2. Michael Martin, *Literature and the Encounter with God in Post-Reformation England* (Farnham, Surrey, UK: Ashgate, 2014), 5.

3. Jacob Bauthumley, *The Light and Dark Sides of God* (London: William Learner, 1650), 1.

4. Bauthumley, *The Light and Dark Sides of God*, 53, 2, 6.

5. On Bauthumley, see Nigel Smith, *Perfection Proclaimed: Language and Literature in English Radical Religion, 1640–60* (Oxford: Clarendon Press, 1989), 53–66; and the DNB entry ("Jacob Bothumley") by Smith; Daniel P. Jaeckle, "The Realised Eschatology and Sweet Style of Jacob Bauthumley," *Journal of Religious History* 35, no. 3 (2011); the accusation of atheism in Helen Stocks, *Records of the Borough of Leicester, 1603–1688* (1923), 386, cited in Edwin Welch, "Bauthumley the Ranter," *Leicestershire Historian* 2, no. 6 (1975): 18–24 (at 20); George Fox, *A journal or historical account* (1694), 131; J. C. Davis, *Fear, Myth and History: The Ranters and the Historian* (Cambridge: Cambridge University Press, 1986), 44–48.

6. Bauthumley, *The Light and Dark Sides of God*, Prefatory epistle, A2r, A4r.

7. Rudolf Otto, *Das Heilige: Über das Irrationale in der Idee des Göttlichen und sein Verhältnis zum Rationalen*, trans. John Harvey, *The Idea of the Holy*, 2nd ed. (1950), 27–28.

8. Otto, *The Idea of the Holy*, xxi.

9. Rowan Williams, *The Edge of Words: God and the Habits of Language* (London: Bloomsbury, 2014); William Franke, *A Philosophy of the Unsayable* (Notre Dame, IN: University of Notre Dame Press, 2014), 18.

10. Sebastian Barry, *World without End* (London: Faber, 2016), 71–72.

11. Gary Kuchar, *George Herbert and the Mystery of the Word: Poetry and Scripture in Seventeenth-Century England* (London: Palgrave Macmillan, 2017), 2–3; c.f., an older tradition of reading "metaphysical poetry" as mysticism, Caroline Spurgeon, *Mysticism in English literature* (Cambridge: Cambridge University Press, 1913); Itrat Husain, *The Mystical Element in the Metaphysical Poets of the Seventeenth Century* (Edinburgh: Oliver and Boyd, 1948). See too Bernard McGinn, *Mysticism in the Reformation (1500–1650)* (Chestnut Ridge, PA: Crossroad Publishing, 2017).

12. Schwartz, *Sacramental Poetics*, 95. Other important studies of the sacramental in early modern poetics include Sophie Read, *Eucharist and the Poetic Imagination in Early Modern England* (Cambridge: Cambridge University Press, 2013); Ryan Netzley, *Reading, Desire, and the Eucharist in Early Modern Religious Poetry* (Toronto: University of Toronto Press, 2011).

13. Ernst Robert Curtius, *European Literature and the Latin Middle Ages* (Princeton: Princeton University Press, 1953), 145–66.

14. E.g., Thomas Wyatt, "Mine owne John Poins," on his exile from court: "I cannot frame my tune to feign, / To cloak the truth for praise, without desert, / Of them that list all vice for to retain," and the opening sonnet of Philip Sidney's *Astrophil and Stella*.

15. See, for instance, Hannibal Hamlin, *The Bible in Shakespeare* (New York: Oxford University Press, 2018), 305–33; Victoria Brownlee, *Biblical Readings and Literary Writings in Early Modern England, 1558–1625* (New York: Oxford University Press, 2018), 79–112.

16. Gilles Deleuze and Felix Guattari, *What Is Philosophy?* (New York: Columbia University Press, 1991), 55.

Index

Abbott, George, 214
Anderdon, John, 227
Aquinas, Thomas, 21, 39, 99, 209, 231, 250
Arbuthnot, John, 219
Aristotle, 48, 53, 97
Arrowsmith, John, 40, 215

Bacon, Francis, 5, 14–15, 27, 28, 90, 104, 105, 118, 124, 127, 133, 139, 208–209, 212, 233, 247
   De Dignitate & Augmentis Scientiarum, 27
   Novum Organum, 14, 28, 105, 118, 208, 212
   Of the advancement and proficience of learning, 27, 105, 212
Barbour, Reid, 97, 230, 238, 239
Baronio, Cesare, 25
Barker, Matthew, 35, 213
Barlow, Thomas, 143, 242
Barton, Thomas, 205
Batt, Timothy, 205
Bauthumley, Jacob, 200–201, 225, 255
Baxter, Richard, 87, 227, 232
Beaumont, John, 213, 217
Beza, Theodore, 39, 214
Blake, William, 33, 63, 73, 180, 221–222, 250
Blount, Thomas, 249
Boehme, Jacob, 8, 10–11, 16, 17, 18, 60–89, 99, 141, 165, 173, 179–182, 199, 207, 220–228, 246, 250
   Aurora, 62, 66, 67, 70, 71, 75, 84, 85, 86, 222–227

Clavis, 68, 223
Four tables of divine revelation, 68
Mysterium Magnum, 60–89, 207, 220–228
Signatura Rerum, 70
Boyd, Zacharie, 39, 214
Boyle, Robert, 5, 12, 15, 41, 44, 92, 115–139, 208, 215, 235–238
   A Discourse of Things above Reason, 12, 15, 208, 235
   Experiments and considerations about the porosity of bodies, 117, 236
   History of Fluidity and Firmness, 41, 119, 129–130, 136, 236, 238–240
   Of the High Veneration Man's Intellect owes to God, 41, 215, 235
   Some Considerations touching the Style of the Holy Scriptures, 117–118, 216
Bradwardine, Thomas, 206
Brett, Arthur, 39, 215
Brinsley, John, 255
Broughton, Hugh, 27, 44, 212, 216
Browne, Thomas, 4, 13, 16–17, 40, 88–89, 90–114, 116, 125, 154, 207, 208, 215, 228–238
   The Garden of Cyrus, 16, 92–95, 97, 101–114, 228–230, 233–234
   Hydriotaphia, or Urne Burial, 92, 114
   Pseudodoxia Epidemica, 91, 94, 208, 215, 229, 230, 238
   Religio Medici, 91, 207, 228, 230
Burnet, Gilbert, 1, 205

INDEX

Burnet, Thomas, 4, 36–38, 54–58, 213–214, 218–219
  An answer to the late exceptions made by Mr Erasmus Warren, 57, 219
  A review of The theory of the earth and of its proofs, 219
  The Theory of the Earth, 36, 54, 58, 213–214, 217–220
Burton, Robert, 7, 208
Buxtorf, Johannes (the Younger), 218
Byrdall, Thomas, 216

Caley, Abraham, 23, 211
Calvin, John, 39, 214
Canes, John Vincent, 34, 213
Caputo, John, 25–26, 66, 212, 223
Cary, Mary, 150, 156, 245
Caryl, Joseph, 35–36, 39, 213–214
Casaubon, Isaac, 25, 98, 211
Casaubon, Meric, 24, 211, 240
  A discourse concerning enthusiasm, 24, 211
  A discourse concerning Christ his incarnation, 240
Cavendish, Margaret, 4, 13–14, 117, 122, 132–139, 199, 240–242
  The Blazing World, 122, 134, 241
  Grounds of Natural Philosophy, 241
  Observations upon Experimental Philosophy, 122, 133–134, 240–241
  Philosophical Letters, 122, 137, 241–242
  Poems and Fancies, 240
Certeau, Michel de, 18, 120, 209, 236
Charleton, Walter, 1, 92, 103, 122, 125, 131, 134, 205, 207, 237, 238, 240
  The darknes of atheism dispelled, 205, 240
  Physiologia Epicuro-Gassendo-Charltoniana, 122, 237, 238, 240
Chidley, Katherine, 156, 246

Clark, William, 31, 34–35, 39, 41, 213, 215, 216
Coccejus, Johannes, 214
Cohen, Leonard, 144–145, 243
Coleridge, Samuel Taylor, 54, 63, 93, 218
Colet, John, 231
Connor, Stephen, 126, 136, 233, 238
Coppe, Abiezer, 243, 245
Cordemoy, Géraud de, 49–50, 217
Cordier, Balthasar, 214, 231
Creech, Thomas, 129, 239
Croese, Gerardus, 87, 227
Croft, Herbert, 58, 220
Cromwell, Oliver, 18, 140, 144–145, 147, 149–150, 152, 156–163, 185, 246
Cudworth, Ralph, 51, 126, 207, 218, 229, 238, 253
Culverwel, Nathanael, 102, 233, 240
Curtius, Benedict, 233
Czepko, Daniel, 99

D'Addario, Christopher, 108, 234
Dallington, Robert, 2, 205
Daneau, Lambert, 47, 143, 216, 242
  A fruitful commentarie upon the twelve small prophets, 242
  The wonderfull woorkmanship of the world, 216
Danielson, Dennis, 176, 249, 254
Davies, Lady Eleanor, 148, 244
Day, Robert, 232
Day, William, 142–143, 242
Dell, William, 87
Descartes, René, 6, 16, 47–50, 55, 75, 120, 127, 130, 209, 217
Digby, Kenelm, 48, 200, 217
Diodati, Giovanni, 242
Dionysius the Areopagite, 20–21, 24–25, 90, 98–99, 101, 112, 209, 211–212, 228, 230–232, 234, 248
Donne, John, 203, 215

258

Drexel, Jeremias, 214
Dunton, John, 214
Du Bartas, Guillaume de Salluste, 39, 214, 249
Du Pin, Louis Ellies, 24, 211

Edwards, John, 214, 219, 234, 239
   A demonstration of the existence and providence of God, 234, 239
   Of the Excellency and perfection of the Holy Scriptures, 214
Elliston, John, 86, 88, 227, 228
Erasmus, Desiderius Roterodamus, 25, 211
Eriugena, John Scotus, 20–21, 210, 231
d'Espagnet, Joannes, 8, 207
Evans, Edward, 102, 232
Evelyn, John, 92, 129, 239

Fairfax, Nathanael, 103–104, 233
Fallon, Stephen, 75, 184, 225, 251, 252, 253
Fernel, Jean, 122, 237
Ficino, Marsilio, 21, 25, 112, 210, 230–231, 234
   On Dionysus the Areopagite, 21, 230, 234
   Platonic Theology, 21, 210
Fifth Monarchists, 17–18, 22, 143, 145, 150, 151, 154, 163, 244, 245
Fish, Stanley, 196–197, 251
Fludd, Robert, 232
Fotherby, Martin, 238
Foscarini, Paolo Antonio, 215
Fox, George, 145, 243, 255
   A distinction between the phanatick spirit and the spirit of God, 145, 244
   A journal or historical account, 255
Franck, Richard, 28–29, 31, 212–213
Franck, Sebastian, 99
Franke, William, 26, 34, 100, 202, 205, 209, 212, 213, 230, 231, 232, 256

Gafferel, Jacques, 108–109, 234
Gale, Theophilus, 34, 213
Galileo Galilei, 125, 197–198, 215, 249, 250
Gassendi, Pierre, 103, 125, 175, 218, 235, 253
Gibbons, B J, 221, 223, 224, 226, 227
Glanvill, Joseph, 2, 5, 125, 205, 212, 237
Godwin, Francis, 58, 220
Gott, Samuel, 47, 217
Greenhill, William, 242
Gregory, John, 40, 215
Gregory of Nyssa, 20, 228, 230, 232
Grew, Nehemiah, 92
Grosseteste, Robert, 99, 231
Guillebert, Nicolas, 214
Gumble, Thomas, 227

Hale, Matthew, 214
Hall, Thomas, 164, 246
Harvey, Gideon, 132–133, 240
Herman, Peter, 172, 248, 250
Hesiod, 34, 67, 196, 254
Heywood, Thomas, 238, 247
Hinds, Hilary, 148, 156, 242, 243, 246
Hobbes, Thomas, 75
Hodson, William, 38, 214
Holland, Philemon, 112, 114, 234, 241
Hooke, Robert, 13, 121, 123, 133, 134, 237, 241
Hooker, Richard, 2, 205
Hotham, Charles, 227
Hotham, Durant, 246
Hugh of Saint Victor, 21, 99, 210, 231
Hughes, George, 48, 217
Hume, Peter, 246–247
Hutcheson, George, 35, 39, 213, 214
Hutchinson, Lucy, 44–45, 129, 130, 216, 239, 248, 253
   Order and Disorder, 44–45, 216
   Translation of Lucretius, 129, 130, 239, 248, 253

INDEX

Jackson, Arthur, 214
Jackson, Thomas, 96–97, 101, 102, 205, 229–230, 232
Johnson, Samuel, 93, 107–108, 169

Keill, John, 219
Keller, Catherine, 65, 223, 232
Kepler, Johannes, 109
Kerrigan, William, 174, 247, 248, 253
Knollys, Hanserd, 232

Lead, Jane, 23, 87
Leonard, John, 175, 248–249, 251, 252, 255
Linche, Richard, 1, 205
Lloyd, Richard, 205, 232
Llwyd, Morgan, 86, 227
Locher, Johann Georg, 249
Locke, John, 211
Longinus, 34, 207, 213, 248
Lucretius, 13, 122, 126–132, 193, 238–240, 248, 253, 255
Lushington, Thomas, 97
Luther, Martin, 88, 176, 220, 223, 229, 251

Maimonides, Moses, 16, 52–53, 57, 209, 218, 230, 231
Manley, Thomas, 214–215
Manningham, Thomas, 217
Mayer, John, 242
Meister Eckhart, 20, 62, 99–100, 101, 124, 181–183, 231, 237, 250–251
Mercerus, Johannes, 214
Milton, John, 4, 11–12, 46, 75, 81, 144, 166–198, 199, 203, 207, 216, 219, 225, 226, 229, 246–255
  De Doctrina Christiana, 171, 182, 251, 254
  Paradise Lost, 11–12, 109, 166–198, 219, 225, 226, 234, 243, 246–255
Mirandola, Pico della, 21
Montaigne, Michel de, 7, 208, 238, 248

More, Henry, 1, 5, 87, 103, 132, 142, 205, 206, 213, 221, 224, 227–228, 238, 240, 242, 253
  Antidote against Atheism, 206
  Censura Philosophiae Teutonica, 227–228
  Conway Letters, 87, 227
  Divine Dialogues, 240
  An explanation of the grand mystery of godliness, 205
  Enthusiasmus triumphatus, 213, 221
  A modest enquiry into the mystery of iniquity, 142, 242
Morton, Thomas, 1, 205, 232
Muggleton, Lodowicke, 87
Muratori, Cecilia, 65, 222, 223, 224, 228

Needham, Marchamont, 145, 243
Newton, Isaac, 54, 218–219, 228, 238
Newton, John, 232
Nicholas of Cusa, 21, 24, 97, 100–101, 164–165, 183, 210, 232, 246, 251
  De Deo Abscondito, 100, 232
  De Docta Ignorantia, 24, 100, 232, 251
  The idiot in four books, 164–165, 183, 246
Nicolson, Margaret, 6, 56, 206, 219
Norbrook, David, 174, 216, 239, 248

Oecolampadius, Johannes, 214
Oldenburg, Henry, 62, 105
Oldham, John, 145, 243
Oley, Barnabas, 230
O'Regan, Cyril, 65, 222
Otto, Rudolf, 202, 256
Ovid, 91, 169, 184, 196, 228

Pareus, David, 225
Parker, Samuel, 103
Patrick, Simon, 214

260

Pepys, Samuel, 122
Perrot, John, 88–89, 228
Plotinus, 21, 234
Plutarch, 94, 111–113, 136, 233, 234, 241
Polhill, Edward, 229
Poole, Elizabeth, 150, 245
Pordage, John, 86–87, 250
Pordage, Samuel, 86–87, 250
Porta, Giambattista della, 233
Power, Henry, 121, 123–125, 133–134, 138, 237–238
Preston, Claire, 5, 92, 108, 116, 206, 228–229, 233, 235

Quarles, Francis, 214

Ramesey, William, 240
Ranters, 17, 22, 88, 143, 154, 163, 199, 245, 255
Ray, John, 92
Reisner, Noam, 95, 171, 229, 247
Reyner, Edward, 38, 214
Richardson, Jonathan (father & son), 189, 249, 253
Ricks, Christopher, 172, 248
Robinson, Thomas, 219
Rosenzweig, Franz, 60, 220
Ross, Alexander, 42, 215, 216
Rossi, Paolo, 14, 55, 208, 219
Rumrich, John P, 194–195, 254

Saltmarsh, John, 87, 197, 255
Salusbury, Thomas, 215
Sanches, Francisco, 100–101, 231
Sandt, Maximilian Van der, 23–24
Sandys, George, 39, 214
Scheffler, Johannes (Angelus Silesius), 100, 251
Scheiner, Christoph, 249, 250
Schwartz, Regina, 175, 195–196, 200, 203, 249, 254, 255, 256
Sennert, Daniel, 125

Shakespeare, William, 39, 203
   King Lear, 39, 203
Smith, John, 205
Smith, Nigel, 22, 62, 86, 88, 154, 210, 221, 227, 228, 250, 255
Sparrow, John, 8, 66–67, 78, 207, 220, 221, 222, 223, 227
Spencer, John, 28, 212
Stillingfleet, Edward, 23–24, 51–53, 57, 98, 144, 211, 218, 243
   An answer to Mr Cressy's Epistle apologetical, 211
   Origines Sacrae, 51, 53, 218, 243
Stirredge, Elizabeth, 156
Swan, John, 213

Tany, Theaurau John, 23, 86, 211, 227
Temple, William, 212
Teskey, Gordon, 11, 170–171, 177, 207, 247, 248, 253
Trapnel, Anna, 4, 17–18, 86, 140–165, 199, 242, 244–246
   The Cry of a Stone, 145–146, 149–163, 242, 244, 246
   A legacy for saints, 149
   Report and Plea, 149, 245
   A voice for the king of saints and nations, 149
Trapp, John, 214
Tufayl, Ibn, 218
Turner, Denys, 19–20, 162, 209, 220, 228, 229, 232
Turner, Jane, 156
Twisse, William, 96–97, 229–230

Valla, Lorenzo, 24, 211
Vane, Henry, 87
Varro, Marcus Terentius, 107, 233
Vaughan, Thomas, 213
Vavassor, François, 214

Ward, Richard, 213
Warren, Erasmus, 57, 219–220

Webster, John, 86, 227
Weeks, Andrew, 67, 70, 207, 220, 223–224
Weil, Simone, 42, 215
Whiston, William, 57, 219
White, Thomas, 48, 54, 217
Wilkins, John, 41–42, 215
Willet, Andrew, 228
Williams, Rowan, 142, 202, 212, 242, 256

Wilson, Catherine, 117, 126, 236, 238
Winstanley, Gerrard, 87, 164, 246
Wiseman, Susan, 149, 151, 244, 246
Wollebius, John, 216
Woodward, John, 57, 219
Wright, James, 239

Xenophon, 57, 233, 234

Zúñiga, Diego de, 40, 215

The authorized representative in the EU for product safety and compliance is:
Mare Nostrum Group
B.V Doelen 72
4831 GR Breda
The Netherlands

www.ingramcontent.com/pod-product-compliance
Lightning Source LLC
Chambersburg PA
CBHW022003220426
43663CB00007B/945